*Studies
in the Organization of
Conversational Interaction*

LANGUAGE, THOUGHT, AND CULTURE: *Advances in the Study of Cognition*

Under the Editorship of: E. A. HAMMEL

DEPARTMENT OF ANTHROPOLOGY
UNIVERSITY OF CALIFORNIA
BERKELEY

Michael Agar, Ripping and Running: A Formal Ethnography of Urban Heroin Addicts

Brent Berlin, Dennis E. Breedlove, and Peter H. Raven, Principles of Tzeltal Plant Classification: An Introduction to the Botanical Ethnography of a Mayan-Speaking People of Highland Chiapas

Mary Sanches and Ben Blount, Sociocultural Dimensions of Language Use

Daniel G. Bobrow and Allan Collins, Representation and Understanding: Studies in Cognitive Science

Domenico Parisi and Francesco Antinucci, Essentials of Grammar

Elizabeth Bates, Language and Context: The Acquisition of Pragmatics

Ben G. Blount and Mary Sanches, Sociocultural Dimensions of Language Change

Susan Ervin-Tripp and Claudia Mitchell-Kernan (Eds.), Child Discourse

Lynn A. Friedman (Ed.), On the Other Hand: New Perspectives on American Sign Language

Eugene S. Hunn, Tzeltal Folk Zoology: The Classification of Discontinuities in Nature

Jim Schenkein (Ed.), Studies in the Organization of Conversational Interaction

In preparation

David Parkin, The Cultural Definition of Political Response: Lineal Destiny Among the Luo

Studies
in the Organization of
Conversational Interaction

EDITED BY

JIM SCHENKEIN

Department of Sociology
Queens College of the City University of New York
Flushing, New York

ACADEMIC PRESS   New York   San Francisco   London
A Subsidiary of Harcourt Brace Jovanovich, Publishers

ACADEMIC PRESS, INC.
111 Fifth Avenue, New York, New York 10003

United Kingdom Edition published by
ACADEMIC PRESS, INC. (LONDON) LTD.
24/28 Oval Road, London NW1

Library of Congress Cataloging in Publication Data

Main entry under title:

Studies in the organization of conversational
  interaction.

  (Language, thought, and culture series)
  Bibliography: p.
      1.   Interpersonal communication—Addresses,
essays, lectures.   2.   Conversation—Research—
Addresses, essays, lectures.   I.   Schenkein, Jim,
Date
HM132.S78   301.11   76-50404
ISBN 0-12-623550-3

None of these studies of conversation would have been undertaken without the work of Harvey Sacks, who introduced each of us to the study of conversation. Although substantial differences in topic and style are evident with just a glimpse through the pages of this volume, the individual studies gathered here share inestimable indebtedness to his teaching. Through his lectures and writings he has had the most profound impact on all our work as well as on the work of many others.

Harvey Sacks died in an automobile accident late in 1975. Acknowledging his special contribution to our independent studies is certainly appropriate here. But of course, it hardly expresses the depth of his influence on us all. And more important, it makes no mention of what a marvelous man he was.

Contents

List of Contributors

M. A. ATKINSON (133), Department of Sociology, Didsbury College of Education, Wilmslow Road, Manchester, England

E. C. CUFF (133), Department of Sociology, Didsbury College of Education, Wilmslow Road, Manchester, England

JO ANN GOLDBERG (199), Department of Sociology, Trinity University, San Antonio, Texas

GAIL JEFFERSON (7, 155, 219), School of Social Sciences, University of California, Irvine, Irvine, California

J. R. E. LEE (133), Department of Sociology, University of Manchester, Manchester, England

ANITA POMERANTZ (79), Department of Sociology, University of California, Los Angeles, Los Angeles, California

ALAN L. RYAVE (113), Department of Sociology, California State College, Dominguez Hills, California

HARVEY SACKS* (7, 249), School of Social Sciences, University of California, Irvine, Irvine, California

EMANUEL A. SCHEGLOFF (7), Department of Sociology, University of California, Los Angeles, Los Angeles, California

JIM SCHENKEIN (1, 57, 155), Department of Sociology, Queens College of the City University of New York, Flushing, New York

W. W. SHARROCK (173), Department of Sociology, University of Manchester, Manchester, England

ROY TURNER (173), Department of Anthropology and Sociology, University of British Columbia, Vancouver, Canada

* Deceased.

Explanation of Transcript Notation

Although contributions have come from many sources, our transcript format is largely the work of Gail Jefferson; over the years, she has developed a system of notation and transcript design intending to produce a reader's transcript—one that will look to the eye how it sounds to the ear. It makes sense to group the symbols by the phenomena they track through the conversation, and to date, we pay particularly close attention to the following:

1. Simultaneous utterances
    Utterances starting up simultaneously are linked together with double left-hand brackets:

    ```
                  TOM:   I used to smoke a lot when I was young
    [[                   [[
                  BOB:   I used to smoke Camels
    ```

2. Overlapping utterances
    When overlapping utterances do not start up simultaneously, the point at which an ongoing utterance is joined by another is marked with a single left-hand bracket, linking an ongoing with an interrupting utterance at the point where overlap begins:

    ```
                  TOM:   I used to smoke a lot
    [                                          [
                  BOB:                         He thinks he's real tough
    ```

The point where overlapping utterances stop overlapping is marked with a single right-hand bracket:

```
                TOM:   I used to smoke a lot more than this
]                                         [     ]
                BOB:                      I see
```

3. Contiguous utterances
    When there is no interval between adjacent utterances, the second being latched immediately to the first (without overlapping it), the utterances are linked together with equal signs:

```
=               TOM:   I used to smoke a lot=
                BOB:   =He thinks he's real tough
```

The equal signs are also used to link different parts of a single speaker's utterance when those parts comprise a continuous flow of speech that have been separated to different lines by transcript design, accommodating an intervening interruption:

```
                TOM:   I used to smoke a lot more than this=
                               [
                BOB:           You used to smoke
                TOM:   =but I never inhaled the smoke
```

Sometimes more than one speaker latches directly on to a just completed utterance, and when this happens, it is marked with a combination of equal signs and double left-hand brackets:

```
                TOM:        I used to smoke a lot=
                BOB:     =[[ He thinks he's tough
=[[             ANN:        So did I
```

When overlapping utterances end simultaneously and are latched onto by a subsequent utterance, this is marked by a single right-handed bracket and equal signs:

```
                TOM:   I used to smoke a lot
]=                                   [    ]=
                BOB:                 I see
                ANN:   =So did I
```

4. Intervals within and between utterances
    When intervals in the stream of talk occur, they are timed in

tenths of a second and inserted within parentheses, either within an utterance:

(0.0)   LIL: When I was (0.6) oh nine or ten

or between utterances:

    HAL: Step right up
       (1.3)
    HAL: I said step right up
       (0.8)
    JOE: Are you talking to me

A short untimed pause within an utterance is indicated by a dash:

–   DEE: Umm – my mother will be right in

Untimed intervals heard between utterances are described within double parentheses and inserted where they occur:

((pause)) REX: Are you ready to order
       ((pause))
    PAM: Yes thank you we are

5. Characteristics of speech delivery
In our transcripts, punctuation is not used to mark conventional grammatical units, but rather, attempts to capture characteristics of speech delivery. For example, a colon indicates an extension of the sound or syllable it follows:

co:lon RON: What ha:ppened to you

and more colons prolong the stretch:

co::lons MAE: I ju::ss can't come
    TIM: I'm so::: sorry re:::ally I am

The other punctuation marks are used as follows:

.   A period indicates a stopping fall in tone, not necessarily the end of a sentence.

,   A comma indicates a continuing intonation, not necessarily between clauses of sentences.

?	A question mark indicates a rising inflection, not necessarily a question.
!	An exclamation point indicates an animated tone, not necessarily an exclamation.
–	A single dash indicates a halting, abrupt cutoff, or, when multiple dashes hyphenate the syllables of a word or connect strings of words, the stream of talk so marked has a stammering quality.

Emphasis is indicated by varieties of italics, the larger the italics, the greater is the relative local stress:

italics	ANN:	It happens to be *mine*
italics	BEN:	It's not either yours it's **mine**
ITALICS	ANN:	*I DON'T KNOW WHY YOU'RE SO HARD ON THIS*

Audible aspirations (hhh) and inhalations (.hhh) are inserted in the speech where they occur:

hhh	PAM:	An thi(hh)s is for you hhh
.hhh	DON:	.hhhh O(hh)h tha(h)nk you rea(hh)lly

Double parentheses are used to enclose a description of some phenomenon the transcriptionist does not want to wrestle with. These can be vocalizations that are not, for example, spelled gracefully or recognizably:

(( ))	TOM:	I used to ((cough)) smoke a lot
	BOB:	((sniffle)) He thinks he's tough
	ANN:	((snorts))

or other details of the conversational scene:

JAN:	This is just delicious
	((telephone rings))
KIM:	I'll get it

or various characterizations of the talk:

RON:	((in falsetto)) I can do it now
MAX:	((whispered)) He'll never do it

6. Transcriptionist doubt
   Other than the timings of intervals and inserted aspirations and
   inhalations, items enclosed within single parentheses are in
   doubt, as in:

   ( )   TED: I ('spose I'm not)
        (BEN): We all (t-   )

   where *spose I'm not*, the identity of the second speaker, and *t–*
   represent different varieties of transcriptionist doubt.

   Sometimes, multiple possibilities are indicated:

   TED: I (spoke to Mark)
            ('spose I'm not)
   BEN: We all try to figure a (tough angle) for it
                                (stuffing girl)

   When single parentheses are empty, no hearing could be
   achieved for the string of talk or item in question:

   TODD: My (   ) catching
   (   ): In the highest (   )

   where the middle of Todd's utterance, the speaker of the subsequent utterance, and the end of the subsequent utterance could
   not be recovered.

7. Other transcript symbols
   The left-hand margin of the transcript is sometimes used to point
   to a feature of interest to the analyst at the time the fragment is
   introduced in the text. Very often the reader is drawn to lines in
   the transcript where the phenomenon of interest occurs by large
   dots (bullets) in the left-hand margin; for example, if the analyst
   had been involved in a discussion of "continuations" and introduced the following fragment,

   ●   DON: I like that blue one very much
       ● SAM: And I'll bet your wife would like it
            DON: If I had the money I'd get one for her
       ● SAM: And one for your mother too I'll bet

   the bullets in the left-hand margin would call attention to Sam's
   utterances as instances of "continuations."

$\uparrow$
$\leftarrow$
$\downarrow$
$\rightarrow$

Other features of the analyst's attention are indicated by a variety of arrows in the left-hand margin, and the analyst will inform the reader of what the arrows specifically call into attention.

. . .

Horizontal ellipses indicate that an utterance is being reported only in part, with additional speech either coming before, in the middle, or after the reported fragment, depending on the location of the ellipses.

Vertical ellipses indicate intervening turns at talking have been taken out of the fragment:

BOB: Well I always say give it your all

.

.

.

BOB: And I always say give it everything

Sketch of an Analytic Mentality for the Study of Conversational Interaction

JIM SCHENKEIN

The studies of conversation in this volume were written more or less independently over the last 5 years in Southern California, in New York and Boston, in British Columbia, and in Manchester, England. I say "more or less" independently because, while each of these separate studies was undertaken without particular regard to the other papers in this collection, they share a number of central methodological commitments and substantive orientations. Although each study examines different features of conversational interaction, and each will be of interest for its own distinctive findings and conceptual models, together they reflect a vigorous research paradigm for the study of natural conversation. Our work, needless to say, is shaped by our commitments, orientations, habits, and more. I would like to offer here a sketch of the analytic mentality governing the collection as a whole.[1]

In the first place, each of these studies is rooted in the close scrutiny of naturally occurring interactions that have been recorded and transcribed. The materials under study were not elicited, remembered, or invented to provide illustration for some analytic design, to exercise some research apparatus, or to examine some prefigured hypotheses. All the materials in this volume are drawn from actual interactions occurring in their natural environments—and that, oddly enough, is kind of a novelty.

The conversational fragments offered for study throughout this volume represent, plainly, the tiniest sample of circumstances in which conversations are found. To begin with, they are all conversations conducted in English, although materials from many regions of North America and England are included here. They are all conversations conducted by persons for whom interactional competency is not obscured by accent, impediment, or other speech distortion, although materials from conversations among adults diagnosed as "mentally retarded" are included here. And they are, for the most part, conversations of the white middle class. Within a phenomenal domain thus limited, however, these studies jointly draw on a wide range of conversational circumstances: There are conversations held over telephones and intercoms; into hidden recorders and open microphones; in living rooms and factories; out of doors and aboard ship; over a meal and under arrest; among strangers, co-workers, intimates, and others; delivering news, conducting business, offering praise, registering complaints, selling insurance, giving instructions, calling the police, telling stories, making excuses, working through therapy, exchanging small talk, and so on. Within obvious limits, it is a highly varied corpus of materials.

To be sure, our analyses are formed by involvement in this particular universe of data. We look directly at varieties of naturally occurring conversational interactions, and our analyses, therefore, are stimulated by attempts to characterize these actual conversational exchanges. In none of these studies are the conversational materials used to bolster, undermine, or perfect any morals, personalities, or politics. In none of these studies is the research conducted by manipulating the natural interactions into scores on some test instrument, codes in some rating scheme, figures in some measurement plan, votes in some judgment exercise, categories in some sorting task, or positions in some scaling device. In none of these studies are the research curiosities satisfied by fine tuning on any erstwhile theory of mankind, society, or communication. Instead, the research in each case has been motivated by taking seriously the details of the natural interactions themselves—and that too, oddly enough, is something of a novelty, particularly for sociologists.

By strict submission to the details of natural conversation, each of these studies is concertedly sensitive to what actually takes place when talk is organized into conversation. For example, since conversation is essentially an interactional activity, our studies necessarily endeavor to offer systematic characterizations of the interaction conducted through conversation; the interactional basis of many of the things people do is taken for granted typically and rarely given rigorous sociological formulation,[2] but in these studies, detailed observations on the interactional unfolding of conversation provide a foundation for the analyses. Since conversation proceeds as speakers arrange their participation through delicately orchestrated sequences of utterances, our studies are necessarily preoccupied with the sequential emergence of conversation; the orderliness of conversational sequences is quite spectacular, and these studies exhibit that orderliness in unprecedented detail. Since conversation is organized through abstract resources and constraints bearing on locally idiosyncratic conversational environments, our studies are necessarily sensitive to the situated fit between abstractly organized structures and the particularities of local context; the descriptions presented here offer promising movement towards an empirically based grammar of natural conversation.

In conducting and reporting these researches on conversation, each of these separate studies makes use of transcripts prepared from audio and/or video recordings of natural interactions. It is, after all, because we can review the recordings and study the transcripts endlessly that we come to see details of conversational organization hidden by real time and ordinary sensibilities. Transcript preparation requires extraordinarily close attention to productional details of the talk under study, and the transcripts and fragments that appear throughout this volume share conventions of design intended to capture and permit access to those details.[3]

Despite other differences in focus or approach, each of these studies is committed to building careful descriptions of the conversational phenomena under investigation. Consider these declarations of topical interest drawn from each chapter:

> Here, on the basis of research using audio recordings of naturally occurring conversations, we attempt to characterize, in its simplest systematic form the organization of turn taking for conversation, and to extract some of the interest that organization has.
>
> —From Sacks, Schegloff, and Jefferson

> After presenting the transcript which will govern our further observations and attentions, I want to coax you into an analytic mentality that aims at describing the systematic procedures with which participants to such encounters can and do juggle their official and abstract identities with informal and personal identities in the course of their ordinary conversation.
>
> —From Schenkein

> A large proportion of compliment responses deviate from the model response of accepting compliments. A close examination of those responses reveals that while rejections are frequent, they are not performed as preferred seconds.

While various sequential features suggest that determination, one indication is that most compliment responses lie somewhere in between (not at the polar extremes of) acceptances and agreements on the one hand and rejections and disagreements on the other.

In this chapter an organization will be described which accounts, in part, for the "in between-ness" of compliment responses.

—FROM POMERANTZ

In the data principally to be focused upon here and in each case presented, there occurs a cluster of two stories and related story commentary, told at separate times by two conversational participants. . . .

The relations displayed between the two stories are not capricious and happenstance, but are instead the products of the conversational participants' attention and careful management. . . .

The study of the various orders of relatedness to be discovered, described, and appreciated presents a fascinating research topic, where often the nature of the relatedness to be discovered functions to render our everyday social intuitions subverted.

—FROM RYAVE

In this chapter we intend to describe and suggest a tentative analysis of some of the ways in which persons talk in a meeting, so as to achieve and sustain the meeting as a social setting. . . .

To this end we shall analyze the following data in order to demonstrate and describe the nature of the recommencement of a meeting as a member's achievement.

—FROM ATKINSON, CUFF, AND LEE

We are, in the end, examining the prospects of a "nonintuitive" analytic mentality for investigating and describing organizational details of conversational interaction, not only thus far undescribed, but thus far unnoticed as resources for conversationalists. . . . We can now take up the organization of conversational interaction around "unexpanded" and "expanded" versions of projected action sequences as a technical accomplishment of conversationalists.

—FROM JEFFERSON AND SCHENKEIN

Under some conditions, tellers can and do find determinate transforms [on their remarks] foreseeable, and engage in interactional work designed to protect their tellings against such metamorphoses. . . . Materials in these calls have been analyzed to display sensitivities that speakers exhibit with respect to structurally founded transformations.

—FROM SHARROCK AND TURNER

Over the course of natural conversational interaction, speakers routinely produce gross shifts in the amplitude level of their successive utterances. There are a range of conversational environments in which the work of such peak amplitude shifts is intuitively apparent. . . .

There may exist another domain in which peak amplitude shifts in speakers' utterances are conversationally organized. An argument will be presented that there exists in conversation an Amplitude Shift Mechanism by which a speaker may mark the relationship of his present utterance to his prior.

—FROM GOLDBERG

This chapter focuses on story beginnings and endings, sketching out two features via which a story can be seen to articulate with turn-by-turn talk: Stories
emerge from turn-by-turn talk, that is, are *locally occasioned* by it, and, upon
their completion, stories re-engage turn-by-turn talk,that is, are *sequentially
implicative* for it.

—FROM JEFFERSON

I'm going to give a presentation that will involve an analysis of a dirty joke,
eventually leading up to a theory of some of the business of dirty jokes.
Roughly, I want to make a case for the dirty joke as a technical object worth
attention.

—FROM SACKS

Across a broad spectrum of topics, each study proposes to describe the
phenomenon of interest. These brief excerpts were chosen to exhibit the
variety of topics brought under descriptive review by the studies gathered
here, so naturally, straightforward commitments to "describing,"
"sketching," "displaying," and "characterizing" will be found in these
topical declarations. But even in these brief excerpts, other features of our
analytic mentality find repeated expression. For instance, there are many
references to the "organization" of conversational phenomena running
through these excerpts (sometimes expressed in terms of the "systematic
form" or "structure" conversational phenomena exhibit as "technical
objects")—these expressions reflect the fact that we are busy describing
the systematic structural form (the "organization") of the various
phenomena we study. There are also several expressions for the "technical accomplishments of member conversationalists" (put in terms of the
"systematic procedures" with which conversationalists transact their
enterprises, the "interactional work" they undertake to have a conversation, and the "speaker sensitivities" they can and do display in their
talk)—these expressions reflect our interest in the artfulness of conversational negotiations. References to the prospects of a "nonintuitive" study
of conversation, and to the interest these "nonintuitive" sensibilities
might have, also appear in these brief excerpts—these expressions reflect
our interest in domains of "organization" and "artfulness" remote from
ordinary sensibilities about interaction or conversation.

In sum, our independent studies of turn taking, identity negotiations,
compliment responses, story clusters, the recommencement of a meeting,
action sequence negotiations, conversational environments for
equivocality, amplitude shifts, story beginnings and endings, and dirty
jokes are all committed to building nonintuitive descriptions of the organization of conversational interaction as the technical accomplishment
of member conversationalists.[4]

This is a collection, then, of more or less independent studies of
conversation that collaborate in several dimensions of policy and proce-

dure. I have come to think of those shared practices as ingredients in an "analytic mentality" since other more familiar terms fail to capture the spectrum of ingredients sketched here. Our particular grouping of shared dispositions is not exactly a "theory" or "method," nor is it merely a "point of view" or some kind of "philosophy." But whatever it is, the result is a research environment for scrutinizing the details of natural conversation; and "analytic mentality" is fuzzy enough to embrace whatever comes up when a closer look at that environment is taken:[5] These studies restrict their corpus of data to naturally occurring interactions; they share materials drawn from a wide range of circumstances in which conversations among the English-speaking, white, middle class take place; they ground their analytic concerns in detailed observations instead of preformed models; they are oriented toward conversation as an essentially interactional activity; they focus on the sequential emergence of turn-by-turn talk; they offer conceptual schemes for characterizing the interface between local context and abstract culture; they employ a standard transcript technology stimulating close attention to the productional details of conversational utterances; they share a commitment to building nonintuitive descriptions of the phenomena under study; and they offer an array of findings on the organization and artfulness of natural conversation.

I hope this introductory sketch illuminates an underlying unity to the separate studies gathered here.

NOTES

[1] This is not the place for an elaborate introduction to the analysis of natural conversation. Some major contours of our research enterprise are outlined here to emphasize a coherence to these separate studies not otherwise readily apparent. A more leisurely introduction to the study of conversational interaction is in the works (Schenkein, forthcoming). Let me also point out that I am never entirely sure of what I mean by an "analytic mentality"—but I will speak more directly about my intentions with it on p. 6.

[2] The work of Erving Goffman (1959, 1961, 1963, 1964, 1967, 1968, 1970, 1971, 1974) stands as an exception to this inattention and has been an important resource for these researches.

[3] A detailed explanation of our transcript notation can be found on pp. xi–xvi.

[4] The work of Harold Garfinkel (1967, 1970, 1972) has influenced these several studies extensively, and the orientations just recited will exhibit our indebtedness quite transparently to those familiar with his work.

[5] Needless to say, an analytic mentality exercised on studies of conversational interaction is not exhausted there. Examples of work undertaken by these authors on topics other than conversation can be found in Ryave and Schenkein (1974), Sacks (1970, 1972b), Sharrock (1974, 1976), and Schenkein (1976a,b, 1977b).

chapter 1

A Simplest Systematics for the Organization of Turn Taking for Conversation*

HARVEY SACKS, EMANUEL A. SCHEGLOFF, AND GAIL JEFFERSON

INTRODUCTION

Turn taking is used for the ordering of moves in games, for allocating political office, for regulating traffic at intersections, for the servicing of customers at business establishments, for talking in interviews, meetings, debates, ceremonies, conversations, etc. (these last being members of the set of what we shall refer to as "speech exchange systems"). It is obviously a prominent type of social organization, one whose instances are implicated in a wide range of other activities. For socially organized activities, the presence of "turns" suggests an economy, with turns for something being valued, and with means for

* This chapter is a variant version of "A Simplest Systematics for the Organization of Turn-Taking for Conversation," which was printed in *Language*, **50**, 4 (1974), pp. 696–735. An earlier version of this paper was presented at the conference on "Sociology of Language and Theory of Speech Acts," held at the Centre for Interdisciplinary Research of the University of Bielefeld, Germany. We thank Dr. Anita Pomerantz and Mr. Richard Faumann for pointing out to us a number of errors in the text.

allocating them affecting their relative distribution, as they do in economies. An investigator interested in the sociology of some sort of activity that is turn organized will want to determine, at the least, the shape of the turn-taking organization's device, and how it affects the distribution of turns for the activities it operates on.

For the investigator of turn-taking systems per se, it is not surprising that there are various ways that turn-taking systems can be workably built. Since they are used to organize sorts of activities that are quite different from one another, it is of particular interest to see whether, how, and how much operating turn-taking systems are characterizable as adapting to properties of the sorts of activities in which they operate. And, once again, an investigator interested in some sort of activity that is organized by a turn-taking system will want to determine whether, how, and how much the sort of activity investigated is adapted to, or constrained by, the particular form of turn-taking system operating on it.

The subject of this report is the turn-taking system for conversation, and the foregoing are among the questions it will be addressed to. Others[1] have noted that the organization of taking turns at talk is one type of organization operative in conversation and have located a range of interesting features and details of that sort of organization. However, no account of the systematics of the organization of turn taking for conversation is yet available. Here, on the basis of research using audio recordings of naturally occurring conversations, we attempt to characterize, in its simplest systematic form, the organization of turn taking for conversation, and to extract some of the interest that organization has.

Aspects of the organization we are calling turn taking have forced themselves on investigators of "small group" behavior, who in addressing problems concerning the distribution of talk among participants in small groups,[2] or the kinds of "acts" that form up sequences in small group sessions,[3] were addressing problems conditioned in central ways by the turn-taking system, although they were not for the most part addressed in that way. Students of "interview" behavior and such two-party conversation as approximates it in form,[4] in concerning themselves with the distribution of talk among the parties, the distribution of silences, the sequences in which the talk shifted from one to another or was retained by a single party and the way such transfer or retention were coordinated were also dealing with questions on which turn taking has a central bearing, but which were only peripherally attacked in turn-taking terms, or were unsatisfactorily accounted for because of weaknesses in the turn-taking models explicitly or implicitly employed. In anthropology, some investigators[5] have explicitly taken note of aspects of turn organization, but the observations were, for the most part, in the service of other interests, for example, stratification and the legal system, and little effort was directed at either gathering or attending materials in sufficient detail to permit appreciation or treatment of turn taking as a central phenomenon in its own right.[6] In all these domains of inquiry, what has attracted investigators' attention has been some particular outcome or product of the operation of turn taking, interpretably relevant to some other problem, but not the organization and operation of the system that allowed or produced such an outcome. Those approaches which have addressed turn taking head on, and with proper appreciation of the depth of its implications and the detailed character of its organization have been largely programmatic or only beginningly empirical; in any case, no systematic account is available.[7]

For the last half dozen years we have been engaged in research, using tape recordings of natural conversation, that has been increasingly directed to extracting, characterizing, and characterizing the interrelationships of, the various types of sequential organization operative in conversation. The disciplinary motivation for such work is sociological.

Our concern with the organization of turn taking has the following base. First, the fact of turn taking and that it must be organized, was something that the data of conversation made increasingly plain: such facts as that one party talks at a time overwhelmingly, though speakers change, though the size of turns varies, though the ordering of turns varies; that transitions seem finely coordinated; that there are obviously techniques for allocating turns that are used and whose characterization would be part of any model that would describe some turn-taking materials; that there are techniques for the construction of utterances relevant to their turn status that bear on the coordination of transfer and on the allocation of speakership; in short, a body of factual material accessible to rather unmotivated inquiry exposed the presence of turn taking and the major facets of its organization. Focusing on facts such as these, rather than on particular outcomes in particular settings, leads to an investigation of the organization of turn taking per se, and not its application and consequences in particular contexts, although the more formal understanding of turn taking illuminates more particular findings.

Reason began to appear for taking seriously the possibility that a characterization of turn-taking organization for conversation could be developed that would have the important twin features of being context-free and also capable of extraordinary context sensitivity.[8]

We look for such a type of organization for the following reasons. First of all, a problem for research on actual conversation is that actual conversation is always "situated," always comes out of, and is part of, some real sets of circumstances of its participants. But there are various reasons why one does not want to have to know or characterize such situations for particular conversations in order to investigate them. And the question then becomes: What might be extracted as ordered phenomena from our conversational materials which would not turn out to require reference to one or another aspect of situatedness, identities, and particularities of content or context.

One reason for expecting the existence of some such type of organization is as follows. Since conversation can accommodate a wide range of situations, since it is a vehicle for interactions in which persons in varieties of identities and varieties of groups of identities are operating, since it is sensitive to the various combinations, and since it is capable of dealing with a change of situation within a situation, there must be some formal apparatus that is itself context-free, that by virtue of the ways in which it is context-free can in local instances of its operations be sensitive to, and exhibit its sensitivity to, various of the parameters of social reality in a local context. Some aspects of the organization of conversation must be expected to have this context-free, context-sensitive status, for, of course, conversation is a vehicle for interaction between parties with any potential identities, and with any potential familiarity. It began to look to us as if the organization of *turn taking* for conversation might be such a thing. That is to say, it appeared to have an appropriate sort of general abstractness and local particularization potential.

In sum, turn taking seemed a basic form of organization for conversation in this sense of basic, that it would be invariant to parties such that whatever variations the parties brought to bear in the conversation would be accommodated without change in the system, and that it could be selectively and locally affected by such social aspects of context. Depiction of an organization for turn taking should fit the facts of variability by virtue of a design that allowed it to be context-sensitive, but should be cast in a manner that requires no reference to any particular context, and nonetheless captures the most important general properties of conversation.

A model, to merit serious consideration, would, it seems to us, have to be capable of accommodating (that is, either be compatible with, or allow the derivation of) the following facts, which seemed grossly apparent to relatively unmotivated examination of conversational materials.[9] In any conversation:[10]

1. Speaker change recurs, or, at least, occurs (cf. p. 15).
2. Overwhelmingly, one party talks at a time (cf. p. 15).

3. Occurrences of more than one speaker at a time are common, but brief (cf. pp. 15–17).
4. Transitions from one turn to a next with no gap and no overlap between them are common. Together with transitions characterized by slight gap or slight overlap, they make up the vast majority of transitions (cf. p. 18).
5. Turn order is not fixed, but varies (cf. pp. 18–19).
6. Turn size is not fixed, but varies (cf. pp. 19–20).
7. Length of conversation is not fixed, specified in advance (cf. p. 20).
8. What parties say is not fixed, specified in advance (cf. pp. 20–21).
9. Relative distribution of turns is not fixed, specified in advance (cf. pp. 21–22).
10. Number of parties can change (cf. pp. 22–25).
11. Talk can be continuous or discontinuous (cf. pp. 25–27).
12. Turn-allocation techniques are obviously used. A current speaker may select a next speaker (as when a current speaker addresses a question to another party); parties may self-select, in starting to talk (cf. pp. 27–33).
13. Various "turn-constructional units" are employed. Turns can be projectedly "one word long," or, for example, they can be sentential in length (cf. pp. 33–38).
14. Repair mechanisms for dealing with turn-taking errors and violations obviously are available for use. For example, if two parties find themselves talking at the same time, one of them will stop prematurely, thus repairing the trouble (cf. pp. 39–40).

With the aim of at least exposing the interest of this area, we shall here offer and consider such a simplest systematics for the organization of turn taking in conversation as does come to terms with the above list.[11] It having been offered, we shall then proceed to show how it deals with the obvious facts, with others that are rather finer, and thereafter proceed to consider its structure and import. With regard to its import, we offer two comments now on the potential interest of some such model: (a) When such facts as those listed above are compared with such as obtain for various of the other speech-exchange systems, such as meetings, interviews, debates, or ceremonies, differences are readily noted. The size of turns and the ordering of turns, in debates, for example, are obviously prespecified. Those differences suggest that different turn-taking systems are involved. Conversation obviously occupies a central position among the speech exchange systems. Perhaps its turn-taking system is more or less explanatory of that centrality. (*b*) Turns are valued, sought, and avoided. The social organization of turn taking distributes turns among parties. It must, at least partially, be shaped as an economy. As such, it is expectable that, as other economies do, its organization affects the relative distribution of that whose distribution it organizes. Until we unravel its organization, we shall not know in what those effects consist and where they will turn up. But, as all sorts of scientific and applied research use conversation now, they all employ an instrument whose effects are not known. This is perhaps unnecessary.

A SIMPLEST SYSTEMATICS FOR THE TURN-TAKING ORGANIZATION OF CONVERSATION

The turn-taking system for conversation can be described in terms of two components and a set of rules.

Component 1—Turn-Constructional Component

There are various unit-types with which a speaker may set out to construct a turn. Unit-types for English include sentential, clausal, phrasal, and lexical constructions.[12] Instances of the unit-types so usable allow a projection of the unit-type under way, and what, roughly, it will take for an instance of that unit-type to be completed.[13] Unit-types that lack the feature of projectability may not be usable in the same way.

For the unit-types a speaker employs in starting the construction of a turn's talk, the speaker is initially entitled, in having a "turn," to one such unit. The first possible completion of a first such unit constitutes an initial transition-relevance place. Transfer of speakership is coordinated by reference to such transition-relevance places, which any unit-type instance will reach.

Component 2—Turn-Allocational Component

Turn-allocational techniques are distributed into two groups: (*a*) those in which next turn is allocated by current speaker selecting a next speaker; and (*b*) those in which a next turn is allocated by self-selection.[14]

Rules

The following seems to be a basic set of rules governing turn construction, providing for the allocation of a next turn to one party, and coordinating transfer so as to minimize gap and overlap. For any turn:

    1. At initial turn-constructional unit's initial transition-relevance place:

(a) If the turn-so-far is so constructed as to involve the use of a "current speaker selects next" technique, then the party so selected has rights, and is obliged, to take next turn to speak, and no others have such rights or obligations, transfer occurring at that place.

(b) If the turn-so-far is so constructed as not to involve the use of a "current speaker selects next" technique, self-selection for next speakership may, but need not, be instituted, with first starter acquiring rights to a turn, transfer occurring at that place.

(c) If the turn-so-far is so constructed as not to involve the use of a "current speaker selects next" technique, then current speaker may, but need not, continue, unless another self-selects.[15]

    2. If, at initial turn-constructional unit's initial transition-relevance place, neither 1(a) nor 1(b) has operated, and, following the provision of 1(c), current speaker has continued, then the Rule-set (a)–(c) reapplies at next transition-relevance place, and recursively at each next transition-relevance place, until transfer is effected.

The ordering of the rules serves to constrain each of the options the rules provide. The fact that 1(a) is the first applying rule does not entail that its option is free of constraints imposed on it by the presence, in the set, of rules which *would* apply if 1(a) did not. Thus, for example, given the applicability of Rule 1(b)'s option if Rule 1(a)'s option has not been employed, for Rule 1(a)'s option to be methodically assured of use it needs to be employed before initial unit's initial transition-relevance place. Thereby, the operation of Rule 1(a)'s option is constrained by Rule 1(b)'s presence in the set, independent of Rule 1(b)'s option actually being employed. Similarly, for Rule 1(b)'s option to be methodically assured of application given the presence in the set of Rule 1(c), it will need to be employed at initial unit's initial transition-relevance place, and before current speaker's option to continue—Rule 1(c)—is invoked. For if 1(c) is thus invoked, Rule 2 will apply, and the Rule-set (a)–(c) will reapply, and Rule 1(a)'s option will take priority over Rule 1(b)'s again. Thereby, Rule 1(b)'s operation is constrained by Rule 1(c)'s presence in the set, independent of Rule 1(c)'s actually being employed. Having noted that lower priority rules thus constrain the use of higher priority options, it should be recalled that the constraints imposed on lower priority rules by higher priority rules are incorporated in the rule-set itself.

    The rules provide an ordering of the application of the technique groups (i.e., the two groups of turn-allocational techniques) that makes the inclusion of the two types of techniques in the rule-set compatible with "one speaker at a time," obviating a violative potential of their joint inclusion were they not ordered. If the technique groups were not ordered, if, for example, both were usable on any occasion on which one was usable, then the very techniques whose operation should yield only one next speaker would provide the possibility of more than one party being selected. That possibility would be provided because each type of technique involves a different party using it, and unless the party doing self-selection were the same party being selected by current speaker, more than one next speaker will have been selected. The rule-set's ordering of the application of the techniques removes this possibility. Furthermore, the "first starter has rights" provision of Rule 1(b) provides an ordering within the possibilities provided by that technique group addressed to the possibility of multiple self-selection that technique opens up.

Minimization of gap and overlap may be seen to be accomplished in two ways, one of which localizes the problem, the other of which addresses it in its localized forms. The rule-set, and the constraints provided on each option in it by the others, cleanses the bulk of conversation of gap and overlap by cleansing the bulk of single turns of gap and overlap. The rules provide for turn transfers occurring at transition-relevance places, wherever the allocational technique's use has been constructionally accomplished. Thus, "current speaker selects next" techniques may be constructionally accomplished at the very beginning of the unit-type employed in a turn (e.g., by the use of an address term for certain unit-types), but the accomplishment of turn transfer does not occur until the first possible transition-relevance place. Since the use of self-selection techniques is contingent on the nonuse of "current selects next" techniques, and those may be done at any point up to the first transition-relevance place, self-selection may not be done (the technique selected or the transfer attempted) until the first transition-relevance place, and since current speaker may continue—Rule 1(c)—if self-selection is not done, thus recycling the rules, self-selection, to be assured, must be done *at* the transition-relevance place.[16] The turn-taking rule-set thus provides for the localization of gap and overlap possibilities at transition-relevance places and their immediate environment, cleansing the rest of a turn's "space" of systematic bases for their possibility.

HOW THE SYSTEM ACCOUNTS FOR THE FACTS

In this section, we bring the system just described to bear on the initially noted, grossly apparent facts to find how the model either produces or is compatible with them. As well, a variety of other, not so readily apparent, findings that attend the model will be examined.

1. Speaker change overwhelmingly *re*curs and at least occurs. This turn-taking system provides a systematic basis for speaker change and speaker change recurrence, while not making them automatic. The possibility of speaker change is built in, recurrently within any single turn's construction, and recurrently for each new turn, because any unit-type instance out of which a turn may be constructed will reach a transition-relevance place, at which the first two priority options involve transfer of turn to a next speaker. Speaker change and speaker change recurrence are not automatic because at each transition-relevance place, the options provided by Rules 1(a) and 1(b) may not be exercised, while the option provided by Rule 1(c) is. For as long as this combination is applied at each encountered transition-relevance place, there will be a sequence in which there is no speaker change. Speaker change *oc*currence is a special case of speaker change *re*currence, being a restriction too complicated to be dealt with here.[17]

2. Overwhelmingly one party talks at a time. This fact is provided for by two features of the system. (*a*) The system allocates *single* turns to *single* speakers, any speaker getting, with the turn, exclusive rights to talk to first possible completion of an initial instance of a unit-type, rights that are renewable for single next instances of a unit-type under the operation of Rule 1(c). (*b*) All turn transfer is coordinated around transition-relevance places, which are themselves determined by possible completion points for instances of the unit-types.

3. Occurrences of more than one at a time are common, but brief. We have already discussed how the rule-set localizes occurrences of overlap. We turn here to the systematic bases for their occurrence and for their briefness.

One obvious source of their briefness is that they occur at transition-relevance places, that is, places where current speakers can or should exit, their exiting removing a constitutive component of the overlap.

There are a number of systematic bases for the occurrence of overlap, of which we can mention only a few.

A. Rule 1(b) in allocating a turn to that self-selector who starts first encourages earliest possible start, and encourages it for each self-selector. It thereby provides for overlap by competing self-selectors for a next turn, when each projects his start to be earliest possible start at some possible transition-relevance place—the case of simultaneous starts.

Data 1–3

[Labov:Battersea:A:7]

PARKY:	*Oo what* they call them dogs that pull the (1)
	sleighs.
	(0.5)

PARKY: S–sledge dogs.
                   (0.7)

OLD MAN: Oh uh :: uh
                        [
● TOURIST: Uh–*Hus*kies.=
● OLD MAN: Huskies. Mm,
                   =[[
● PARKY: *Hus*kies. Yeh Huskies.

[Labov *et al.*:Travel Agency:2]
    LIL: Bertha's lost, on *our* scale, about fourteen   (2)
                   pounds.
    DAMORA: Oh::no::.
                        [
● JEAN: *Twelve* pounds I think wasn't it.=
● DAISY: Can you be*lieve* it?
                   =[[
● LIL: *Twelve* pounds on the Weight Watcher's
                   scale.

[Frankel:67]
● MIKE: I know who d'guy is.=   (3)
● VIC: He's ba::d.
                   =[[
● JAMES: You know the gu:y?

It is notable that such simultaneous starts testify to the independent-for-
each-party projectability of possible completion points of the talk that
occupies current turn.

    B. Another basis of overlap derives from the projectability of possi-
ble completion or transition-relevance places. Variation in the articulation
of the projected last part of a projectably last component of a turn's talk,
which is in fact a consequential locus of articulatory variation, will expectably produce overlap between a current turn and a next.

Data 4–8

[Crandall:2-15-68:93]
    A: Well if you knew my argument why did you   (4)
                   bother to a: sk.
                        [
    B: Because I'd like to defend *my*
                   argument.

[Civil Defense Headquarters.2:88]

B: Well it wasn't me :: (5)
              [
A: No, but you know who it
was.

[NB:I:6:7]

A: Sixty two feet is pretty good si: ze. (6)
               [
            Oh:: boy.

[GTS:1:2:24]

A: Terr::*i*fi:: c. (7)
           [
B: I think it's much better than about
a:: black 'n white *nuns* going down stai:rs.

[GTS:1:2:28]

A: So yer not a Pontiac People any- (8)
mo(hh) re.
        [
B: They're gonna hit you with a bi:::ll,

The addition of such optional elements that can specifically go after first possible completion without intending continuation (e.g., address terms, etiquette terms) will be productive of similarly structured overlaps (and their absence, for that matter, can be productive of similarly structured gaps).[18]

Data 9–11

[NB:III:3:5]

A: Uh *you* been down here before havenche. (9)
                        [
B: Yeh.

[Trio:II:12]

P: Yeh alright dear (10)
         [
J: Okay

[FD:IV:35]

A: What's yer name again please sir, (11)
                    [
B: F. T. Gallo-
way.

4. Transitions from one turn to a next with no gap and no overlap are common. Together with transitions characterized by slight gap or slight overlap, they make up the vast majority of transitions. The components and the rule-set, in organizing transfer exclusively around transition-relevance places, provide for the possibility of no gap—no overlap transitions. We have described some structural bases for the occurrence of some gap, and some overlap, bases that also provide for such gap or overlap being slight, and bases that are consequences of the very rule set that otherwise secures no gap—no overlap transitions.[19]

5. Turn order is not fixed, but varies. This fact is produced by the system via a combination of two of its features: (a) single turns are allocated at a time; and (b) for each such allocation, a series of options are provided, each of which can provide for different next speakers. Thereby, ordering of speakers, being locally (i.e., turn by turn) controlled, can vary.

We can add to the initial observation that, while turn order varies, it does not vary randomly. For example, one bias that is particularly important is for speaker just prior to current speaker to be selected as next speaker.

Data 12

[From GTS:2:2:70]

●	ROGER:	((To Jim)) Are you just agreeing because you (12) feel you wanna uh
●	JIM:	Hm?
●	ROGER:	You just agreeing?
●	JIM:	What the hell's *that*.
	AL:	It's– Agree ing?
		[
●	ROGER:	Agreeing.
●	JIM:	A*gree*::n.
●	ROGER:	Yeah.
	AL:	With us. Just going along with us.
●	JIM:	No.
●	ROGER:	Saying "yes, yes" hehheh hh hehhh hh heh-heh hh
		[
●	JIM:	Well, i–i–it's–it–s true. Everything he sai(h)d is *true*, so

Roger as last and next for Jim, and Jim as last and next for Roger work across this whole sequence, with Al's first entry not coming off as the effective turn, and his second being initially shaped as an addition to another's turn. See also Data (ix), (p. 52) and (14).

The sources of this bias are external to the turn-taking system's basic organization and cannot be detailed here.[20] What *is* to be noted here is that the rule-set allows such a bias to operate, via the ordering of the options that make up the rule-set. It is the priority of the "current speaker selects next" option that allows the bias to occur.

An importance of the bias is this. Because of it, the possibility of "colloquy" is systematically provided, that involving, in the first instance, the possibility of local (i.e., turn-by-turn) monitoring for hearing, understanding, agreement, and so forth. It is, indeed, directly after any turn that dealing with problems of hearing, understanding, for example, concerning it are preferably raised, their means of being raised involving the selection of the last speaker to be next, to repeat, clarify, and so on.[21]

6. Turn size is not fixed, but varies. The variability of turn size has its grossest sources in two features of the system we have described: (*a*) The availability of a range of unit-types out of which turns may initially be constructed (a range that varies on the parameter of length), and the availability to a current speaker of free selection among them, provides that for a set of turns, each of which will have contained but the single unit to which a speaker is initially entitled by virtue of having a turn, the turns in the set may have varying turn sizes.[22] In this regard, sentential constructions are the most interesting of the unit-types because of the internally generated expansions of length they allow, and, in particular, allow *before* first possible completion places.

Data 13

[GTS:2]

KEN: I still say though that– if you take if you take   (13)
uh a big fancy car out on the road and you're
hotroddin around, you're– you're bound to
get– you're bound to get caught, and you're
bound to get shafted.
(For short, single-sentence turns, cf. Data [ii]
and [x].)

Thus, sentential constructions alone do provide for turn-size variability.

It is in terms of this expandability property of sentential construction before first possible completion that the "projectable completion" feature of Component 1 of the turn-taking system is to be understood. Sentential constructions are capable of being analyzed, in the course of their production by a party/hearer able to use such analyses to project their possible directions and completion locii. In the course of its construction, any sentential unit will rapidly (in conversation) reveal projectable directions and conclusions, which its further course can modify, but will further define.[23]

(b) A second, and additional, source for turn-size variation is this. Rule 1(c) provides for the possibility that any current speaker may get a chance to produce more than a single instance of a unit-type—cf. Data (xiii). The possibility of Rule 1(c)'s operation means that the system does not define maximum turn size, while the turn-constructional component does determine minimal turn size. Rule 1(a) providing any current speaker with a turn-termination technique usable at any transition-relevance place, the variability of turn size is systematically provided for by this route, independent of the aforementioned one.

Together, these two sources provide for a considerable range of variability in turn size.

7. Length of conversation is not specified in advance. The turn-taking system itself says nothing directly about length of conversation or closing conversation. It does, however, put constraints on how any rules, or system of rules, for achieving conversational closing, and thus length, could operate. For example, by virtue of Rule 1(a), ending ought not, and rarely does, occur after a turn in which a "current speaker selects next" technique has been used.

Length of conversation (or closing conversation) is governed by other kinds of organization than the turn-taking system. One such organization has already been described elsewhere;[24] about it we can note that the close of conversation, and therefore its length, are generated in a manner internal to its developing course (as turn length has been earlier described as having its eventual length determined internally, in the course of its development). Not all conversational activity for which the turn-taking system is relevant occurs in instances of the unit "a single conversation" for which that closing structure is relevant. The turn-taking system is, in the first instance, a system for "sequences of talk." There is an order of organization for "types of sequences," by reference to which length of conversation for units of that sort may be determined. The turn-taking system itself is compatible with varying lengths, and does not pre-fix any length.

8. What parties say is not fixed or specified in advance. In ceremonies, what is said by the participants in it may be specified in advance to any degree desired. In debates, the order in which the participants talk is directly related to the character of what they are to say, the parties being characterizable as "pro" and "con," and the turns in which they

talk as, for example, "rebuttal" and "counterrebuttal." The turns an "interview system" organizes alternatingly are "questions" and "answers." In these and other speech-exchange systems, the turn-taking organization employs, as part of its resources, the grosser or finer prespecification of what shall be done in the turns it organizes.

By contrast with these other speech-exchange systems, the turn-taking organization for conversation makes no provision for the content of any turn, nor does it constrain what is (to be) done in any turn. Neither the components nor the rule-set includes features that bear on this matter. That is not to say that there are no constraints on what may be done in any turn, for that is clearly not the case. "First turns" in a structurally characterizable set of circumstances properly take "greetings," and "next turns" can in a variety of closely describable ways be constrained by "prior turns." We note only that in conversation such constraints are organized by systems external to the turn-taking system. One aspect of conversation's flexibility is a direct and important consequence of this feature of its turn-taking organization: Its turn-taking organization and thus conversational activity per se operate independent of various characterizations of what occupies its turns, the "topic(s)" in them.

As with other of the points we have made about variance, the nonfixedness of what parties say should be modified by noting a bias operative in it. The group of allocation techniques we have called "current speaker selects next" cannot be done by any utterance, or any utterance-type whatsoever. Rather, there is a set of utterance-types—adjacency pair first parts[25]—that can be used to accomplish such a selection, and in being constrained to employ one of those, there are constraints on what a party can say. But note: (a) No party is constrained in any turn to use a "current speaker selects next technique"; and (b) any party interested in doing so has a considerably sized set of utterance-types to choose from, each of which may accomplish the selection. And while a party selected by the use of such a technique will be constrained in what he says in the turn so allocated (e.g., being under some constraints to "answer" if the technique employed to select him was "question"), these constraints are given by the organization of the "types of sequences"[26] whose first parts serve as the "current speaker selects next" techniques, and not by the turn-taking system per se. That the conversational turn-taking system does not constrain what occupies its turns, frees the turns for use by other systems, those systems' components then being subject to the organizational contingencies of the turns that they occupy.

9. Relative distribution of turns is not fixed, but varies. The rule-set maximizes the set "potential next speakers." That is: Rule 1(a) allows current speaker to select any other party as next speaker; Rule 1(b) allows

any party other than current speaker to self-select as next speaker. The combination provides alternative routes whereby any current nonspeaker can be next speaker, and is thus potential next speaker. Furthermore, Rule 1(c) has the consequence of not excluding even current speaker from next speakership, except that the system permits the treatment of the use of that option as a within-turn event, it counting not as an instance of a turn allocation to a same speaker, but as an increment to turn size. Since the rule-set operates at each transition-relevance place, and at each such place any party to the conversation can speak next, the rule-set provides for the possibility of any distribution of turns overall, and thereby frees turn distribution for manipulation by such interests as can be realized with the distribution of turns.[27]

As relative distribution of turns is the cumulative outcome, at any current point in a conversation, of the determinations of turn order done turn-by-turn, the biases operative in turn-order determination, one of which was noted earlier (point 5), may issue in skewings intrinsic to the turn-taking system, in the overall distribution of turns to any point.

10. The number of parties to a conversation can change. Conversation can take different numbers of parties. The turn-taking system provides for that in a manner similar to that by which it provides for conversation of varying lengths. As it is built to organize but two turns at a time, current and next, and the transition from the one to the other, and does not restrict the number of such "current and nexts" it can serially organize, so it organizes but two speakers at a time, "current and next," and is not overtly directed to the size of the pool from which current and next are selected. In not providing for number of speakers beyond current and next, the system is compatible with different numbers of participants from conversation to conversation. Further, in being compatible with differing numbers of participants, it is compatible with varying numbers of participants within any single conversation, since there are mechanisms for entry of new participants and exit for current participants (though we will not describe them here).

While the turn-taking system does not require restrictions on the number of parties to a conversation it organizes, and number of participants can, therefore, vary between conversations and within any conversation, the system favors, by virtue of its design, smaller numbers of participants. This is related, most centrally, to the bias operative on mechanisms of turn ordering, discussed in point 5. Most simply put: The rule-set refers to only two speakers, "current" and "next," and the turn-order bias, when it operates selects "just prior to current" to be "next." In two-party conversation, the two speakers the rule-set refers to, and for whom the turn-order bias works, comprise all the parties to the conversation, and it is not in point to speak of a turn-order "bias." The "last as next" bias, however, remains invariant over increases in the number of parties, and with each additional increment in number of parties tends to progressively concentrate the distribution of turns among a subset of the potential next speakers. With three parties, one might be "left out" were the bias to operate stringently; with four parties, two would be "left out," and so on.

It can be noted that some of the variabilities we have been discussing are connected (as, for example, in the preceding, number of parties and turn order) and have a range of differential relevancies, whose partial ordering we may illustrate by reference to the "number of parties" parameter.

So, for example: For two parties, the relevant variability is not differential distribution of turns (given that they will have alternating turns), but differential turn size.

With three parties, differential distribution of turns becomes relevant. While turn size remains relevant, a bias toward smaller turn size is introduced. With the introduction of a third party, "next turn" is no longer guaranteed to (or obliged for) any current nonspeaker. While in two-party conversation, a current nonspeaker can pass any given transition-relevance place that is nonobligatory (i.e., where "current selects next" technique has not been used) with full assurance of being "next speaker" at some point, with three or more parties this is not assured. Should a current nonspeaker interested in speaking next not self-select at a next transition-relevance place, then some other current nonspeaker might self-select, and in his turn select someone else, and so forth; or, current speaker might continue, and in his continuation select some other current nonspeaker, for example. Therefore, a current nonspeaker interested in speaking next will be under constraint to self-select at first possible transition point, and each successive such point. Furthermore, a current speaker interested in choosing among potential next speakers will be under constraint to accomplish the selection before first possible transition place (at which transition-relevance place transfer then occurs, via Rule 1[a]), lest an undesired current nonspeaker self-select at that point. From both directions, then, there will be a pressure for minimization of turn size, distinctively operative with three or more parties.

With four parties, a type of variability we have not so far considered is introduced: that is, variability in the number of turn-taking systems in operation. There are mechanisms for the schism of one conversation into more than one conversation. Those mechanisms can operate when at least four parties are present, since then there are enough parties for two conversations. With four parties, then, schism is a systematic possibility. We earlier noted that the turn order bias of "last speaker being next speaker" becomes a relative distributional bias with three or more parties. With four or more parties, a possible check on it is introduced by the possibility of schism. If there is an interest in retaining, in a single conversation, some current complement of parties (where there are at least four), then the turn-taking system's means for realizing that effort involve "spreading turns around," because any pair of parties not getting or taking a turn over some sequence of turns can find their mutual accessibility for getting into a second conversation.

Data 14

[From Schenkein:II:13—drastically simplified version]
Ethel, Ben, and Max are visiting Bill and Lori. They've brought a lot of food, including a salami Max took out of his refrigerator. Ben is wearing his new combination eyeglasses/hearing aid. At this point, Lori is offering drinks.

ETHEL:	I'll take Scotch, if you have it,	(14)
● BEN:	You're gonna have to quit yelling, you see,	
ETHEL:	Oh lookit his *ear!*	
	[[	
● LORI:	Oh that's *right.* You got– I know I noticed when he came in.	
● BEN:	Did you notice it?	
● LORI:	Yeah how do you like it.	
● BEN:	It's *fan*tastic.	
ETHEL:	Except the thing presses into his head.	
● BEN:	It–it hurts me terrible I have to go down and get it adjusted.	
● LORI:	Yeah.	
● BEN:	It kills me right here.	
● LORI:	It's,	
● BEN:	The glasses are tight I *feel* it.	

LORI:	What happens if somebody else puts it on,	MAX:	Is the salami dry?
		MAX:	Bill,
BEN:	Nothin,	MAX:	Did it get dry?
LORI:	Will I hear it?	BILL:	A *li*ttle bit,
LORI:	Will I *hear* it?	BILL:	But it's good that way.
BEN:	You gotta put this inside the *ear.*	BILL:	(Because) all the fat evaporates.

LORI: And then will it be
real loud?
BEN: Well, *yeah*. Probably
will be because you're–   ETHEL: Y'know *we* had–
LORI: It won't be *too* loud,   ETHEL: *We* knew somebody who
BEN: Well *I* could adjust the   used to hang–
*vol*ume, I have it,   ETHEL: hang it–
BEN: *I* have it down almost   ETHEL: leave it out*side*
all the way.   all the time
LORI: Okay   ETHEL: so it *would* dry out
BEN: Yeah. Because see I   ETHEL: The fat would dry
have *per*fect *hear*ing   all out.
in *this* ear.

In that regard, an interest in retaining the full complement of parties encourages a distribution of turns different than that which would be the distributional product of the turn-order bias.

It should be noted that the schism possibility introduced by a fourth party can serve as a check on turn distribution introduced by a third party, just as the turn distribution introduced by a third party serves as a check on turn size mechanisms operative for two parties.

It should also be noted that the schism possibility's service as a "check" on turn distribution is equivocal, for turn distribution can, by the same measure, be used as a means by some parties for encouraging schism by others.

11. Conversation can be continuous or discontinuous. Talk is continuous when, for a sequence of transition-relevance places, talk continues (by another or by a same speaker continuing) across a transition-relevance place, with a minimization of gap and overlap. Discontinuities occur when at some transition-relevance place,[28] a current speaker having stopped, no speaker starts (or continues), the ensuing space of nontalk constituting itself as more than a gap; not a gap, but a lapse.

Data 15

[C-J:2]
J: Oh I could drive if you want me to.   (15)
C: Well no I'll drive (I don' m in')
                                          [
J: hhh
              (1.0)
J: I meant to *off*ahh.
●   (16.0)

J: Those shoes look nice when you keep on put-
             ting stuff on 'em.
C: Yeah I 'ave to get another can cuz cuz it
             ran out. I mean it's a lmost(h) ou(h) t=
                                [   ]
J: Oh:::   ah he
             •hh heh=
C: =yeah well it cleans 'em and keeps
             'em clean.
             [
J: Yeah right=
C: =I should get a brush too and *you* should
             getta brush 'n you=
                        [
J: Yeah suh::
C: =should fix your hiking bo ots
                                     [
J: my hiking boots=
C: =which you were gonna do this weekend.
J: Pooh, did I have time this wk– well::
C: Ahh c'mon=
J: =wh'n we get– (uh::kay), I haven't even sat
             down to do any– y'know like •hh today I'm
             gonna sit down 'n read while you're doing yur
             coat,
                   (0.7)
J: do yur– hood.
C: Yehhh=
J: =(ok)
                   (2.0)
J: I haven't *not* done *any*thing the whole
             *week*end.
C: (okay)
•   (14.0)
J: Dass a rilly nice swe::der, (•hh) 'at's my favo-
             rite sweater on you, it's the only one that
             looks right on you.
C: mm huh.
•   (90.0)

That talk can be continuous is provided for in the rules by each option
providing some procedure whereby some next speaker can be located at

any transition-relevance place. The exercise of any option to talk, in the ordered fashion in which they become available, at each transition-relevance place yields a sequence of continuous talk. Each of the rules, however, providing an *option* (and the last of the ordered set of rules, in particular, providing an option, rather than, for example, a backstop, providing a speaker, should no other option have provided one), the possibility of discontinuity is also given. At any transition place at which none of the options to speak has been employed, the possibility of a lapse, and thus discontinuous talk, arises.

A variety of constraints may operate on the possible placement of lapses. An important one is given by the turn-taking system itself. If the Rule 1(a) is employed in a turn's talk, in selecting a next speaker to talk upon its possible completion, no lapse can properly occur; that is, a silence after a turn in which a next has been selected will be heard not as a lapse's possible beginning, not as a gap, but as a pause before the selected next speaker's turn beginning. We are saying: Among the means used for reducing gap are classificatory decisions that seem themselves orderly with respect to the alternative applicability of "gap," "pause," and "lapse" as ways of conceiving the appearance of silence in a conversation.[29]

If Rule 1(a) has been employed in a current turn's talk, then, a lapse is ruled out as a possibility immediately following it. A lapse occurs when Rule 1(a) has not been employed, by a recycling of the options provided by Rules 1(b) and 1(c). That is, Rule 1(a) not having been employed, next turn is available to a self-selecting next speaker. Should no one self-select, then current speaker may self-select to continue (in his continuation possibly applying Rule 1[a]). Should current speaker not self-select to continue, Rule 1(a) remains not in operation, and there is further space—another round—available for self-selection, and in the absence of self-selection by another, self-selection by current speaker to continue. That is, a series of rounds of possible self-selection by others and self-selection by current to continue—Rules 1(b) and 1(c)—may develop, in none of which are options to talk exercised, with the thereby constituted development of a lapse in the conversation.[30]

12. Turn-allocation techniques.[31] An initial observation that next-speaker selection techniques operate in conversation can be made from "obvious cases," such as an addressed question selecting its addressee to speak next, or that in starting to speak when not selected, a party selects himself to speak.[32] Those obvious cases can suggest two consequences to begin with: (*a*) Obvious cases having suggested that there are selection techniques in operation, there is warrant for searching out techniques that are less obvious, but expectably used; (*b*) the obvious cases suggest that

the techniques may be grouped, and suggest a kind of grouping, which can organize the search for other techniques.

There are, indeed, other allocation techniques, and they do, indeed, appear to be grouped as "current selects next" and "self-selection." The most we can do here is to briefly describe several techniques from each group, so as to suggest that the groups indeed have more than a member each, and that they naturally fall into groups so differentiated.

A. The "obvious" case of an addressed question is but a special case of a class of utterance types, or "type of sequence" parts, which share the property of possibly selecting next speaker. That is, "question" is one instance of the first part of a sequential unit elsewhere termed[33] "adjacency pairs." That class of units includes as well such sequences as "greeting–greeting," "invitation acceptance/decline," and so on.

Data 16–19

[GTS:1] Complaint/denial

| KEN: | Hey yuh took my chair by the way an' I don't think that was very nice. | (16) |
| AL: | *I* didn' take yer chair, it's *my* chair. | |

[FN] Compliment/rejection

| A: | I'm glad I have you for a friend. | (17) |
| B: | That's because you don't have any others. | |

[   ] Challenge/rejection

| A: | It's not break time yet. | (18) |
| B: | I finished my box, so shut up. | |

[Barker & Wright, 1951] Request/grant   (19)

7:19 Raymond sat back in his chair. He was nearly finished with his breakfast. He said in a slightly complaining tone, "Mommie, I don't want this other piece of toast." His mother said casually, "You don't? Well, O.K., I guess you don't have to eat it." He finished eating his breakfast [p. 23].

See as well, Data (viii) for offer/accept and offer/reject, (ix) et passim for question/answer, (15) for offer/reject, two compliment/accepts, and others throughout the data in this paper, Goldberg (1977) on instruct/receipt and the papers cited in note 26 for others.

Some features of this class of units have been described elsewhere, and others will be described in later reports. Their first components can be termed "first pair-parts"; first pair-parts set constraints on what should be done in a next turn (e.g., a "question" making "answer" specially relevant for next turn); they do not by themselves allocate next turn to some candidate next speaker. They are, nonetheless, the basic component for selecting next speaker. For it is primarily by affiliation to a first pair-part that the most apparently effective device for selecting next speaker—addressing someone—in fact works.[34] Thus, an important, perhaps the central, general technique whereby current speaker selects next, involves the affiliating of an address term (or some other device for achieving "addressing," e.g., gaze direction) to a first pair-part.[35] That technique will select the addressed party as next speaker. But addressing a party per se will not necessarily select him as next speaker. Thus, addressing a question to a party selects that party as next speaker; but, when that party speaks next, and addresses an answer (a second pair-part) to prior speaker, the addressee is not necessarily selected as next speaker. For example,

Data 20–21

[SN-4:3]

SHARON:	You didn' come tuh talk tuh Karen?	(20)
MARK:	No, Karen– Karen' I 're having a fight,	
	(0.4)	
MARK:	after she went out with Keith an' not with (me).	
● RUTHIE:	hah hah hah hah	
● KAREN:	Wul Mark, you never asked me out.	

[Toni-6:372-380]

S:	Oscar did you work for somebody before you worked for Zappa?	(21)
O:	Yeh, many many.	
	(3.0)	
	Canned Heat for a year.	
S:	Didya?	
O:	Poco for a year.	
● T:	ooh when they were good?	
O:	Bangor Flunt Madura fer a y– couple years	
T:	Bangor Flunt Madura?	
O:	Bangor Flying Circus.	
● J:	Oh: yeh I remember Bangor Flying Circus	
	[	

and the data cited in note 35. In each case, note that the speaker after an answer is not the questioner to whom the answer was addressed, although in Data (21) there are also sequences in which the questioner goes again after the answer.

B. One variant of the use of the first pair-part to select a next speaker will accomplish a next-speaker selection without addressing or any such other related technique, but will select only a particular other as next speaker. That variant is a variant of the "question," a type of first pair-part, such as repetitions of parts of a prior utterance with "question" intonation,[36] a variety of "one-word questions," for example, "what?" "who?" and other "repair techniques."

Data 22

[Schenkein:II:38]

BEN:	They gotta– a ga*rage* sale.	
● LORI:	Where.	(22)
BEN:	On third *a*venue.	

See also Data (i)–(vi), (12) (JIM: Agree::n), (21) (T: Bangor Flunt Madura?).

This question-type may be done without any affiliated technique for selecting a particular other, and thereby select a speaker of just prior turn as next speaker. These repair techniques constitute a central device that introduces the turn-order (and, cumulatively, the turn-distribution) bias noted earlier. For the only systematic mechanism available for next speaker selection that can prefer, formally, a next speaker identified only in turn-taking (and thus context-free) terms is one that selects prior speaker as next speaker.

C. The technique described under heading A above, the use of a first pair-part addressed, might appear to sharply constrain the talk of a turn in which a "current speaker selects next" technique was to be used. That is, it might appear that any such turn would have to be constructed to be a first pair-part; and "current selects next" techniques would then seem to not have a general operability, but be tied to utterances constructed as first pair-parts. It should, therefore, be noted that a turn's talk, whether it initially be constructed to be a first pair-part or not, can be made into a locus of "current selects next" by adding to it of a "tag question" addressed, for example, "you know?" and "don't you agree? "

The availability of the "tag question" as affiliatable to a turn's talk is of special importance, for it is the generally available "exit technique" for a turn. That is, a current speaker having constructed a turn's talk to a possible transition-relevance place without having selected a next, and finding no other self-selecting to be next, may, employing his option to continue, do a tag question, selecting another as next speaker upon the tag question's completion, and thereby exiting from the turn. In this regard, the tag question is one member of a class we may call "recompleters," a class that supplies one major source of the talk done when Rule 1(c)'s option is exercised. The effectiveness of tag questions in this regard is that they invoke Rule 1(a), and make the start of a particular next speaker's turn relevant on *their* completion. It should be noted that this sort of use of Rule 1(a) via tag questions is sequentially quite different from the invocation of Rule 1(a) via turns constructed from their starts to be, for example, addressed questions. For the former are instances of Rule 1(a) being applied, only given that Rule 1(b) has not been exercised. While turns that employ Rule 1(a)'s options from their starts thus project turn transfer at first transition-relevance place, tag questions (i.e., what we might term "1[c]–1[a]'s") come after an initial transition-relevance place. They thus operate in a second cycle of the rule-set's options.

D. The list of "current speaker selects next" techniques can be extensively expanded by inclusion within it of such techniques that employ social identities in their operation. For example, in a conversation composed of two couples, an invitation, for example, to go to the movies made by a speaker will be heard to select as next speaker a member of the "other couple," excluding "own spouse." The problem of introducing particular social identities into our description of the technology is particularly complex because it is one of the major aspects of conversation's flexibility that it is compatible with multiplicities of, and changes in, the social identities of some "same" participants. A formal characterization of how participants' social identities are made relevant and changed in conversation does not now exist, though work is proceeding on that problem. It is clear enough that some "current selects next" techniques are tied to the issue such a formal characterization will deal with, but are for now too cumbersome to be introduced in detail.[37]

E. The basic technique for self-selection is "starting first." Rule 1(b) explicitly incorporates this technique in its provision that "first starter gets the turn." That formulation should not primarily be heard to refer to a circumstance in which, upon one turn's completion, several parties begin to talk, among whom "first starter goes." Rather it invites noticing that regularly, after a very brief pause, only one starts. That is, that the interutterance pauses are very brief shows that one regularly starts fast; and the *single* starter should be thought of as "first starter," succeeding in being single starter because of the "first starter goes" provision, and being "dispensable" in that had he not started and started fast, someone else would have. Here it is appropriate to recall the earlier discussion of the pressure Rule 1(b) and its "first starter" provision place on turn size:

The first starter provision motivates any intending self-selector to start as early as possible at an earliest/next transition-relevance place, and a current speaker oriented to that will so construct a turn's talk as to allow its intact formation in the fact of this pressure. Thus, from both sides there is a pressure for turn-size minimization.

. The pressure for early starts on self-selectors produced by the "first starter goes" provision is constrained by a feature of the unit-types out of which a turn's talk is constructed. It was noted (p. 12) about the unit-types, that they project from their beginnings, features of their construction, their direction, and what it will take to complete them.[38] A self-selector aiming for an earliest start, one projected in the course of the ongoing utterance so as to follow closely on its completion, has the problem that his earliest start will have to begin with a unit-type's beginning, a beginning which, given its projectability, will need to reflect some degree of planning for the turn's talk, and will itself project that planning. That will be involved, though current turn is still in progress, and may be internally extended with its extensions modifying its direction. There are, as well, the earlier mentioned (pp. 16–17) additions to prior turn, after first possible transition place, of articulatory extensions and optional postcompletion elements. A next turn's beginning is thus subject to multiple sources of overlap—an overlap of a unit-type's beginning possibly impairing its part in the turn's utterance construction and its projection of the turn's plan. Therefore, the need to begin with a sentence's beginning (where a sentence is the planned unit) constrains the relative timing of its turn's start, for its analyzability will be affected if it overlaps.

With regard to the "begin with a beginning" constraint and its consequences, a familiar class of constructions is of particular interest. Appositional beginnings, for example, "well," "but," "and," and "so," are extraordinarily common, and do satisfy the constraints of beginning. However, they do that without revealing much about the constructional features of the sentence to follow: That is, they do not require that the speaker have a plan in hand as a condition for starting. Furthermore, their overlap will not impair the constructional development or the analyzability of the sentence they begin. Appositionals then are turn-entry devices—prestarts, just as the earlier discussed tag questions are exit devices—postcompleters. Appositionals and tag questions are heavily used devices, though the basis for their use is by no means self-evident linguistically. We are proposing that they are to be understood as devices with important turn-organizational uses.

F. While the basic technique for self-selection is "starting first," and it is by virtue of its operation that regularly first starters are only starters, it is obvious enough that self-selection *is* done when another self-selector has already started, and that such self-selectors *do* in fact start a turn's talk. Aside from the case of "more than one at a time," which is produced by simultaneous starts by self-selectors aiming for earliest possible start, there are multitudes of instances of "more than one at a time," where one clearly started first. There are, then, techniques for "second starters" or "subsequent starters."

The first starter provision for self-selection operates without respect to the type of utterance thereby started. Second starter techniques—more accurately, their efficacy in superseding the operation of the first starter provision—are contingent on the type of utterance they can, from their starts, reveal themselves to be. We cannot here begin to detail the constraints under which second starter supersession operates. We can, however, recall one basis for such a supersession which was discussed earlier. It was noted in the discussion of turn-order bias that prior speaker could systematically be selected to be next speaker, and that techniques for accomplishing this were overtly directed to problems of understanding prior utterance, *that* furnishing the basis for the possibility of colloquy. Now we can note that such addressing of problems of understanding is a priority activity in conversation. A self-selector whose turn beginning reveals his turn's talk to be prospectively addressed to a problem of understanding of prior utterance may, by virtue of that, get the turn, even though at the turn transfer another started before him, and his start is, then, second.

Data 23

[KC-4:2]

R:	Hey::, the place looks different.	(23)
F:	Yea::hh.	
● K:	Ya have to see all our new–	
	[ ]	
● D:	It does?	
R:	Oh yeah	

Note that D starts well after K, and that K does not withdraw until enough of D's turn is out (here all of it) to exhibit that he is raising a problem of understanding.

13. Various turn-constructional units are employed for the production of the talk that occupies a turn. The turn-taking system we are describing is one for conversation, that is, for talk in interaction. We have

proposed that the allocation of turn space is organized around the construction of talk *in* the turns. That organization appears to key on one main feature of the construction of the talk in a turn, namely, that whatever the units employed for the construction, and whatever the theoretical language employed to describe them, that they have points of possible unit completion, points that are projectable before their occurrence. That being the better part of what the turn-taking system asks of the language materials out of which its turns are fashioned, it will be compatible with a system of units that has this feature.

The discussion (p. 12) of the turn-constructional component of the turn-taking system identifies the types of turn-constructional units as sentential, clausal, phrasal, and lexical—that is, syntactically. The discussion of appositionals and tag questions, and most importantly, the way in which the prospect of turn transfer at "first possible transition-relevance place" conditions decisions as between left-embedded and conjoined sentence structures, should indicate the deep ways in which syntax matters to turn taking, albeit a syntax conceived in terms of its relevance to turn taking. If one examines empirical materials to see where in an ongoing turn next speakers begin (or try to begin) next turns, one finds that such starts do not occur continuously over the developmental course of a turn, but discretely over its development. That is, possible transition-relevance places recur discretely in the course of a turn (this is the import of Rule 2 in the rule-set). Examination of *where* in current turns such "next-turn starts" occur shows them to occur at "possible completion points." These turn out to be "possible completion points" of sentences, clauses, phrases, and one-word constructions,[39] and multiples thereof.

Data 24–28

[Trio:II]

● PENNY: An' the fact is I– is– *I* jus' thought it was so kind of   (24)
          stupid I didn' even say anything when I came ho:me.
                    [[
● JANET: Y–   Eh–
              (0.3)
    JANET: Well Estelle jus' called'n . . .

[T. Labov: Battersea:B:1]
    TOURIST: Has the park cha:nged much,   (25)

PARKY: *Oh::* ye:s,
        (1.0)
● OLD MAN: Th'*Fun*fair changed it'n ahful lot didn' it.
                                [[
● PARKY: Th–   That–
PARKY: *That* changed it,

[GTS 5:9]
● KEN: I saw 'em last night at uhm school.   (26)
                         [
● JIM: They're a riot

[GTS 1:MC1:7]
● LOUISE: I think it's really funny to watch.   (27)
                           [
● ROGER: Ohhh God!

[CDHQ:2:82]
A: Well we just wondered,   (28)
A: We just came in from Alexandria,
A: Just got home
● A: and these winds were so bad we're gettin scared again heh
    [
● B: Mm hm,
● B: No, we doh–
    [
● A: And we wondred whether we should go to a motel
   or something.
B: No, you stay right where you are . . .

Note that in Data (24)–(27) the next turn starts come at first possible transition-places and next possible transition places; in Data (28), A gets a number of turn-constructional units before B comes in, A comes back in after a first lexical unit, and B comes back in at first possible completion of a first sentential unit. See also Data (33) below, et passim.

The empirical materials of conversation, then, lead to the observation about the facticity of the use of such components, and to their inclusion in the model of turn taking as the elements out of which turns are built.

Clearly, as well, some understanding of "sound production" (i.e., phonology, intonation, etc.) is very important to turn-taking organization. For example, discriminations between "what" as a one-word question and as the start of a sentential (or clausal or phrasal) construction are made not syntactically, but intonationally. When, further, it is realized that any word can be made into a "one-word" unit-type,[40] and that via intonation, then, the character of the unit-types' description in syntactic terms can be appreciated as partial.

While the rule-set itself appears to treat as central only the "projectable completion" feature of its host's language materials, it seems productive to assume that, given conversation as a major, if not *the* major, locus of a language's use, other aspects of language structure will be designed for conversational use, and, *pari passu*, turn-taking contingencies. The interaction of syntactic and turn-taking structures, however, awaits serious investigation, perhaps along lines such as the following.

We earlier noted that the turn-taking system is a system for se-quences of turns. A "turn" is to be thought of as a turn-in-a-series, with the potential of the series being made into a sequence. Turns display gross organizational features that reflect their occurrence in a series. They regularly have a three-part structure: a part which addresses the relation of a turn to a prior, a part involved with what is occupying the turn, and a part which addresses the relation of the turn to a succeeding one. These parts regularly occur in that order, an obviously rational ordering for an organization that latches a turn to the turns on either side of it.

Data 29–33

[TZ:21-23]

    A: It would bum you out to kiss me then, (29) hunh

           [

    B: Yeah well we all know where that's at.
            ((pause))

    A: (   )

           [

    B: I mean you went– you went through a– a long rap on that one.=

•   A: =Yeah, so I say that would bum you out then, hunh

Where "yeah" is a formal affiliator to last turn, and "hunh" is a tag question, projecting a link to next turn.

[Fat tape:1]

    D: Jude loves olives.   (30)

    J: That's not bad.

• D: She eats them all the time. I understand they're fattening, huh?

Where the first sentence relates to a prior via multiple proterm use, and a tag question projects a link to next turn.

[Fat tape:6]

    J: But by the time you get out of the (31) shower and get your d– self ready,

                               [

• M: Well I'm *not* ready. I haven't kept you waiting yet though, have I?

    J: Michael, You will, I know you will

Where the first sentence relates to the prior at least by contrast, and the tag question relates to a next.

[Ladies:12:13]

    B: Maybelle's takin' this week off, and she– you (32) know something, she looked kinda tired.

• A: Uh huh. (2.0) Uhm well I guess she's been working pretty steadily, hasn't she.

                                 [

    B: Yeah, she's been working pretty steady, and she's had some difficult cases.

[HG:2-3]

    N: Yah an' an' the fact that you're you feel guilty (33) about eating them *that's* what makes you break out, because it's– it's all inside you.

    H: So people who've broken out they're just very emotional people, huh,

                           [

    N: Heh heh heh, and they're worried about it.

                   [

    H: heh heh heh heh heh heh

• N: I don't know. It sounds kinda crazy, bu:t

    H: •hh just a little.

The turn-taking system, it should now be clear, exerts pressure to have these systematically potential turn parts, or turn jobs, be accomplished before first possible completion, for example, in a single sentence.

Data 34–35

[TZ:57-59]

A: So it could happen to:: some people. ·hh   (34)
But I: I wouldn' uh I wouldn': I wou– I
say I wouldn' uh ((pause)) I don' know of
anybody– that– 'cause anybody that I really
didn't *di:g* I wouldn't have the *ti:me,*
uh: a:n: to waste I would say, unh if I
didn' (   )
                         [
● B: And you consider it wasting to jist be–
you know– to jist like talkin' an' bein' with
somebody.

A: Yeah. If you haven't got nothin' goin' (you're)
jist wastin' your time. ·hh You could be doin'
somethin' important to you. You know an–=

Where B links to prior via the conjunction and the cross reference, and links to a next by building the turn as a first part of an adjacency pair—confirmation request/ confirmation—getting a confirmation next.

[HG:3]

N: So what   ti me–   (35)
                    [   ]
H: Now what–
● N: Oh so we we get the tickets when we get
there, right?
                         [
H: yeah yeah they're reserved seats.

Where the interruption marker "oh" exhibits a relationship to prior, and the tag question to next. See also Data (33), second turn, which is similar to (34).

It is expectable, then, that some aspects of the syntax of a sentence will be best understood by reference to the jobs that need to get done in a turn-in-a-series, turns being a fundamental place for the occurrence of sentences.

14. Repair mechanisms for dealing with turn-taking errors and violations obviously are available for use. The various organizations that are operative in conversation are susceptible to errors, violations, troubles, and for them repair devices are available. We cannot here enter into a full discussion of repair.[41] We mean to touch on three themes.

First, among the variety of repair devices in conversation are ones directed to, and designed for, turn-taking problems. No special theoretical motivation is needed to observe that questions such as "who, me?"[42] the lore and practices of etiquette concerning "interruption" and complaints about it, the use of interruption markers such as "excuse me" and others, false starts, repeats or recycles of parts of a turn overlapped by others, as well as premature (i.e., before possible completion) stopping by parties to simultaneous talk, are repair devices directed to troubles in the organization and distribution of turns to talk.

Second, at least some of the mechanisms for turn-taking repair are intrinsic to the very system whose troubles they repair. Thus, for example, the basic device for repairing "more than one at a time" involves a procedure which is itself otherwise violative in turn-taking terms—namely, stopping a turn before its possible completion point;[43] it involves, then, a transformation of a central feature of the turn-taking system, the use of turn-constructional units to their next possible completion, and not some device quite external to it. In that regard, we can further note that there are places in the rule-set itself designed for repair, in particular the cycle of options provided by Rules 1(b) and 1(c). What we earlier called "1(c)–1(a)'s," a current speaker continuation after the nonoccurrence of turn transfer at a transition-relevance place, a continuation that selects a next speaker to go,[44] should be appreciated as a repair of a failure of turn transfer, provision for which is directly incorporated in the turn-taking system's basic organization. It is a major feature of a rational organization for behavior that accommodates real worldly interests, and is not susceptible of external enforcement, that it incorporates resources and procedures for repair of its troubles into its fundamental organization.

Third, the turn-taking system constrains repairs of other than a turn-taking sort. For example, repairs by "other than current speaker" are not done until a turn's completion, respecting the turn-taking system's allocation of rights to a turn even where repair is found necessary. In fact, most repair (e.g., correction of a word) is done within the turn in which the repairable occurs. But when repair spills over the boundaries of a turn, when, for example, "other than speaker" initiates a repair in the turn following the one in which the repairable occurred, then the sequence so initiated is organized by the same turn-taking system, and the repair sequences exhibit the same features of turn taking as we have been discussing, including the feature currently under discussion—that is, repair sequences can take repair.[45]

The compatibility of the model of turn taking with the facts of repair is thus of a dual character: The turn-taking system lends itself to, and incorporates devices for, repair of its troubles; and the turn-taking system is a basic organizational device for the repair of any other troubles in conversation. The turn-taking system and the organization of repair are thus "made for each other" in a double sense.

THE TYPE OF MODEL THIS IS

So far, we have touched on a variety of literature in which materials relevant to turn-taking organization in conversation are collected, addressed, or analyzed, although not necessarily in explicit turn-taking terms; we have proposed a set of grossly observable features of conversation with which a model of turn taking should be able to come to terms, if it is to merit serious consideration; we have proposed a model of a turn-taking system for conversation, or at least some major components of such a model; and we have sketched that, and how, that model comes to terms with the facts we had proposed as constraints, hopefully in the course of that discussion displaying some interesting features and uses of that model. It is certainly the case that the proposed model is in several respects incorrect or insufficient. However this particular model may be defective, we do think that the foregoing discussions support the claim that the appropriate model for turn taking in conversation will be this *sort* of model. In this section, we try to characterize what that *sort* is, by citing a few of its most important features with some elaborations. Those features are (*a*) that it is a "local management system," and (*b*) that it is an "interactionally managed system." Having characterized the sort of system it is, we will offer a formulation of the sort of problem it seems designed to serve as a solution to.

In characterizing the turn-taking system we have been dealing with as a "local management system," we take note of the following clear features the rule-set and the components have: (*a*) The system deals with single transitions at a time, and, thereby, with only the two turns a single transition links at a time; that is, it allocates but a single turn at a time; (*b*) the single turn it allocates on each occasion of its operation is "next turn"; (*c*) while the system deals with but a single transition at a time, it deals with transitions comprehensively (i.e., it deals with any of the transition possibilities it methodizes the use of), exclusively (no other system can organize transitions independent of the turn-taking system),[46] and, via its dealing with "next turn," it deals with transitions serially, in the order in which they come up. These features by themselves invite a characterization of the system of which they are part as a local management system, in that all the operations are "local," that is, directed to "next turn" and "next transition" on a turn-by-turn basis. It should be noted, however, that this much constitutes local management only with respect to turn order. The system is, however, locally managed with respect to turn size as well. Not only is the allocation of turns accomplished in each turn for a next, but the determination of turn size is locally accomplished, that is, accomplished in the developmental course of each turn, under constraints imposed by a next turn and an orientation to a next turn in the current one. While the earlier discussion pointed out a range of features in conversation that are not fixed but vary, the two that the system directly and explicitly concerns itself with in its machinery are turn size and turn order. The turn-taking system is a local management system, then, in the sense that it operates in such a way as to allow turn size and turn order to vary, and be under local management, across variations in other parameters, and while achieving the aim of all turn-taking systems—the organization of "n at a time"—and the aim of all turn-taking organizations for speech-exchange systems[47]—"one at a time while speaker change recurs."

The turn-taking system under examination can be further characterized for the kind of local management system it is. The character and organization of the rules that constitute the system as a local management system themselves determine its more particular organization in not only allowing and/or requiring turn size and turn order to vary, but in subjecting their variability to the control of the parties to the conversation for any conversation. It is, therefore, among local management systems, a "party-administered" system. Furthermore, it makes turn size and turn order interdependent by interlocking the mechanisms for their respective determination, turn-allocation mechanisms having consequences for turn size, and procedures for regulating or determining turn size employing turn-allocation techniques (as in the use of tag questions as turn exit, and therefore, turn stopping, devices). The system then integrates the machinery for turn-size and turn-order organization, and subjects that machinery to the administration of the parties to any conversation. The mechanism by which the system lends itself to party administration, by which turn-size and turn-order determinations are integrated, and by which the system achieves comprehensiveness for any turn transition is the option cycle that the ordered set of rules provides. For that rule-set provides options for "speakers" and "potential next speakers," putting itself thereby at the disposal of participants; it interconnects "stopping by current'' and "starting by next," thereby connecting turn size with turn order; and is abstractly formulated, so as to not exclude any transition place from its scope.

A set of further features of the system, collected under the rubric "interactionally managed," concerns the way in which the turn-taking system, in its local management, participant-administered form fits to, and is a specific adaptation of turn taking for, conversational interaction.

Party administration need not be interactive. In the turn-taking system for conversation, however, it is. The party-administered, local management of turn order is effected through the rule-set, whose ordered property provides a cycle of options in which any party's contribution to turn order determination is contingent on, and oriented to, the contributions of other parties. The basis of this contingency is given by the ways in which the operation of any of the options the rules provide is contingent on higher order options not having been exercised, and constrained by the prospective operation of lower-order options, a point discussed after the description of the rule-set (p. 13).

Turn size is also the product of not only party-administered local management, but of interactional production. That involves the sort of turn unit the turn-taking system uses, a facet which can here be used to explicate further what we intend in characterizing the system as an "interactionally managed system." The turn unit is of a sort which employs a specification of minimal sizes, but which provides for expansion within a unit, that is stoppable (though not at any point), that has transition places which discretely recur within it and can themselves be expanded or contracted—each of these features except the first being loci of interactional determination. By virtue of this character, it is misconceived to treat turns as units characterized by a division of labor in which the speaker determines the unit and its boundaries, and other parties to the conversation have as their task the recognition of them. Rather, the turn is a unit whose constitution and boundaries involve such a distribution of tasks as (as we have noted): That a speaker can talk in such a way as to permit projection of possible completion to be made from his talk (from its start), and to allow others to use its transition places to start talk, to pass up talk, to affect directions of talk, and so on, and that their starting to talk, if properly placed, can determine where he ought to stop talk. That is, the "turn" as a unit is interactionally determined.[48]

For conversationalists, that turn size and turn order are locally managed (i.e., turn-by-turn), party-administered (i.e., by them), and interactionally controlled (i.e., any feature being multilaterally shaped), means that these facets of conversation, and those that derive from them, can be brought under the jurisdiction of perhaps the most general principle particularizing conversational interaction,[49] that of "recipient design." With "recipient design" we intend to collect a multitude of respects in which the talk by a party in a conversation is constructed or designed in ways which display an orientation and sensitivity to the particular other(s) who are the coparticipants. In our work, we have found recipient design to operate with regard to word selection, topic selection, the admissibility and ordering of sequences, the options and obligations for starting and terminating conversations, and so on, which will be reported in future publications.[50] It is a major basis for that variability of actual conversations that is glossed by the notion "context-sensitive." By "the particularizing operation of recipient design on turn size and turn order," we are noticing that parties have ways of individualizing some "this conversation"; their collaboration in turn allocation and turn construction achieves a particular ordering of particular-sized turns and turn-transition characteristics[51] of the particular conversation at the particular point in it. In evolving a machinery by which turn organization is subjected to recipient design in a workable way, turn taking, abstractly conceived, is adapted specifically for conversation.

SOME CONSEQUENCES OF THE MODEL

In this section, we hope to state briefly some consequences of the type of organization we have described. We will consider only such sorts of consequences as are of "general interest."

1. An intrinsic motivation for listening. In its turn-allocational techniques, the turn-taking system for conversation builds in an intrinsic motivation for listening to all utterances in a conversation, independent of other possible motivations, such as interest and politeness. In the variety of techniques for arriving at a next speaker, and in their ordered character, it obliges any willing or potentially intending speaker to listen to, and analyze, each utterance across its delivery. Thus, a participant willing to speak next, if selected to do so, will need to listen to each utterance and analyze it at least to find whether or not he is selected as next speaker with it. And any potentially intending speaker will have to listen to any utterance after which he might want to speak to find, at the least, that no other has been selected as next speaker with it. Under either of these circumstances, a willing or potentially intending next speaker will have to listen through current utterance's end in order to be able properly to effect turn transfer, and perhaps in order to secure the turn. Given the mechanism for selecting "last speaker as next," a current speaker will

also be subject to this motivation upon completion of his turn. By maximizing the set of potential next speakers for any next turn,[52] the system translates a willingness or potential desire to speak into a corollary obligation to listen.

2. Turn-taking organization controls, at least partially, the understanding utterances get. There are a variety of candidate proposals with regard to the question: How is talk understood? The investigation of turn taking contributes to this problem in various ways. One is: The basis furnished by the turn-taking system for listening, just discussed, may be amplified in the following respect. A participant potentially willing to speak, if selected to do so, will need to listen to any utterance to find if, with it, he is being selected to speak next. A major class of "current selects next" techniques being constituted by "first pair-parts," that is, by type-characterized utterances such as "greeting," "question," "insult," and "complaint," a willing speaker will need to analyze utterances to find if an instance of such an utterance-type is being employed, and is being employed in a way that possibly selects him as next speaker. And a potentially intending speaker will need to examine any utterance after which he might want to speak to find whether such a thing was being done to him or to some other party.

3. A methodological consequence. The turn-taking system has, as a by-product of its design, a proof procedure for the analysis of turns. When a speaker addresses a first pair-part, such as a "question," or a "complaint" to another, we have noted, he selects the other as next speaker, and selects for him that he do a second part for the "adjacency pair" he has started, that is, to do an "answer," or an "apology" (among other possibilities), respectively. The addressee, in doing a second pair-part, such as an "answer" or "an apology" next, not only does that utterance-type, but thereby displays (in the first place to his coparticipants) his understanding of the prior turn's talk as a first part, as a "question" or "complaint."

Therein lies a central methodological resource for the investigation of conversation (by contrast with the investigation of literary and other "text" materials), a resource provided by conversation's thoroughly interactional character. For it is a systematic consequence of the turn-taking organization of conversation that it obliges its participants to display to each other, in a turn's talk, their understanding of other turns' talk. More generally, a turn's talk will be heard as directed to a prior turn's talk, unless special techniques are used to locate some other talk to which it is dircted. Regularly, then, a turn's talk will display its speaker's understanding of a prior turn's talk, and whatever other talk it marks itself as directed to.[53]

In the first place, of course, such understandings are displayed to coparticipants, and are an important basis for conversation's local self-correction mechanism. Clearly, they also supply another important basis for the "last as next" turn-order bias, a prior speaker being motivated to self-select as next speaker if he finds the understanding of his prior utterance, displayed by current speaker in current turn, unacceptable.

But while understandings of other turn's talk are displayed to coparticipants, they are available as well to professional analysts, who are thereby afforded a proof criterion (and a search procedure) for the analysis of what a turn's talk is occupied with. Since it is the parties' understandings of prior turns' talk that is relevant to their construction of next turns, it is *their* understandings that are wanted for analysis. The display of those understandings in the talk in subsequent turns affords a resource for the analysis of prior turns, and a proof procedure for professional analyses of prior turns, resources intrinsic to the data themselves.

THE PLACE OF CONVERSATION AMONG THE SPEECH-EXCHANGE SYSTEMS

The use of a turn-taking system to preserve one party talking at a time while speaker change recurs for interactions in which talk is organizationally involved is not at all unique to conversation. It is massively present for ceremonies, debates, meetings, press conferences, seminars, therapy sessions, interviews, trials, and so on. All of these differ from conversation (and from each other) on a range of other turn-taking parameters and in the organization by which they achieve the set of parameter values they organize the presence of.[54]

Such a sort of comparative investigation of the speech-exchange systems available to members of a same society, conceived of in terms of differential turn-taking systems has barely been looked into by us. However, certain striking arrangements may be noted, if only to suggest the possible interest this area shall have.

It seems, as noted, correct to say that generally, the allocational techniques for conversation do one turn allocation at a time. Alternatives to such a mode of operation are readily found. In debates, for example, the ordering of all turns is preallocated, by formula, by reference to "pro" and "con" positions. In contrast to both debates and conversation, meetings that have a chairperson partially preallocate turns, and provide for the allocation of unallocated turns via the use of the preallocated turns. Thus, the chairperson has rights to talk first, and to talk after each other speaker, and can use each such turn to allocate next speakership.

The foregoing suffices to suggest a structural possibility; that turn-taking systems, or at least the class of them whose members each preserve "one party talks at a time," are, with respect to their allocational arrangements, linearly arrayed. The linear array is one in which one polar type (which conversation instances) involves "one turn at a time allocation"; that is, the use of local allocational means, and the other pole (which debates instance) involves "preallocation of all turns," and medial types (which meetings instance) involve various mixes of preallocational and local allocational means.

That the types can be so arrayed permits them to be compared, directly, in relevant functional terms. Thus, one pole (local allocation of turns) permits maximization of the size of the set of potential speakers to each next turn, but is not designed organizationally to permit the methodical achievement of an equalization of turns among potential speakers; whereas the other (preallocation of all turns) is designed to permit the equalization of turns (or can be; it can be designed for other ends) which it does by specifying (and thereby, minimizing the size of the set of potential) next speaker. If the range of turn-taking systems is arrayed on a continuum ranging from full preallocation of turns to one allocation at a time, then any system may be found to maximize, minimize, or not be organizationally relevant to a range of functions (such as equalization of turns among participants, maximization of potential next speakers, etc.). The functions which any system is design-relevant for may then be explored, and the various systems compared with respect to their consequences on any given function of interest. On the two we have mentioned, equalization of turns and maximization of set of next speaker candidates, local allocation and full preallocation are polar types, as, indeed, it might turn out they are for any function for which turn allocation is systematically relevant.

Given the linear array, the polar position of conversation, and the functions that position permits maximization of, a characterization of the organization of turn taking in conversation takes on more than merely ethnographic interest. Occupying such a functionally interesting structural position, conversation is at least one representative of the means by which one polar possibility is organizationally achieved.

All positions on the linear array use turns and preserve the feature "one party talks at a time." While they each specify these differently, and while our systematic characterization was for conversation only, one further generalization—and the orderliness of the difference it leads to noticing—may be mentioned. For all positions of the linear array, "turns" are at least partially organized via language-specific constructional formats, for example, syntactic construction (of which sentential construction is a most important and familiar, but not sole, instance). Turn size may be characterizable by two different aspects of sentential organization: (*a*) multiplication of sentence units in a turn, and (*b*) increasing complexity of syntactic construction within single sentence units. Two observations can be made about turn size and its relation to position on the linear array. First, turn size increases with increasing degrees of preallocation on the linear array; second, the metric employed for gauging, and for constructionally increasing, turn size may shift with position on the array, multiplication of sentence units being the central mode for the preallocational pole, and increasing internal complexity within single (or minimized) sentence units being the central mode for local allocational systems. Both of these observations can be seen to be natural products of the design of the turn-taking systems at various points on the array.

While we have referred to conversation as "one polar extreme" on the linear array, and "ceremony" as possibly the other pole, we should not be understood thereby to be proposing the independent, or equal status of conversation and ceremony as polar types. For it appears likely that conversation should be considered the basic form of speech-exchange system, with other systems on the array representing a variety of transformations on conversation's turn-taking system to achieve other types of turn-taking systems. In this light, debate or ceremony would not be an independent polar type, but rather the most extreme transformation of conversation, most extreme in fully fixing the most important, and perhaps nearly all, of the parameters that conversation allows to vary.

NOTES

1. For example, Goffman (1955, 1964, 1971), Albert (1964), Kendon (1967), Yngve (1970), Duncan (1972a,b, 1973). Thus Goffman (1964, pp. 135–136):

> Card games, ball-room couplings, surgical teams in operation, and fist fights provide examples of encounters; all illustrate the social organization of shared current orientation, and all involve an organized interplay of acts of some kind. I want to suggest that when speaking occurs it does so within this kind of social arrangement; of course what is organized therein is not plays or steps or procedures or blows, but turns at talking. Note then that the natural home of speech is one in which speech is not always present.
> I am suggesting that the act of speaking must always be referred to the state of talk that is sustained through the particular turn at talking, and that this state of talk involves a circle of others ratified as coparticipants. (Such a phenomenon as talking to oneself, or talking to unratified recipients as in the case of collusive communication, or telephone talk, must first be seen as a departure from the norm, else its structure and significance will be lost.) Talk is socially organized, not merely in terms of who speaks to whom in what language, but as a little system of mutually ratified and ritually governed face-to-face action, a social encounter. Once a state of talk has been ratified,

cues must be available for requesting the floor and giving it up, for informing the speaker as to the stability of the focus of attention he is receiving. Intimate collaboration must be sustained to ensure that one turn at talking neither overlaps the previous one too much, nor wants for inoffensive conversational supply, for someone's turn must always and exclusively be in progress.

2. Stephan and Mishler (1952); Bales (1950, 1970); Coleman (1960).

3. Bales (1950).

4. Jaffe and Feldstein (1970); Matarazzo and Wiens (1972).

5. For example, Mitchell (1956, p. 79):

Important headmen also have the right of walking in front of their juniors. If there are three or four headmen returning from, say, a court case, they arrange themselves in the pathway in an order which reflects their rank. As they file down the narrow field paths the leader is the most senior among the group. After him come the other headmen and last of all the commoners. This order of precedence is also followed when initiands pass through the tribal initiation ceremonies.

Or Beardsley, Hall, and Ward (1959, p. 88):

Father and mother take the small children in to bathe with them, granny scrubs the men's backs, and relatives or neighbors who have no bath (three houses in Nilllke) come to chat while waiting their turn at the end of the day. The senior male of the household finishes his bath first and the family follows in regular order of sex and age precedence. The first bather gets the hottest water.

And in 1933, Isaacs (1933, pp. 222–223), a psychologist doing what amounts to an ethnography of children, wrote:

"Taking turns" is one of the hardest lessons for children under five years to learn . . . the young child cannot without much experience believe that "his turn" really will come in due time. All that he knows is that the others "have got it" and he hasn't. A few minutes is an eternity when one is eagerly waiting for a prized pleasure such as riding on a tricycle or a see-saw. Nor does one believe in the goodwill of the others who are enjoying their turns first—one knows only too well how readily one would exclude *them* if one were allowed! Only the proved evenness of justice of the controlling adult will make a transition possible from the impetuous assertion of "I want it *now*" to that trust in the future which makes "taking turns" possible.

6. Among anthropologists, Albert (1964) has come the closest to addressing turn taking per se:

The order in which individuals speak in a group is strictly determined by seniority of rank. If the eldest present is lower in social rank than some other individual, age gives way before social status. Thus, a nephew may be older than his uncle but the uncle is of higher rank and will speak before him. A prince or chief may be younger than others present but speaks first by virtue of his higher rank. There are no recorded instances of confusion or conflict in the matter of determining order of precedence, even in very large groups.

In public, the rule for servants, females, and other inferiors is to speak when spoken to but otherwise to maintain silence. Nevertheless, the pattern is so arranged that younger or socially inferior persons are in due course able to express their views. Thus, the senior person will speak first; the next in order of rank opens his speech with a statement to the effect, "Yes, I agree with the previous speaker, he is correct, he is older, and knows best, etc." Then, depending on circumstances and issues, the second speaker will by degrees or at once express his own views, and these may well be diametrically opposed to those previously expressed. No umbrage is taken, the required formula of acknowledgment of the superior having been used. If the *umukuru*, senior person, is truly very aged and weak his son may speak first, explaining his departure from the rules at the outset; "My father is old, his memory is not good, he wishes me to speak for him," or some other appropriate excuse is given. It is not unusual for the formal order of precedence to be abandoned in the latter part of a protracted discussion, and for loud voices to be heard even among upper-class individuals.[Reproduced by permission of the American Anthropological Association from the *American Anthropologist, 66* (6, part 2), 1964. Pp. 40–41.]

7. Except perhaps, for Samuel Beckett's *The Lost Ones* (1972).

8. When we speak of "context-free" and "context-sensitive" we cannot say the scope of reference of "context" that is relevant. For now, let it suffice to employ a longstanding understanding of "context" in the social sciences, one that attends the various places, times, and identities of parties to interaction. What we mean to notice is that major aspects of the organization of turn taking are insensitive to such parameters of context, and are, in that sense, "context-free," while it remains the case that examination of any particular materials will display the context-free resources of the turn-taking system to be employed and disposed in ways that are fitted to particulars of context. It is the context-free structure that defines how and where context-sensitivity can be displayed; the particularities of context are exhibited in systematically organized ways and places, and those are shaped by the context-free organization.

We understand that linguists use a different sense of context-free and context-sensitive, in which "context" refers to syntactic or sound environment, and "context-free" and "context-sensitive" are mutually exclusive possibilities. Our usage goes, in the first instance, to social contexts; whether it has a bearing on sound or syntactic ones we cannot say.

9. There are obvious structures involved in this list: historical structures by reference to which some facts would be noted only after others had; and substantive structures, in which various of the points are variously related to each other. The list is presented as to override any of these structures. Much might be learned from a consideration of these structures, but we are not interested in such uses of these points here (just as more can be made of the turn-taking model we propose than we will be making here). The list of points is intended as a set of empirical constraints on the model we propose, and, for now, nothing more, just as most of the attention we will give the model of turn taking we propose will be addressed to showing that the model meets the constraints set by these empirical observations. The list should be read with these intended uses in mind. For example, each item might be read as following not the item that preceded it in the list, but following the sentence preceding the list as a whole.

10. The heading "in any conversation" has raised for several readers of this paper in manuscript the question of cross-cultural validity. Such a question can, of course, be settled only empirically, by examining varieties of conversational materials. We can report the validity of our assertions for the materials we have examined, and apparently for Thai materials examined by Moerman (1972), New Guinea creole materials examined by G. Sankoff (personal communication), and for an undetermined number of languages within the competency of a substantial number of linguists at the Linguistic Institute in Ann Arbor, Michigan (Summer 1973), and elsewhere, who have found what follows consistent with what they know of their languages, or illuminating of otherwise recalcitrant problems in their understanding. Furthermore, examination of cross-cultural conversation, that is, where parties do not share a language of competence but a *lingua franca* in which all are only barely competent, is consistent with what follows (cf. Jordan & Fuller, in press). Finally, the cross-cultural question, as we understand it, asks how the structures on which we report

vary across languages (lexically or syntactically conceived), or language communities, or across social organizations, structures that are thereby cast as more basic ones. That ordering is not at all clear to us. We do find that aspects of turn-taking organization may vary in terms of other aspects of the sequential organization of conversation. And, as we suggest in the final section of the paper, there are various turn-taking systems for various speech-exchange systems, for example, conversation and debate.

11. There are other gross empirical features of conversation that could be added to the list. The ones we have noted are all important aspects of the organization of turn taking for conversation, and are therefore critical tests of a model of that organization. Space considerations preclude developing for each point the ways in which it is critical. One evidence of the crucial character of at least some of the points is that when other than the observed feature is the case, the turn-taking system that it is correct for is not a turn-taking system for *conversation*, but for some other speech-exchange system. In that sense, any such feature (e.g., of turn-order's or turn-size's non-prespecification) is criterial for the organization of turn taking for *conversation*, and it is critical that a proposed model be shown to be compatible with it.

12. See the following section, point 13.

13. It is empirically evident from sequential materials, that projectability is the case; that is, we find sequentially appropriate starts by next speakers after turns composed of single-word, single-phrase, or single-clause constructions with no gap—that is, with no waiting for possible sentence completion. For example, single-word turns:

[FD:IV:191]:

	DESK:	What is your last name Loraine	(i)
		[	
•	CALLER:	Dinnis.	
•	DESK:	What?	
•	CALLER:	Dinnis.	

[Trio:18]

	JEANETTE:	*Oh* you know, Mittie– *Gor*don, eh– *Gor*don, Mittie's	(ii)
		*hus*band died.	
		(0.3)	
	ESTELLE:	Oh whe::n.	
	JEANETTE:	Well it was in the paper this morning.	
	ESTELLE:	It *wa*::s,	
•	JEANETTE:	Yeah.	

[Ladies:3:2:5]

	FERN:	Well they're not comin,	(iii)
•	LANA:	*Who.*	
	FERN:	Uh Pam, unless they c'n *find* somebody.	

[NB:I:5:4]

	GUY:	Is *Rol* down by any chance dju know?	(iv)
•	EDDY:	*Huh?*	
	GUY:	Is uh Smith down?	
	EDDY:	*Yeah he's* down,	

Single-phrase turns:
[TG:]

| | A: | Oh I have the– I have one class in the e:vening. | (v) |
| • | B: | On *M*ondays? | |

A:	Y–uh::: Wednesdays.=
B:	=Uh–Wednesday,=
A:	=En it's like a *M*ickey *M*ouse course.

[Ladies:2:8:5]

ANNA:	Was last night the first time you met Missiz Kelly?	(vi)
	(1.0)	
● BEA:	Met whom?	
ANNA:	Missiz Kelly.	
BEA:	*Yes.*	

Single-clause turns:
[NB:III:3]

A:	Uh *you* been down here before havenche.	(vii)
	[	
B:	Yeh.	
● A:	Where the sidewalk is?	
B:	Yeah,	
● A:	Whur it ends,	
B:	Goes all a' way up there?	
	[	
A:	They c'm up tuh the:re,	
A:	Yeah.	

For another sort of evidence on this point, see pp. 34–35, and Data (24)–(28) cited there. For additional data and discussion of the precise placement of talk starts, cf. Jefferson (1973). How projection of unit-types is accomplished, which allows such "no-gap" starts by next speakers, is an important question on which we have been working. It seems to us an area to which linguists can make major contributions. Our characterization in the rules, and in the subsequent discussion, leaves the matter of how projection is done open (cf. pp. 33–38).

Several observations are in order here concerning data citations: (*a*) An explanation of the symbols used in the transcriptions appears in the introduction to the book (for a more complete explication of notational symbols, the reader should consult the original paper in *Language*); (*b*) the data excerpts cited in this paper are illustrative. They are representative of large collections of data on the various points we have assembled out of a substantial number of conversations. The data cannot be presented more extensively because of space limitations, but all the data in the paper can be examined for points other than those in whose service they are initially cited, and in many cases we have selected such data excerpts for a point as would illustrate other points in the paper independently (bullets (●) indicate the location of the phenomenon for which the data excerpt is introduced). Similarly, all the data in all our other papers can be inspected for their bearing on the points made in this one. And any materials of natural conversation (transcribed to an appropriate level of detail and precision) collected by others may be examined as well. All this, of course, is appropriate if, indeed, what is proposed in the paper is so "for any conversation."

14. For example,

[Schenkein:II:49]

SARA:	Ben you want some ( )?	(viii)
BEN:	Well, *al*right I'll have a,	
	((untimed silence))	
SARA:	Bill you want some?	
BILL:	No,	

In which Ben and Bill's turns are allocated by Sara (instances of current—Sara—selecting next), and Sara's turns are by self-selection.

Or:
[Adato:2:9]

SY:	See Death'v a Salesman las'night?	(ix)
JIM:	No.	
	((untimed silence))	
SY:	Never see(h)n it?	
JIM:	No.	
SY:	Ever *seen* it?	
JAY:	Yes	

in which Jim and Jay are selected as next speakers by Sy, and Sy's turns are allocated by self-selection (about Sy's selections of next speaker, note that whether or not the first interchange involves a glance-selected recipient, the second and third are at least partially lexically accomplished, in the uses of "never" and "ever").

That the preceding should not be taken to evidence that questions are always self-selected and answerer turns the product of "current selects next" techniques may be seen in the following;

[GTS:5:25]

JIM:	Any a' you guys read that story about Walter Mitty?	(x)
KEN:	*I* did,	
ROGER:	Mm hmm	

all the turns in which are allocated by self-selection.

For further discussion, and additional data, concerning turn allocation, see pp. 27–33.

15. Thus:

[TG:JFr:20]

AVA:	*He*, he'n Jo were like on the outs, yihknow?	(xi)
	(0.7)	
● AVA:	So uh,	
	[[	
● BEE:	*They* always are (hh)hhh	

[Ladies:2:2:3:14]

CLAIRE:	So then we were worse o– 'n she and' she went down	(xii)
	four,	
	(0.5)	
● CLAIRE:	But uhm	
	(1.5)	
● CLAIRE:	Uh	
	[[	
● CHLOE:	Well then it was *her* fault Claire,	
	[	
CLAIRE:	Yeah she said one no trump,	
	and I said two, an' then she went back t'two . . .	

[GTS:1:2:86]

ROGER:	*That's a joke* that police force. They gotta hunderd cops	(xiii)
	around the guy en so(h)me guy walks in and says I'm	
	gonna shoot you and *shoots* him.	

- ROGER: :hhmhhh heh
- ROGER: En it's the president's as*sas*sin y'know,
                    (0.9)
- ROGER: They're *won*der ful.
                                [
- LOUISE: Hm–Now they're not even sure.

16. We use the term "transition-relevance *place*" in order to avoid choosing, with a term, between alternative and possibly compatible features of transition coordination we are currently investigating. There are aspects of transition coordination that seem to require the notion of a "space" for transitions. To take an easily accessible example, interturn silences that are not treated by participants as gaps or pauses. And there are aspects of transitions for which the notion of a transition "point" seems correct. For example, the end of a question that selects a next speaker seems often to constitute a transition point, a new turn starting there whether or not talk by another is immediately begun. The two are not necessarily mutually incompatible as later discussion will indicate. The concerns of this paper seem to us not to depend on this order of detail, and we avoid prejudicing the issue by the use of "place," of which both "space" and "point" are possible specifications.

17. Speaker change *oc*currence is the case of a two-turn sequence, e.g., just: A: Hello; B: Hello, with nothing following.

18. Cf. Jefferson (1973), which deals specifically with this matter.

19. The relationship between the brief gap that may characterize an accomplished transition and such extended silences as do occur within conversations, characteristically between sequences, will not be considered here beyond noting that Rule 1(b) does provide that self-selection is optional, and that Rule 1(c) provides that "same speaker continuing" is also optional. This combination allows the possibility of a lapse, which will be considered below (in our discussion of point 11).

20. For some discussion, see below, point 12(*b*), p. 30.

21. As in Data (12) above, and in (i)–(vi), (21)–(23).

22. Data (i)–(x) and scan the rest of the data for varying sizes of single-unit turns.

23. Cf. Schegloff (forthcoming).

24. Schegloff and Sacks (1973).

25. See p. 28 ff., and for further elaboration Schegloff and Sacks (1973).

26. Discussions of a number of types of sequences have been published or are in press; for example, summons–answer sequences (Schegloff, 1968), side sequences (Jefferson, 1972), insertion sequences (Schegloff, 1972), closing sequences (Schegloff & Sacks, 1973), story sequences (Sacks, 1974), expanded sequences (Jefferson & Schenkein, 1977), and various others (e.g., Jefferson, 1973).

27. For example, it is sometimes suggested in the literature on small groups that relative distribution of turns (or some similar measure) is an index of, or medium for, power, status, influence, etc. For example, Bales (1970):

> Who speaks how much to whom in the group is a "brute fact" characterizing the actual present situation. Speaking takes up time. When one member speaks it takes time and attention from all other members of the group, some of whom may want to speak themselves. To take up time speaking in a small group is to exercise power over the other members for at least the duration of the time taken, regardless of the content. It is an exercise of power that may not coincide at all with the status position of the individual based on outside criteria, or even on special criteria developed within the group. . . .
> Within the small group the time taken by a given member in a given session is practically a direct index of the amount of power he has attempted to

exercise in that period [*Personality and interpersonal behavior*. New York: Holt, Rinehart, and Winston. Pp. 76–77].

The next paragraph in the text above suggests another kind of care, in addition to those which researchers in this area undoubtedly already take, to be taken in such uses of relative turn distribution by professional analysts.

28. What follows is not true for any transition-relevance place at all, but for certain classes of transition places, characterizable by reference to the organization of sequences, not the organization of turn taking.

29. That is, parties' treatment of silence in conversation is contingent on its placement. Roughly, intraturn silence (silence not at a transition-relevance place) is a "pause," and initially not to be talked in by others; silence after a possible completion point is, initially, a gap, and to be minimized; extended silence at transition-relevance places may become lapses. But some silences are transformable. For example, if a developing silence at a transition place, which is a (potential) gap is ended by talk of the same party who was talking before it, the "gap" may be transformed into a "pause" (being now intraturn); that is one way that "gap" is minimized (cf. Data [xii], [xiii], [1]).

30. The option cycle relationship between Rules 1(b) and 1(c) depicted here may help to explain such results as are reported in Matarazzo and Wiens (1972) to the effect that "reaction time latencies" (the time intervening between one speaker's completion and a next speaker's start in two-party conversation) are shorter, on the average, than are "initiative time latencies" (the time intervening between one speaker's "completion" and the start of a "follow-up" utterance by same speaker, the other participant not having talked). It was, in part, the encountering of similar data in our materials that prompted that formulation of the rules.

31. Since turn allocation has appeared both as an empirical fact about conversation and as part of the components and rule-set, the discussion of it is more extensive than that in other sections, and is concerned to, at least partly, explicate that part of the rule-set.

The theme of showing the compatability of the model with the gross facts is different in the case of turn allocation than in the case of other of the facts; for it is a central design outcome of the model to make multiple allocation techniques compatible with "one speaker at a time" by its ordering of them (see pp. 13–14).

32. See note 14, and the data therein; also Data (21).

33. See notes 24 and 25.

34. "Addressing" itself can be done as a first pair-part, e.g., as in summoning; cf. Schegloff (1968).

35. As, for example, in Data (viii), (14), or (21).

36. Cf. Jefferson (1972).

37. Cf. Sacks (1972c).

38. For example, one large group of turn beginnings are sentence starts, all of which are informative to some degree about the character of the sentence or turn so begun, some of them extremely so. For example, a turn's talk beginning with a *Wh*-word powerfully projects the possible involvement of a "question" character to that turn, with familiar consequences by now, for example, that it will be possibly selecting a next speaker, possibly selecting last speaker as next speaker, and given the availability of the one-word question form, the possibility of a rapid turn transfer.

39. See note 13.

40. See p. 30, discussion in point 12(B) for partial repeats and the citation there.

41. For discussion of two different aspects of repair, see Jefferson (1972) and Sacks and Schegloff (1974).

42. For example:

(L&M:7) Mother, 11-year-old daughter, and dog are in bed, putting the daughter to sleep; the dog has been addressed earlier in the conversation.

M:	wha'd are you doin.	
• L:	me?	
M:	yeh, you goina go ta sleep like that?	
L:	nothing	(xiv)
L:	no, hh heh hh hh	
M:	with your rear end sticking up in the air, how you gonna sleep like that.	
L:	heh heh I'm n(h)ot(h)	

43. See Data (23) et passim.

44. Above in the discussion of 12(C), pp. 30–31.

45. Earlier work on repair, for example, Jefferson (1972), Schegloff (1972), and Sacks and Schegloff (1974) encountered the ordering of repair by the turn-taking system, not having especially looked for it. Cf. in particular the data in Jefferson (1972) in regard to the present discussion.

46. Thus, while an addressed question requires an answer from the addressed party, it is the turn-taking system, and not syntactic or semantic features of the "question," that requires the answer to come "next."

47. Cf. Miller (1963), p. 418.

48. Prior researchers, for example, Bales (1950), Jaffe and Feldstein (1970), in looking for a unit that could be "recognized," possibly for good technical reasons in their research, have focused on its self-determined, independent, recognizable completeness. This appears to contrast with the main turn-organizational character of conversation, which is the interactional shaping of turns.

49. We owe the possibility of ever having seen the importance of the particularization theme to our acquaintance with Harold Garfinkel. See Garfinkel (1967) and Garfinkel and Sacks (1970).

50. For word selection, cf. Sacks and Schegloff (1974).

51. Jefferson (1973) pp. 56–71, et passim.

52. See point 9, p. 21f.

53. Cf. Moerman and Sacks (1974).

54. Nor is the feature unique to a particular linguistic or social community. It is evidently exhibited in conversation, meetings, etc., in societies whose languages and systems of social organization quite drastically differ. Cf. for example, Albert (1964), and note 10.

chapter 2

Identity Negotiations in Conversation

JIM SCHENKEIN

INTRODUCTION: THE CURIOSITY AND THE DATA

The transcript reproduced below represents the opening few moments of an eventually lengthy conversation between a life insurance salesman and a prospective client. The identification categories of "life insurance salesman" and "prospective client"—focused as they are within a notorious sort of business encounter—already provide considerable information about the nature of the encounter whose opening utterances we will be examining in close detail. That information, of course, was available to the participants no less richly than it is to us now. On the strength of the interactional parameters which "salesman" and "prospective client" appropriately conjure for us all, we are already alive to formulatable boundaries of likely, and even preferable, and even fantastic behavior for such encounters.

Whatever else they might or might not share, such encounters are made up of talk between strangers who know one another only as local versions of some abstract identity like "salesman" or "client." For these encounters, strangers not only conduct their business under the auspices of their official identity relations, but they also negotiate into the unfolding of their encounter eminently personal identities from their separate biographies. After presenting the transcript which will govern our further observations and attentions, I want to coax you into an analytic mentality that aims at describing the systematic procedures with which participants to such encounters can and do juggle their official and abstract identities with informal and personal identities in the course of their ordinary conversations.

The Data[1]

ALAN:	((knocks on door: BAM BAM BAM BAM))	1
	(2.0)	2
PETE:	((opens door))	3
ALAN:	Hi, Pete?	4
PETE:	' Ye:s.	5
ALAN:	*Oh.* Good. My name is Alan Pritt, hi.	6
PETE:	Hi.	7
ALAN:	I see yur back here in Bohemia.	8
PETE:	Yeah. ((closes door))	9
ALAN:	Ye:ah. ((walks to couch))	10
	(Boy.) W– ((sits))	11
PETE:	((walking to chair opposite couch))	12
	Where didju, say you lived, inda,	13
	inna– San Clemente?	14
	[	
ALAN:	San Clemente! Yeah.–Whatiyou	15
	teach.	16
PETE:	At–tuh Crayton.	17
ALAN:	O:h. Whattiyou teach.	18
PETE:	Well, I really don'teach I, I'm a	19
	graduate student there, I taught,=	20
	[	
ALAN:	O:h.	21
PETE:	=A couple of quarters lass quarter but	22
	I'm not really a teacher I'm working	23
	on my degree. ((sits in chair))	24
ALAN:	*Oh.* Okay.	25
	(2.0)	26

ALAN:	This is, a handbook of life insurance,	27
	((gives handbook to Pete))	28
	(3.0)	29
ALAN:	An' if you, figure it out you're a	30
	better man than I am hhh.	31
	[	
PETE:	O(h)h it's,	32
	difficult heh hhh.	33
ALAN:	No(h) it's not really, if you have	34
	prob– uh I should say it depends on	35
	what area you get into. I mean, you're	36
	not probably gonna go into advanced	37
	state–estate planning for yourself.	38
	Y'know like you don't have, y'know,	39
	eight nine, hunnerd thousand dollers	40
	do ya?	41
PETE:	No.	42
ALAN:	Oka(hh)y heeh heeh.	43
PETE:	Not today. hehh heh	44
ALAN:	Not today, well then it won't be	45
	y'know, extrordinarily difficult to	46
	figure out.	47
PETE:	Yeah, *o*kay. Well that'll be good I'll	48
	learn something about it,	49
ALAN:	Mm hmm. It just tels you some of the	50
	basic concepts. And, I give a memobook,	51
	out. And also let me put my magic card	52
	innit.	53
PETE:	Your magic card?	54
ALAN:	My magic card, this makes the whole	55
	thing a s– sort of a kaleida–scopic	56
	experience–not really it's just,	57
	y'know, uh two dimensional a(hh)c-	58
	tually hehh hehh hehh hehh heh ih– it	59
	all depends on y'know, what you've	60
	been doing right before you, look at	61
	the card I guess if it's two dimen-	62
	sional.	63
PETE:	Righ(h)t.	64
	(2.0)	65
ALAN:	Uhh,	66

PETE: I gather you also wanna try t'sell me   67
        some insurance.   68
              (2.0)   69
ALAN: Now– that doesn't sound like a bad   70
        idea–no, ih– it *would* be nice. But   71
        what I'd *like* to do,   72
              (3.0)   73
ALAN: Uhh, do you *have* any insurance.   74
PETE: No *life* insurance.   75
ALAN: No life insurance, yeah you have car   76
        and that don' chu.   77
                    [
PETE: Yeah.   78
ALAN: We all have car, an– and s–stuff like   79
        that. Uh, what I would *like* to do is   80
        set some time to uh, get tuhgether   81
        with ya becuz, I have to go to summer   82
        camp.   83
PETE: Oh you're in the reserves.   84
ALAN: Yeah.   85
PETE: Oh.   86
ALAN: An that's, fer two weeks, in uh,   87
        y'know for the nex'two weeks.   88
        Actually tuh go into it tonight, I   89
        like to be able to s'down an'prepare   90
        something specific'ly *for* a person I   91
        talk to.   92
              (2.0)   93
ALAN: Umm,   94
              (4.0)   95
ALAN: Umm in thinking about it in that terms–   96
        er in those terms preparing something   97
        specific'ly for you do you have any,   98
        amount of money, thet you could set   99
        aside monthly, that would not, y'know   100
        cramp your style so much you can enjoy   101
        life while you live–*hehhehh*ehhh Y'know,   102
PETE: Well, it's really– that's a difficult   103
        question it would depend on what kinds   104
        of benefits I would get forrit.   105
ALAN: Yeah   106

PETE:	Like–uh, f'I got fantastic benefits I	107
	could find something to set aside, but,	108
ALAN:	Mm hmm,	109
	[	
PETE:	I can't jus'say I have, ten dollers	110
	or a hunnerd dollers to set aside for	111
	things,	112
ALAN:	Mm hmm,	113
	[	
PETE:	Y'know without knowing what they are.	114
ALAN:	Well, see, when I ask you *this,*	115
	(3.0)	116
ALAN:	What I'm gonna show you is the	117
	regular– uh, life contract. Now the	118
	reason I show that is becuz it's the	119
	lowest premium permanet type of life	120
	insurance. Instead of showing you	121
	something thet, would have a *lot* of	122
	cash–This is what I show young people–	123
	this is what I own *myself.*	124

.

.

.

TOWARD A DESCRIPTION OF THE DATA:
THE NEGOTIATION OF OFFICIAL IDENTITIES

Even a casual review of the transcript will provide us with a variety of sequences in which the negotiation of participant identities is more or less transparent. For example, as the encounter begins to unfold, a wide range of biographical details—touching on such topics as place of residence (8, 13–15),[2] occupation (15–23), education (24), personal wealth (39–42, 98 ff.), other insurance coverage (74–80), and military obligations (82–88)—are laced into succeeding exchanges between Alan and Pete. It is plain enough: The sort of greeting exchanged, the sort of description offered, the sort of biographical details exhibited, all reflect facets of participant identities. And these are by no means the only resources for negotiating identities here of course; not only appearance, carriage, and gesture, but also the kind of humor tendered, the style of authenticity enacted, and the degree of interactional grace commanded will surely provide other varieties of resources for negotiating identities through this or any other encounter. Needless to say, the kinds of phenomena we choose to mull over will depend on our own "identities" as participant or observer of this conversation, analyzing the interaction as a lay conversationalist or a student of conversational interaction, informed by metaphysical or practical sophistications, and so on. While participant identities may very well be engineered or enlivened through such things as "greetings," "descriptions," "biographical details," "appearance," "carriage," "gesture," "humor," "authenticity," and "interactional grace," I want to begin by looking elsewhere.[3]

After the greetings are exchanged, seats are taken, and the promotional gift from the life insurance company (a handbook on life insurance) is delivered (4–51), both the salesman and the client are left with transacting entry into the buying/selling project which all the rest has been poised to promote.[4] Their entry into the buying/selling project is organized around systematic identity negotiations, and we can start our examination of these by taking a closer look at the alternative formulations the client and the salesman offer for that upcoming project:

| PETE: | I gather you also wanna try t'sell me | 67 |
| | some insurance. | 68 |

and, a little later:[5]

ALAN:	Actually tuh go into it tonight, I	89
	like to be able to s'down an'prepare	90
	something specific'ly *for* a person I	91
	talk to.	92

Both the client and the salesman formulate the anticipated next project with identity-rich characterizations: While the client's "I gather you also wanna try t'sell me some insurance." (lines 67–68) invokes generally impersonal categorical identifications for "anybodies" interacting in the bounds of this kind of event as a "salesman" and a "prospective client," the salesman's ". . . I like to be able to s'down an'prepare something specific'ly *for* a person I talk to." advances the prospect of personal categorical identifications for "somebodies" interacting with one another in particular. I want to examine more closely the juxtaposition and fit of these alternative formulations.

Proposing that the next project can be characterized by the work involved for a salesman wanting to sell an insurance policy, the client's formulation locates the encounter as but a current instance of a more generally distributed phenomenon whose salient features, moreover, can be abstracted in ways that apply invariantly to all such encounters. The client's formulation is not an invention of this client for this particular salesman, nor is it made applicable via some special examination of this salesman's interests and practices. Rather, the client's formulation "I gather you also wanna try t'sell me some insurance." (67–68) draws upon a generally available description of the interests and practices of an abstract identity category like " salesmen," and it is made applicable here under the auspices of something like "what anybody knows" about the interests and practices of "salesmen" generally. In short, the client's formulation presumes to capture the interests of this particular "salesman" and to confront him with those interests by invoking impersonal identity characteristics of "salesmen."

By contrast, the salesman's formulation proposes that the next project is not the one supposed by the client on the basis of "what anybody knows" about encounters such as this one. Instead, the salesman's ". . . I like to be able to s'down an'prepare something specific'ly *for* a person I talk to." (89–92) informs the client that the next project is an interview that this salesman will conduct so that later, presumably on some other occasion, the buying/selling project can be tailored to the client's particular circumstances. This is a delicately designed counterformulation. A proposal to treat this client in some exclusively personal fashion would be suspect by its achieved ultrafittedness to the idiosyncratic features of this encounter; but on the other hand, in these circumstances an announced practice of treating any prospective client personally is a more credible, precedented, and indeed professional orientation towards the client by its achieved insensitivities to the particularities of this encounter. If treating anybody like a somebody is an impersonal personalization, it is nonetheless the kind of personalization Alan proffers in this instance.[6] So while Alan's counterformulation does not deny the relevance of official identification categories, there is a movement from the "salesman" toward the "agent" as an official version of Alan's identity in his alternative formulation of the upcoming project.

Now the emerging analysis of these alternative formulations may tempt us into viewing Alan and Pete as engaged in some kind of interactional combat (e.g., their opposing formulations represent a confrontation between impersonal "anybody" identity categories and personal "somebody" identity categories). There is an exceedingly strong temptation to depict these gross features of the two formulations strategically: We can assign the interactional victory to the client for having caused the salesman trouble with his "let's get down to business" remark, or to the salesman for having taken conversational control with his "that sounds

nice, but what I'd like to do is . . ." remark. Although we could surely
furnish each remark with strategic advantages for its respective speaker,
and although our interest in the strategic bases of interactional negotiations is both popular and serious, the juxtaposition of these alternative
formulations need not encourage us to catalogue details of their opposition. And while each of these formulations (67–68, 89–92) portrays the
participants with alternative identities, the second portrayal is deeply
fitted to the first. The fit of the second formulation with features of the first
formulation, after all, distinguishes that remark from all the intervening
utterances (69–88) as the "response" to the initial formulation. Let us now
draw out some of the features which the salesman's second formulation
repeats from the client's first formulation.

The client initially formulates the interests of the salesman in terms of
interests that would characterize *any* salesman; the salesman subsequently formulates his intended treatment of the client in terms of a
service he would perform for *any* prospective client. Each formulates the
encounter as a local instance of a more generally experienced interactional scene, and the identities invoked in each for the conversational
personnel are invariant to a change in the formulator's interlocutor. Each
formulation describes an activity appropriate as a "salesman's" business,
and the identity achieved in each for Alan is consequently generated from
alternative business he might have for the current encounter as a "salesman" (e.g., making a sale versus conducting an initial interview). Each
formulation implies an identity for Pete from the would-be eyes of the
alternatively identified "salesman" (e.g., as a possible sale versus as a
possible interview subject).

As we all know, there are other ways to formulate the upcoming
business of the encounter, and some of these, by their poor fit with the
client's first formulation, would attract attention as "ignoring," "evad-
ing," "being stumped by," "just plowing through some spiel," "on the
way to a response," and the like. The design of Alan's second formulation, however, recognizably responds to materials initially exhibited in
Pete's first formulation. Most strikingly, both formulations select identifications from versions of the official identities abstractly governing the
conduct of the interaction between Alan and Pete. Although each formulation enlivens alternative identifications for Alan and Pete, the juxtaposition and fit of these alternatives negotiates among versions of official
identity categories.

But conversationalists are very busy. They also have procedures for
developing *un*official identity categories. I want now to develop some
appreciation of the sequential unfolding of these unofficial identity negotiations with which Alan and Pete multiply their identity resources and

bring into conversational play identities more or less remote from their official identity prospects.

IDENTITY MULTIPLICATION: THE NEGOTIATION OF UNOFFICIAL IDENTITIES

As it happens, the official identity negotiations we have just considered are initiated by Pete's first formulation (67–68) in a conspicuous turn at talking. Pete not only usurps a turn already begun and then abandoned by Alan:

	(2.0)	65
ALAN:	Uhh,	66
PETE:	I gather you also wanna try t'sell me	67
	some insurance.	68
	(2.0)	69

but the turn is surrounded by silence. Moreover, this turn at talking comes as the "next" to a four-turn action sequence in which the giving of a memobook and business card becomes a display of unofficial identity potentialities:

ALAN:	. . . And, I give a memobook	51
	out. And also let me put my magic card	52
	innit.	53
PETE:	Your magic card?	54
ALAN:	My magic card, this makes the whole	55
	thing a s– sort of a kaleida–scopic	56
	experience–not really it's just,	57
	y'know, uh two dimensional a(hh)c–	58
	tually hehh hehh hehh hehh heh ih– it	59
	all depends on y'know, what you've	60
	been doing right before you, look at	61
	the card I guess if it's two dimen–	62
	sional.	63
PETE:	Righ(h)t.	64
	(2.0)	65
ALAN:	Uhh,	66
PETE:	I gather you also wanna try t'sell me	67
	some insurance.	68
	(2.0)	69

As a "next" turn to this prior sequence, Pete's officially preoccupied first formulation (67–68) initiates the official business on the heels of some unofficial conversation. Let us now direct our attention to the unofficial identity negotiations of this just prior sequence. The display of unofficial identities is developed, in this case, through the course of a four-turn action sequence distributing two alternating turns at talking to Alan and Pete.

The action sequence is generated by Alan's description of his business card as "my magic card" (52). Whatever assessments might be made on the allusive description by Pete or any of us, "my magic card" excites a confrontation with bits and pieces of an extensive array of identity-rich issues (of which "What does he mean?" or "Why did he say that?" are gross but recognizable examples). There may well be an official relationship between "magic" and "business" (for example, as a characterization of the "magic" Alan can perform on behalf of Pete's life insurance needs), but that relationship remains vague and quite unknown to beholders of Alan's utterance at this point. There may well be an unofficial relationship between "magic" and "business" (for example, as a characterization of the "magic" Alan believes to be empowered by an anagrammatic variation of his business card), but that relationship remains vague and quite unknown as well. It makes sense to think of the utterance as an *Identity-Rich Puzzle* since however "magic card" speaks to the business at hand (metaphorically, explicitly, digressively, creatively, indirectly, and so forth), the tie cannot be made by merely consulting the official "salesman" and "client" identity categories, nor by examining their relationship to "magic card."

In the next turn at talking in the action sequence, Pete's "Your magic card?" (54) returns all those identity-rich matters back to Alan for further development. Whatever "magic card" could be for Alan or Pete or any of us, its repetition with a rising inflection in the second turn sends the Puzzle back to Alan for resolution. Although "why did he say that?" could well be posed to Pete's "Your magic card?" (54) and could excite an abiding curiosity with Pete's unfolding biography at this point, that question, like so many others, somehow does not come up for these passes ordinarily, and we, like the conversational participants, are caught up in resolving the issue of the prior turn. Securing the position currently out of central focus can actively participate in enforcing the attentions on someone else of course, but curiously, it has been popular to view repetitions like "Your magic card?" for their so-called "passive" or even "nondirective" characteristics. Plainly, among the variety of things Pete could have done there, following Alan's Identity-Rich Puzzle with a Pass is a full-blooded, vigorously directive, and wonderfully interesting action that confronts Alan with the disposition of his own Puzzle.[7]

The third turn in the action sequence is filled with Alan's treatment of the issue raised by his earlier Identity-Rich Puzzle (". . . my magic card . . .") and now passed back to him ("Your magic card?"); the turn starts off with a repeat of the Puzzle ("My magic card . . ."), and is then used to deliver an *Identity-Rich Solution:*

However sharply or vaguely Alan or Pete or any of us can now see the *magic* in "my magic card," it is subsequently shaped by Alan into some kind of key which "makes the whole thing a s– sort of kaleida–scopic experience– not really it's just, y'know, uh two dimensional a(hh)actually hehh hehh hehh hehh. . . ." Now the jump from "my magic card" to "the whole thing" begins this Solution by locating the magic in another, blazingly allusive, mystery: Whatever the *magic* might be, it has something to do with "the whole thing," whatever *the whole thing* might be. Of course, whether *the whole thing* intends to describe the business card, the card and memobook, the buying and selling of life insurance, life and death, and/or whatsoever else, there are appropriately relevant identity determinations to be made about Alan and the link he is invoking between his "magic card" and "the whole thing." It may well be that Alan's link is forged from solidly commercial interests, and that those interests are transparent to you, and that you have already decided certain identity characteristics about Alan as a consequence; but plainly, there are other determinations and other sides of Alan uncontrolled by the local business at hand that might also be made more visible. In short, the Solution to the original Identity-Rich Puzzle is ushered in with an Identity-Rich Puzzle of its own:[8] The clues Alan now develops to solve this new mystery will likewise serve to solve the *magic* of his business card.

Just as the jump from "my magic card" to "the whole thing" replaced one indeterminate reference with another, Alan's subsequent "a s– sort of kaleida–scopic experience–not really . . ." sustains an allusionary flow of talk with more allusions. A kaleidoscope is, after all, an optical delight, a perceptual trick, a toy, a work of art, a magical invention that turns reflected facets into an orderly version of a wonderful vision; but, on the other hand, the kaleidoscope holds forth only temporary order and is vulnerable to infinite and unfathomable change from both planned and unplanned disturbances—just the sort of universe insurance happens to service. The use of "kaleida–scopic" here appears to be a marvelously apt way of sustaining both official and unofficial identity potentialities through a continuously allusive flow of talk. Although policies on the hazards faced by some kaleidoscopic order are currently unavailable to the general public (and the potential for developing identity categories ungoverned by the interests of a "salesman" or a "client" is invigorated considerably as a consequence), as a metaphoric representation of the uncertainties confronting any apparently orderly universe (and the insurance tailor-made for it), Alan's "a s– sort of kaleida–scopic experience– not really . . ." is not altogether incognito, just wearing sunglasses. The rush to amend this remark at once, without interruption for breath, silence, or comment from Pete, underscores the metaphorical intention of this "kaleida– scopic experience" remark by opposing it to what "it" really is: "–not really it's just, y'know, uh two dimensional a(hh)ctually . . ." Just as the mystery about what "it" is survives in the juxtaposition of "kaleida–scopic experi- ence" and "two dimensional," so does the potential for both official and unofficial identity developments. Again, whether *two dimensional* intends to

describe the business card, the card and memobook, the buying and selling of
life insurance, life and death, and/or whatsoever else, Alan has disclosed
magical possibilities involving kaleidoscopic manipulations of real and actual
dimensions. While insurance is a very real business built upon actuarial
studies, Alan has developed his utterance in a direction simultaneously pro-
vocative of unofficial identity potentialities that consort with disturbances of
reality and actuality.

Alan's final remark carries the *magic* still closer to the unofficial identities
solving his initial Puzzle: ". . . heh ih–it all depends on y'know, what you've
been doing right before you, look at the card I guess if it's two dimensional,".
This is as close as Alan comes to formulating what you have to do to transform
a two-dimensional business card into a kaleidoscopic experience, but the
relevance of perception-altering drugs looms vividly hidden there. The identity
potentialities surrounding the use of drugs are, at last, concertedly unofficial
for the business at hand; indeed, the official identity categories of "salesman"
and "client" have been embedded in a more lively context characterized by
the potential for perceptual magic with the current dealings.[9]

Alan has delivered an Identity-Rich Solution which carefully introduces
the somewhat risky topic of drugs and the identities and activities drugs
make relevant by stacking one indeterminate referent upon another and
another. In the end, the utterance is poised not merely to excite the
unofficial identity categories accompanying perceptual distortions of reality and actuality; but also, by its exclusively allusive delicacy with these
unofficial "salesman" and "client" identities. Risky topics like "what
you've been doing right before you look at it" are made risky by such
careful introduction of course; it is remarkable that this broker of risks is
filling his unofficial identity horizons with risky topics.

In the next turn at talking, Pete's "Righ(h)t." brings closure to the
action sequence initiated four turns earlier by Alan's Identity-Rich Puzzle.
Although "Righ(h)t." acknowledges the materials of the Identity-Rich
Solution in the prior turn, it offers no elaboration on the unofficial
identities forwarded by Alan there. The turn at talking following an
Identity-Rich Solution is ripe for demonstrations of affiliation with
the identity categories enlivened by the solution, but while Pete's
"Righ(h)t." does·not distance itself thoroughly from the unofficial identities alluded to in Alan's prior Solution, neither does it jump to affiliate with those identities. In fact, if Alan's ". . . a(hh)ctually hehh hehh
hehh hehh heh . . ." displays animated enthusiasm over the identity negotiations conducted through the action sequence, then Pete's subsequent
"Righ(h)t." is considerably more reserved and steps down the animation
markedly.

Now it is plain enough that the identity implications of this action
sequence could receive more elaborate treatment than I offer here. Step
by step through the action sequence both official and unofficial identity

categories are sustained in interesting ways, and we might well treat the relations between the negotiated identities as our continuing research interest. Of course, other interests can be enlivened by close scrutiny of these materials, and some of those interests are not especially exercised by continued musings over allusive identity categories. Whatever the particulars of the identity negotiations, for example, the negotiations exhibit an organization of sequentially arranged turns at talking. Based on the sketch we have just been through, the action sequence generated by Alan's "magic card" description of his business card can be schematized as follows:

ALAN	Identity-Rich Puzzle
PETE:	Pass
ALAN:	Identity-Rich Solution
PETE:	Comment

This four-turn action sequence is very common. In the materials I have examined, it occurs in a wide variety of conversational environments, occupies a place in the conversational repertoire of persons who are otherwise "different" by traditional sociological variables, and can be used for an endless parade of interactional projects. In the following excerpt from a conversation between a "therapist" and a "patient" another identity negotiation is organized through a four-turn Puzzle–Pass–Solution–Comment action sequence:

MIKE:	We used t'have a good time around the ginny.
STAN:	The ginny?
MIKE:	Yeah, the ginny. People'd jump innit 'n get all nice 'n cooled off, and–duh, v'course it was no place t'get caught skinny dipping since ol' man Walters was church council president r'something hee heh, but we, y'know, managed t'spend part of every hot day dipping in the ginny hehh hehh heh
STAN:	Sounds like fun.

While in the earlier excerpt Pete's Comment ("Righ(h)t.") seems to be a disengagement from Alan's unofficial identity allusions ("it all depends on y'know, what you've been doing. . ."), in this instance Stan's Comment ("Sounds like fun.") seems affiliative with Mike's "dipping in the ginny." To be sure, ironic inflection could wrest any affiliation from "Sounds like fun." or a gestural display could sweep "Righ(h)t." into an intimate affiliation. I want to underscore, and not trivialize, the endless varieties of tinted interactional displays that do in fact occur in otherwise structurally identical action sequence positions. Whatever else may be their similarities and differences in topic, style, intent, and grace, and however else we might decide their relative artistry, both instances are organized as a four-turn Puzzle–Pass–Solution–Comment action sequence.

Sometimes, as in the following excerpt from a conversation between two "sisters," a four-turn Puzzle–Pass–Solution–Comment action sequence is generated when the "fine" part of a "How are you"/"Fine" exchange is built as an Identity-Rich Puzzle:

ELLEN: Fine, jus'fine thank you cept for this fucking *infec*tion.

PATTY: Infection?

ELLEN: I can't seem to get rid of this fucking, uh *ur*inary track infection–it's been dragging on now for a couple a'months– and it's driving me up a *wall* hehh hehh heh

PATTY: They're impossible I know all about it deary believe me– have you been, uh y'know to a doctor cause some penicillin or something was what finally knocked it outa'me.

Not only can this four-turn action sequence organize the burgeoning of a topic, and indeed stimulate the beginnings of a conversation as in this exchange between Ellen and Patty, but it can also organize the dénouement of a topic, and indeed transact closure to an encounter. In the following excerpt from a conversation between a "telephone operator" and a "businessman" an apparently unhappy interaction is brought to a close with a four-turn Puzzle–Pass–Solution–Comment action sequence:

B: . . . my problem, if you would jus'listen for a second has to do with what I need here.

O: What you need?

B: What I need. I've been trying for more than a month now to get installed one of your multiple input systems?

O: You're talking to the wrong department sir. Let me connect you with Sales.

It is not at all uncommon for the four-turn Puzzle–Pass–Solution–Comment action sequence to be "expanded" into a six-turn action sequence by the addition of a second Pass and the second Solution it generates. Most often, the second Pass repeats an item in the first Solution, rendering it an Identity-Rich Puzzle requiring its own interrogation before the Comment is delivered. In the following excerpt from a conversation between a "brother" and a "sister," the four-turn sequence is expanded to six turns by the insertion of a second Pass and the second Solution it generates:

LILLY: I'd love to come but–tuh, I'll be down at Mullard all week*end*,

RALPH: At Mullard?

LILLY: Y'know Mullard Space Lab in London. We're we're in the middle of a sort of a–experiment there?

● RALPH: A sort of experiment.

● LILLY: Yes, y'know they've launched this orbiting observatory carrying three grazing incidence uh X-ray telescopes, and this weekend, uhh, some important data from a, uh supernova's coming in.

RALPH: Bernice will be very unhappy about it y'know that don'tchu . . .

Now in all of these instances, an initial Identity-Rich Puzzle generates an action sequence organized around solving the referent it noticeably glosses over (viz., "my magic card," "the ginny," "this fucking infection," "what I need here," "at Mullard," and "a sort of a–experiment"); and, as we have seen, in the second position in each of these instances the Puzzle is repeated, passing it back to the prior speaker (viz., "Your magic card?" "The ginny?" "Infection?" "What you need?" "At Mullard?" and "A sort of experiment."). Upon the occurrence of an initial Identity-Rich Puzzle, there are of course other next action possibilities; but when an Identity-Rich Puzzle succeeds in generating subsequent talk about it, it appears as though a four-turn action sequence is a preferred interactional form. Consider the following from the Pete and Alan encounter with which we began:

ALAN:	Uhh, do you *have* any insurance.	74
PETE:	No *life* insurance.	75
ALAN:	No life insurance, yeah you have car	76
	and that don' chu.	77
	[	
PETE:	Yeah.	78

ALAN: We all have car, an– and s–stuff like   79
        that.   80

In this instance, Pete answers Alan's question (74) with an Identity-Rich
Puzzle ("No *life* insurance.") which not too mysteriously points to other
sorts of insurance Pete has. In the next turn Alan starts off with a repeat
of the Puzzle ("No life insurance,") which, we have seen, could serve to
pass the elaboration of that Puzzle back to Pete; but Alan continues his
utterance with the obvious Solution to the Puzzle himself (". . . yeah you
have car and that don' chu."). When Pete confirms Alan's Solution in the
next turn ("Yeah."), Alan is given the floor and uses this next turn for an
affiliative Comment on the discovered identity ("We all have car, an– and
s–stuff like that."). We can schematize the progress of this sequence as
follows:

ALAN: Identity-Rich Puzzle
PETE: Candidate Solution
ALAN: Confirmation
PETE: Comment

As it happens, this four-turn Puzzle–Solution–Confirmation–Comment
action sequence occurs again in the adjacent turns at talking:

ALAN: . . . Uh, what I would *like* to do is   80
        set some time to uh, get tuhgether   81
        with ya becuz, I have to go to summer   82
        camp.   83
PETE: Oh you're in the reserves.   84
ALAN: Yeah.   85
PETE: Oh.   86

where this time it is Alan who delivers an Identity-Rich Puzzle with his
reference to "summer camp" (82–83). Pete next offers a candidate Solution (84),[10] Alan then confirms the Solution (85), and Pete fills the fourth
turn in the action sequence with a Comment (86) that is not especially
affiliative, but nonetheless properly occupies that action sequence position.

    There are surely interactional uses for both the salesman and the
client in identity multiplication, and each can surely turn the generation of
unofficial identities by the other (namely the client's involvement with
other kinds of insurance and the salesman's involvement with military
obligations) into an occasion for affiliation or disaffiliation, approval or
disapproval, curiosity or incuriosity, and so on.[11] But what is being

underscored here is that both are deeply involved in the reciprocal generation of unofficial identities for one another through a four-turn Puzzle–Solution–Confirmation–Comment action sequence; in these adjacent action sequences, Alan and Pete trade places to occupy reciprocal positions so that the initiator of the first Puzzle (75) offers the Solution and Comment for the second Puzzle (82–83), and vice versa.

Now that we have developed some appreciation for the organization of these identity negotiations through discrete action sequences, let us consider briefly how they are woven together into an unfolding conversation for the systematic display of both official and unofficial identity potentialities.

CONCLUSION: SEQUENTIAL RESOURCES IN CONVERSATION

I have been describing a collection of sequential resources out of which speakers, hearers, and other beholders of conversation build their connections. Examining a little stretch of talk between a life insurance salesman and his prospective client has revealed that their exchange of remarks—remarks that are interestingly delicate in their negotiation of identities for Alan and Pete—is organized into characteristic action sequences. The relationships between these discretely packaged blocks of interaction exhibit a layer of sequential resources for making and breaking connections.

For example, Pete's "I gather you also wanna try t'sell me some insurance." (67–68) comes off as directly getting down to business because it comes as a next utterance to an Identity-Rich Puzzle sequence devoted to the elaboration of Alan's "magic card" description of his business card (51–64). This just prior package of talk is organized with sequential resources widely used by ordinary conversationalists, and we observed the four-turn Puzzle–Pass–Solution–Comment action sequence in a number of other circumstances. After this pointedly *un*official identity negotiation, Pete usurps the next turn at talking from the appropriate next speaker, and initiates a sequence pointedly contrastive by its devotion to the official business with his "I gather you also wanna try t'sell me some insurance." (67–68). In this instance, Pete follows an action sequence organized around the introduction of unofficial identities with one devoted to the official business of the encounter, and in this way, he displays an unwillingness to engage in identity multiplication. When it is identities that are being negotiated, the apposition of one kind of action sequence with another provides conversationalists with an arena for connecting or disconnecting from the identities promoted in each chunk of

interaction. In the Alan and Pete conversation, Pete disconnects by returning to official identities germane to the business at hand; but he only
asserts his disconnection after participating in the full Puzzle–Pass–Solution–Comment sequence in which an unofficial connection is developed. It may be that some action sequences are organized to resist
interruption, and with even an unwilling participant, they run to completion, whereupon a *next* action sequence is specifically organized to display the unwillingness buried in prior complicity. In any event, the interface between discretely organized packages of interaction (what I have
been calling "action sequences") can be systematically engaging *or* dis-
engaging, but it appears to be an environment—a specific sequential
locale—in which conversationalists negotiate their reciprocal identities.

Now we began with a consideration of the juxtaposition and fit
between Pete's first-formulation of the upcoming business (67–68) and
Alan's second formulation (89–92). The exchange of these intimately
coordinated utterances, we noted, does not occur in adjacent turns at
talking. In reviewing now the progress of the action sequence beginning
and ending with alternative versions of official identifications, we can
observe that the intervening interaction (69–88) orients to the propriety of
a successively forestalled second formulation from Alan:

PETE:	I gather you also wanna try t'sell me	67
	some insurance.	68
	(2.0)	69
ALAN:	Now– that doesn't sound like a bad	70
	idea–no, ih– it *would* be nice. But	71
	what I'd *like* to do,	72
	(3.0)	73
ALAN:	Uhh, do you *have* any insurance	74

Alan's "Now– that doesn't sound like a bad idea–no, ih– it *would* be
nice." (70–71) ironically underscores the conventional propriety of Pete's
just prior "getting down to business" remark (67–68) by characterizing it
as a novel idea, then ratifying his interest in it; but he goes on with a
response-start that asserts the availability of a counter formulation with
his "But what I'd *like* to do," (72). When Alan interrupts his own
response-start with silence (73), and then a direct question about the
business between them (74), his question and the answer it projects in a
subsequent turn at talking from Pete have been packaged as a side
sequence[12] merely "on the way" to a temporarily postponed second
formulation.

Engineering legitimate intrusions to an ongoing action sequence like first formulation/second formulation is an artful interactional enterprise sensitive to the sequential organization of conversation: and plainly, elaborate projects can be negotiated over the course of such side sequences. In this instance, as we have seen, the Identity-Rich Puzzle with which Pete answers Alan's question—"No *life* insurance." (75)—then generates a four-turn Puzzle–Solution–Confirmation–Comment sequence concerned with the other kinds of insurance Pete must have. The postponement of Alan's forthcoming second formulation has been extended still further, but through the course of this Identity-Rich Puzzle interruption, Pete can exhibit the unofficial domains of his biography he is willing to introduce in this conversation (Pete's unofficial other insurance policies are considerably more formal than Alan's prior "magic card" references to perception-altering drugs), and Alan can exhibit the domains of affiliation he is willing to exercise with Pete (Alan's affiliation with Pete's car insurance seems somehow less thrilling than *could* have been Pete's affiliation with Alan's "magic card" allusions). When this intervening Identity-Rich Puzzle sequence is brought to closure, Alan recalls his original response-start:

ALAN: . . . Uh, what I would *like* to do is. . . 80

where now on its second use, this response-start is used to develop a second Identity-Rich Puzzle sequence:

ALAN: . . . Uh, what I would *like* to do is 80
       set some time to uh, get tuhgether 81
       with ya becuz, I have to go to summer 82
       camp. 83

This time, as we have seen, Alan's reference to "summer camp" generates another four-turn Puzzle–Solution–Confirmation–Comment sequence through which one of Alan's unofficial identity positions enters the conversation. When this second intervening action sequence is played out, Alan develops his twice interrupted second formulation and moves, inevitably, into the dollars and cents of the encounter.

ALAN: An that's, fer two weeks, in uh, 87
       y'know for the nex'two weeks. 88
       Actually tuh go into it tonight, I 89
       like to be able to s'down an'prepare 90
       something specific'ly *for* a person I 91
       talk to. 92
         (2.0) 93

ALAN: Umm,   94
      (4.0)
ALAN: Um in thinking about it in that terms–   96
     er in those terms preparing something   97
     specific'ly for you do you have any,   98
     amount of money, thet you could set   99
     aside monthly. . .   100

Here then is a stretch of talk between Alan and Pete composed as an expanded two-turn first formulation/second formulation sequence. There were three successive expansions of that sequence: First, Alan's initially interrupting preliminary question projected at least an intervening question/answer sequence; then a return to the postponed sequence is extended by adjacent Identity-Rich Puzzle sequences punctuated by the repeat of Alan's first response-start in their midst.

I have been describing a collection of sequential resources and some of the systematic relations among them. In about a minute's worth of talk between Alan and Pete (51–92) we can finely describe the relations among a variety of discretely organized action sequences—one of them abruptly contrasting with a prior sequence, three of them legitimately expanding an ongoing sequence, and all of them organizing the reciprocal negotiation of official and unofficial identities. Naturally, over the course of these delicately enlaced action sequences other connections can surely be seen by private eyes.[13]

NOTES

1. These materials were collected in southern California in the summer of 1970 under a grant from the National Institutes of Health (1 F01 MH 44093).
2. Numbers within parentheses refer to specific lines of data.
3. Like many other things, so many of the "elsewheres" I look were shown to me by Harvey Sacks.
4. Although the encounter has been ostensibly arranged for the delivery of the life insurance handbook, neither Alan nor Pete, nor any of us, will be surprised when no mere delivery takes place. In another conversation I have studied, another life insurance salesman, delivering another promotional gift (this time, a free leatherette wallet), remarks about the initial direct-mail contact sent out by the company: "Y'know we send these *out* (2.0) –N'feel that– y'know, f'a guy's innerested enough t'even t'talk t'us, he– y'know, it's worth it t'us. Jus–tuh *get* the guy, y'know." That a delivery of some promotional gift will be turned into a sales attempt is known in advance by the client, counted on by the salesman, invested in by the company, and somehow known to all of us even though the prospect of the buying/selling project need never be formulated in advance by any of the participants to this tacit anticipation. There are, apparently, abstract features of encounters such as this one that organize the unfolding interaction from such things as deliveries towards such things as

the business at hand. The progress of these conversational movements is linked to the negotiation of various interactional enterprises. For these life insurance materials, "getting to" the buying/selling project is organized around systematic identity negotiations, and these will be elaborated here; but for a detailed consideration of "getting to" as a structural unit of these conversations see Schenkein (1971), particularly Chap. 2.

5. We will examine closely the space between these two formulations shortly (cf. p. 69 et seq.).

6. It seems to be the case that for encounters such as this one, the local experience of its unfolding is significantly constrained to come off as a version of some standard, unlived interaction. Personalizing the official formulation of the upcoming business with an impersonal policy declaration ("I treat anybody like a somebody") plugs Alan's second formulation into a guarantee of the conventional unfolding of the upcoming business; not only does Alan's declared policy invoke some abstract standard for encounters like this, but within this particular encounter, Alan's policy declaration marks a return to the standard unfolding from his just prior "summer camp" (82–88) and earlier "magic card" (52–64) informalities. I will have more to say about this contrast later (cf. p. 73 et seq.).

7. We have been looking at Passes for some time now. They figure in the "expansion" of action sequences, and come in very handy when jockeying for some later position in a projected action sequence. A more elaborate discussion of some other instances can be found in Jefferson and Schenkein (this volume, pp. 155–172).

8. The repetition of resources drawn from prior talk within the ongoing conversation is very common, and it is not at all unusual for something like an initial puzzle format to generate groups of Puzzle formats in subsequent talk (even in subsequent talk orienting to solving an earlier Puzzle). For an initial report on structural, topical, inflectional, thematic, and, in particular, sequential features of prior talk that are systematically repeated in the conduct of subsequent interactional enterprises, see Schenkein(1975b). See Jefferson(1977).

9. In the end, tracking down referents in any stream of talk rests on insight or interpretation of continuously equivocal meanings. I have used a smaller typeface for this portion of the discussion to mark clearly its position in my analysis as an instance of semantic tracking. In my attempt to introduce the notion of "Identity-Rich Solution," I was committed to describing the actual twists and folds of this particular turn at talking, but since this turn never becomes a straightforward declaration like "Let's talk about drugs," my description must inevitably rely on my interpretations of the allusions. I take it that I am not having a kaleidoscopic experience that dazzles me with an other-dimensional, freakish, interpretation; and moreover, I take it that many of us can see the drugs not mentioned there. We can see many things that are not there, of course, and unmentionables are among them. If, for some reason, you cannot see the drugs absent in Alan's Solution, at least you can see that his utterance is identity-rich, whatever his referent might otherwise be.

10. The Solution Pete comes up with, "Oh you're in the reserves" (84) involves a review of the kinds of activities Alan might reasonably be engaged in that require his having to go to summer camp. There are some other reasonable possibilities (e.g., Alan is going as an executive trainee, or a therapy session participant, or a camp counselor), and there are varieties of less likely possibilities (e.g., Alan is going as an Explorer Scout, or as an honor-farm parolee, or as a family spy on his younger sister); but all of the other possibilities would penetrate Alan's biography more deeply than biographies have been penetrated up until now in the conversation. As an excuse for interrupting normal routine, "summer camp" for a college-age male before the expiration of the Viet Nam draft calls simply meant "Oh you're in the reserves." Only a cultural stranger or other eccentric interlocutor could fail to come up with it. Pete's Solution is not especially perceptive, but it exhibits his

participation in multiplying identity categories for the salesman within generally available boundaries.

11. The phenomenon of "identity multiplication" is considered more elaborately in Schenkein (1971); see Chap. 6 particularly.

12. I am borrowing the term "side sequence" from Gail Jefferson (1972).

13. Some of the many benefits I enjoy from knowing Sheila Klatzky and Roland Wulbert have certainly found their way into the previous pages.

chapter 3

Compliment Responses

NOTES ON THE CO-OPERATION OF MULTIPLE CONSTRAINTS

ANITA POMERANTZ

INTRODUCTION

DEAR ABBY:

My wife has a habit of down-grading sincere compliments.

If I say, "Gee, Hon, you look nice in that dress," her reply is likely to be, "Do you really think so? It's just a rag my sister gave me."

Or if I tell her she did a great job cleaning up the house, her response might be, "Well, I guess you haven't seen the kids' room."

I find it hard to understand why she can't accept a compliment without putting herself down. And it hurts me a little. How do you explain it, Abby?

PERPLEXED

DEAR PERPLEXED:

Your wife lacks self-confidence and feels some-

what embarrassed to accept praise. Don't be hurt.
Most people have difficulty accepting compliments
with grace.[1]

"Perplexed" opens his letter with a description of something his wife purportedly does, namely, she downgrades sincere compliments. The description of the wife's downgrading of compliments is shaped into a description of how that behavior affects him.[2] The shaping of her behavior as a puzzle for him is illustrated in the selection of the closing identification, "Perplexed," which purportedly refers to what the writer is *relative to* his wife's responses to compliments.

The problems that the writer describes are problems which are presented to Abby for solution. The writer claims that he does not understand his wife's responses to compliments ("I find it hard to understand why . . .") and that he is hurt by those responses ("And it hurts me a little "). The problem behavior, i.e., that which he finds "hard to understand" and which "hurts" him, is his wife's not accepting (his) compliments.

Abby, in turn, treats the husband's request for an explanation of the problem behavior as legitimate by proffering, right off, an explanation: "Your wife lacks self-confidence . . . ." With that answer, the wife's rejecting of compliments is turned into a symptom, or manifestation, of her low self-esteem.

Within both the husband's letter and Abby's response, the problem behavior is referred to in terms which suggest the nonattainment of the preferred response—*accepting* compliments, for example, ". . . *can't* accept a compliment *without putting herself down*," ". . . *embarrassed* to accept praise," ". . . *difficulty* accepting compliments" (emphasis added).

The problem behavior, then, is behavior which does not conform to a model or standard. Deviations from that model, that is, the *not* accepting of compliments, may constitute noticeable, reportable, puzzling, troublesome, and symptomatic phenomena.[3]

Yet it is also known that compliments are very regularly either rejected, downgraded, or only qualifiedly accepted. As Abby suggests, "Most people have difficulty accepting compliments with grace."

To examine compliment responses, then, is to examine behavior where actual performances are often discrepant from ideal or preferred performances, and where actual performances are often reported as, at least, somewhat problematic.

RESEARCH PROBLEM

A large proportion of compliment responses deviate from the model response of accepting compliments. A close examination of those responses reveals that while rejections are frequent, they are not performed as preferred seconds.[4] While various sequential features suggest that determination, one indication is that most compliment responses lie somewhere in between (not at the polar extremes of) acceptances and agreements on the one hand and rejections and disagreements on the other.

In this chapter an organization will be described which accounts, in part, for the "in between-ness" of compliment responses. That organization involves the co-operation of conflicting preferences on compliment responses, that is, preferences which are concurrently relevant but not concurrently satisfiable.[5]

Compliment responses will be seen to be subject to separate systems of constraints. One system which is relevant is that of recipients' agreements or disagreements with prior compliments. Responses to compliments often find expression as second assessments which are formed as agreements or disagreements with the prior compliments. In the agreement/disagreement system, agreements are generally performed as preferred seconds and disagreements as dispreferred seconds.

A second system of constraints has already been mentioned: accepting or rejecting prior compliments. In this system, acceptances are generally performed as preferred seconds and rejections as dispreferred seconds.

The two systems, agreement/disagreement and acceptance/rejection, are interrelated. While the subtleties of their interrelatedness will be dealt with subsequently, as an initial statement it can be said that there is an affiliation between the preferences and the dispreferences of each system. That is, agreements are associated with acceptances and disagreements with rejections.

Given the general operation of the agreement/disagreement system and the acceptance/rejection system and the interaction between them, one would expect a high representation of agreements and acceptances as compliment responses. The data, however, run contrary to this expectation. The prevalence of disagreements and rejections is proposed to be an outcome of yet another system of constraints which co-operates along with the other systems on compliment responses. That system involves speakers' minimization of self-praise.

For recipients of compliments, the preferences to (*a*) agree with

and/or accept compliments and (b) avoid self-praise stand in potential
conflict. Various "solutions" to, or "resolutions" of, these conflicting
constraints are available to recipients of compliments. The remainder of
this paper will be devoted to descriptions of constraint systems which
bear on compliment responses, and solution types to conflicting constraints as displayed by compliment responses.

CONSTRAINT SYSTEMS

Compliment responses are coordinated with the compliments which
they follow. One kind of system that links compliment responses with
prior compliments is that of chained actions. An action chain may be
characterized as a type of organization in which two ordered actions,
$Action_1$ and $Action_2$, are linked such that the performing of A_1 provides
the possibility of performance of A_2 as an appropriate next action.[6] A
given utterance which is an instance of an $Action_1$ in a particular action
chain may simultaneously be an instance of a different $Action_1$. That is, it
may provide the possibility of actualization of one of several specifiable
$Action_2$s as an appropriate next action.

One action chain for compliments consists of:

A_1:   A compliments B.
A_2:   B accepts/rejects the compliment.

Upon receipt of a compliment (A_1), a recipient may perform an acceptance or rejection of it (A_2). In this action chain, compliments have the
status of "supportive" actions. Supportive actions, including offers, invitations, gifts, praise, and so on, are organized as having acceptances/
rejections as relevant next actions.

A second action chain which is relevant for compliments as $Action_1$s
consists of:

A_1:   A compliments B.
A_2:   B agrees/disagrees with the complimentary assertion.

Upon the production of a complimentary assertion (A_1), a next speaker
may perform an agreement or disagreement with it (A_2). In this action
chain, compliments have the status of assessments, and as such, they
engender recipients' agreements and disagreements.[7]

To reiterate, two sets of $Action_2$s which are linked with prior compliments are acceptance/rejection and agreement/disagreement. The members of the two sets are interrelated, acceptances with agreements and rejections with disagreements. Some features of the relatedness of these members will be explicated in the following sections.

Acceptances

Acceptances and rejections are A_2 alternatives subsequent to a number of supportive actions, including the class, compliments. The alternatives, however, are nonequivalent, with acceptances preferred and rejections dispreferred. One basis for the claim of nonequivalency has already been suggested: that the action of accepting compliments is referred to in talk as model behavior and that of rejecting compliments as puzzling, troublesome, symptomatic, and so forth. In addition to being considered nonequivalent, the alternatives are sequentially organized nonequivalently. They inhabit differently shaped turns and sequences and differ in their potential for termination of sequences.[8]

The preferred action chain, that is, the chain with a preferred A_2, for a compliment as a supportive action, is:

A_1:   A compliments B.
A_2:   B accepts the compliment.

The acceptances are regularly accomplished with appreciations. Erving Goffman has elaborated on some aspects of such supportive interchanges:

> When a ritual offering occurs, when that is, one individual provides a sign of involvement in and connectedness to another, it behooves the recipient to show that the message has been received, that its import has been appreciated, that the affirmed relationship actually exists as the performer implies, that the performer himself has worth as a person, and finally, that the recipient has an appreciative, grateful nature . . . the giving statement tends to be followed immediately by a show of gratitude.[9]

Subsequent to compliments, appreciations regularly take the form of *appreciation tokens,* for example, "thank you," "thanks," "thank you so much," and "well thank you." A feature of an appreciation token is that it recognizes the status of the prior as a compliment without being semantically fitted to the specifics of that compliment. That is, it does not, itself, contain a focus upon the referent of the compliment.[10]

If an appreciation token is to be performed as an A_2, it should be performed in a next turn to a compliment.

[SBL:2.2.4.-3]
    A: Why it's the loveliest record I ever heard.   (1)
                 And the organ–
                 [
●   B: Well *thank* you.

[KC4:33]
    F: That's beautiful It really is   (2)
                            [
    R: Yah
●   K: Thank you

[HS:S:11]
    A: You look so nice.   (3)
    B: I got a new shirt.
    A: It's very pretty.
●   B: Thank you.

[SBL:2.2.4.-3]
    A: Well I–I wannid to say I enjoyed your class so   (4)
                 this morning, and *too*.
●   B: Well, thank you.

It seems plausible that in doing an appreciation, a recipient recognizes the prior not merely as a compliment, but as that sort of compliment which warrants an acceptance, that is, that *should* be accepted; that with his acceptance–appreciation, he may be seen to be implicitly agreeing with the prior compliment.

The evidence for the connectedness between acceptances and agreements is rather stronger than "plausibility."

Agreements

Subsequent to assessments, agreements are A_2s. A major type of agreement in this environment is one achieved with a second assessment. The referent assessed in a prior assessment is again assessed in a current turn such that current speaker's assessment (the second) stands in agreement with prior speaker's. Referent preservation across the pair of assessments is a feature of such agreements. This very prevalent agreement construction is illustrated in the instances below:

[MC:1]
    B: Isn't he cute   (5)
    A: O::h he::s a::*dor*able

[JK:3]
    C: . . . She was a nice lady––I liked her   (6)
    G: I liked her too

[GJ:1]
    A: She's a fox!   (7)
    L: Yeh, she's a pretty girl.

The affiliation between acceptances of compliments (appreciation tokens) and agreements (second assessments in agreement) is demonstrated by the relative positioning between those components.

Acceptance components may be followed by agreement components within responses to compliments. Those two components may co-occur in recipient's next turn to a compliment; for example,

[SBL:2.2.4.-3]
    A: Oh it was just *beau*tiful.   (8)
●   B: Well *thank* you + Uh I thought it was quite
                       nice . . .

[JS:II:6]
    L: *Those*'r jus' *beau*tiful.⌈(They're great.)   (9)
    E: ⌊Well–
●   E: Thank– + It's juh– This is *just* the *right*
                       (weight).

or in recipient's successive turns within a compliment sequence, e.g.,

[SBL:2.2.4.-3]
    A: Why it's the loveliest record I ever heard.   (1a)
●   B: Well *thank* you.
                       [[
    A: And the organ–
    A: The organ music came out so beauti-
                       fully in it.
                       [
●   B: I thought it did *too*,

[KC4:33]

F:	That's beautiful. It really is	(2a)
	[	
R:	(Yah)	
K:	Thank you	

      .

      .

      .

F:	That is beautiful
	[
K:	'n that nice

Acceptance and agreement components, then, may be used in combination and/or as alternatives by recipients within compliment sequences.

Rejections

Subsequent to instances of some classes of supportive actions, for example, offers and invitations, rejections often contain appreciation components, including negated appreciations (e.g., "No thanks") and/or accounts for the rejection. The accounts are frequently formed with reference to the occasion at hand, that is, provides something which stands as an explanation of why this particular invitation, offer, etc., at this particular time is not being accepted. A few illustrations of rejections containing both components are presented below:

[BC:1]   (10)
JOHN:	You wanna sandwich?	[offer]
DAVE:	No thanks,	[neg. appreciation]
	I ate before I left.	[account]

[JS:II:142]   (11)
L:	Bill? Whaddiyou drink.	[offer]
( ):	Thank you dear	[appreciation]
	I'm not– not drinking right now.	[account]

[SBL:1.1.10.-14]   (12)
| B: | Uh if you'd care to come over and visit a little while this morning, I'll give you a cup of coffee. | [invitation] |
| A: | Hehh! Well that's awfully sweet of you, | [appreciation] |

I don't think I can make it this   [account]
morning um, I'm running an ad in the
paper and–and uh I have to stay near
the phone.

In contrast to the type of rejection construct above, rejections to compliments are not formed with (negated) appreciations plus account. Rather, the primary way in which compliments are rejected is with disagreements or qualifications of the prior complimentary assertions.

Disagreements

As illustrations of rejections accomplished with disagreements, the two responses reported in the "Dear Abby" letter will be briefly discussed.

H: Gee, Hon, you look nice in that dress   (A)
W: Do you really think so? It's just a rag my sister
            gave me.

In response to the husband's complimentary assessment, the wife does a second evaluation, that is, *her* evaluation, which stands in some disagreement with the prior. Disagreement machinery is utilized at least with respect to recipient's selection of a contrastively classed (negative) evaluative term, "just a rag," from the positive one contained in the prior, "nice."

H: (You) did a great job cleaning up the house.   (B)
W: Well I guess you haven't seen the kids' room.

In (B), the wife presents an argument in response to H's compliment. She locates an intended "exception": "The kids' room" is what she proposes invalidates his favorable assessment. As in (A), the wife's response in (B) is a kind of disagreement with the prior positive characterization ("great job").

Some aspects of the interrelatedness between acceptances and agreements, and rejections and disagreements may be summarized as follows: While appreciations and agreements are affiliated components (as evidenced by their co-occurrence in local environments), they are not sequentially interchangeable. Agreements tend to occur less frequently than appreciations and seem to have more restrictive conditions for their productions. When agreements do co-occur with appreciations, they are proffered routinely after initial appreciations. In short, while appreciations and agreements are interrelated, appreciations over agreements seem to be preferentially selected for accepting compliments.

Rejections are routinely performed with disagreements.

The suggested interrelatedness is shown below:

For acceptances	For rejections
(P) Appreciation tokens	
(S) Agreements	(P) Disagreements

Note: (P) indicates preferential selection. (S) indicates an affiliated though secondary selection.

The interactions between acceptances, appreciations, and agreements, and between rejections and disagreements, do not account for the prevalence of rejections and disagreements and the relative infrequency of acceptances, particularly of agreements, which occur subsequent to compliments. That configuration is an artifact of a co-operating constraint system which stands in opposition to the satisfaction of acceptances and agreements.

Self-Praise Avoidance

When a recipient agrees with a prior compliment, he affiliates his position with the prior asserted position; when he disagrees, he disaffiliates his position from that of the prior. Subsequent to compliments, agreements/disagreements which retain prior referents are agreements/disagreements with praise of self.

A: Praise of B
B: Agreement/disagreement with praise of self

There is a system of constraints governing how parties may credit or praise themselves. *Self-praise avoidance* names a system of constraints which is enforceable by self and/or other, in that order. Some illustrative materials of enforcements by self and by other are presented below.

If self-praise is performed by a speaker, that is, if a speaker does not enforce upon himself self-praise avoidance, a recipient may in next turn make notice of the violation and enforce the constraints. One way is with critical assessments of the self-praiser:

[GTS:2:17]

K:	. . Y'see I'm so terrific,	(13)
● A:	Y'see folks, he is *very vain*, an' he realizes his mature talents compared to our meager contents of our minds.	

[HS:S]

A:	Just think of how many people would miss you. You would know who cared.	(14)
B:	Sure. I have a *lot* of friends who would come to the funeral and say what an intelligent, bright, witty, interesting person I was.	
● A:	They would*n't* say that you were *humble*	
B:	No. Humble, I'm not.	

[v.D.II]

J:	I heard that on my radio that night Richie.=I–I *knew* I (was hearing) your voice coming into my bedroom.	(15)
R:	O::h. Could you have taped that?=I'd've *loved* t'hear my voice ( )	
● S:	"M(hh)odesty is o(hh)ne of my gr(h)eatest virt(hh)ues"hhh	

While self-praise may not be publicly noticed on any given occasion, it is, nonetheless, a class of action which is noticeable and collectible with the possibility, on a subsequent occasion, of being turned into a complaint, a gossip item, an unfavorable character assessment, and so on.

[W.1]

C:	They got this one girl that they're always talking about you know	(16)
	.	
	.	
	.	
● R:	They probably say she thinks she's cute she's this, she's that	

Self-praise constraints may be enforced by the speaker, himself, in a variety of ways. One way is to incorporate a disclaimer within self-praising talk, e.g.,

[BC:III:28]

B: So he– so then, at this– y'see, *––I don' like to* (17)
         brag but see he sorta like backed outta the
         argument then.

or qualification, e.g.,

[S.2]

G: Ken gave that internship to Peter?! I'm much (18)
         better than he is! *Well maybe I shouldn't say*
         that.

[JG:5]

A: . . I wonder if they're, you know, lurking (19)
         around trying to think of somebody who's you
         know can manage it.

B: Yeah. You'd be *per*fect.

A: Well you know as far as *I'm* concerned I
         would plus the fact that everybody else that
         they've, you know–that we've got at the store
         I've gone *through* throughly uhh

A: . . and I don't figure anybody else can do it
         only–

● A: *not from the standpoint that they can' handle*
         the job=

B: Umhum.
       =[[

● A: *don't misunderstand me.*

B: Right.

A: Bu–like Janet Brown, she's goin' to school in
         Northridge.

B: Oh:

A: An holding down a full time job here . . .

[AA:2.1]

         ((Overlapping talk which is not a part of this (20)
         conversation has been omitted.))

J: Well wuh– whadduz uhm, what did Rourke
         say tuh you.
         ((pause))

S: What– did he *say?*

S: Uh,
         ((pause))

S:	Thet I w'z the most fan*tas*tic employee he ever *ha:d*.
● S:	Well. Not exactly.
● S:	He jus' tol' Jim en I thet (we're getting a raise).

The system of *self-praise avoidance* is not limited to violation markers by self and other. It also bears on how crediting is done. The constraints on *self*-praise are collaboratively oriented to and interactionally satisfied with *coparticipant* praise activities. That is, an orientation that coconversationalists display with respect to each other is to see that others are properly credited. For example, announcements of accomplishments are often initiated by one in behalf of another present:

[v.D.II]

● R:	*You* should *see* this paper she wrote. –Eighty (21) pages.
	(1.0)
● R:	I have to brag about you Dotty.
	(1.5)
● R:	Quite a masterpiece
D:	Thank you.

[JS:II:142]

● E:	Jo– this's, this's one *Jon* made, (22)
M:	He *di::d* you mean the em*broi*dery?
E:	*Ye:::s*
	.
	.
	.
M:	( ) so ta:lented::d.

Credit may also be shifted *to* coparticipant subsequent to that coparticipant's praise of other-than-self.

[SBL:1.1.12.-27]

B:	. . I really think it was *the C.F.O. Camp that* (23) *worked this out for me.*
A:	Uh huh, Uh huh, Well, (it's true)–You mean–
	(1.0)
A:	you were in*spired* there,

B: Yeah, I think was uh huh, I–
                [[
● A: But it was with– it was with– *It was within*
                yourself,

[SBL:1.1.12.-35]
A: *So*, they'll be nice to have in the house there,   (24)
B: Mm hm,
                            [
A: I won't– I won't worry about things.
                                            [
B: No,
● B: Uh and I think it's– and Bea, you know, well,
                I think it's awfully nice of you to r–rent to a
                family with children.

[NB:4.-7]
B: So ev'rybuddy's been nice in the 'partmint   (25)
                just like with my leg ehh heh hah hah!
                                    [
A: Ye::a::uh.
● A: Well you– People *should* be nice tuh you
                Agnes, yer a, thoroughly nice person tuh be
                nice to.

Subsequent to compliments, the preferences of (*a*) avoiding self-
praise and (*b*) accepting and agreeing with the compliment are at odds
with one another. If a compliment were to be agreed with, a recipient
would be, at the same time, praising himself. And since agreements and
acceptances are co-implicated, the satisfaction of the acceptance preference is in potential conflict with the satisfaction of self-praise avoidance.

Instances of actual compliment responses display a sensitivity to
these potentially incompatible sets of constraints. An analysis of compliment responses suggests that they may be seen as types of "solutions" to
the multiple preferences described above.

SOLUTION TYPES

Praise Downgrades

One solution type includes responses which display a sensitivity to,
and partial satisfaction of, the two conflicting preferences: to accept/agree

with prior compliment and to avoid self-praise. These responses exhibit features of both agreements and disagreements, that is, the agreements display some features of disagreements and vice versa.

An apparatus which allows for the "in between-ness" of these responses is one that includes ordered agreement and disagreement forms.

One type of agreement, an upgrade, can be called "optimal" on sequential grounds.[11] Upgrades are prevalent in environments in which agreements are preferred; they occur in agreement turns and sequences and typically not in combination with disagreements. Upgrading techniques include the incorporation of stronger second evaluation terms, for example,

[JS:II:28]

J:	T's– tsuh beautiful day out isn't it?	(26)
● L:	Yeh it's just gorgeous . . .	

[MC:1]

A:	Isn't he *cute*	(27)
● B:	O::h he::s a::*dor*able	

and added intensifiers, for example:

[SBL:2.1.8.-5]

B:	She seems like a nice little lady	(28)
	[	
● A:	Awfully nice little person.	

[JS:I.11]

E:	Hal couldn' get over what a good *buy* that was, (Jon),	(29)
	[	
J:	Yeah	
● J:	=That's a r– a rerry good buy.	

The counterpart of an upgrade as optimal agreement is a contrastive opposite as optimal disagreement. Contrastive opposites are produced in environments in which disagreements are preferred, for example, subsequent to self-depreciations; they occur in disagreement turns and sequences and typically not in combination with agreements. The following instances are of that type: They have contrastively classed evaluative terms relative to the priors, that is, negative, critical evaluations are followed by positive, complimentary ones.

[JG:2]
    R: Did she get my card.   (30)
    C: Yeah she gotcher card.
    R: Did she t'ink it was terrible
•   C: No she thought it was very adohrable.

[NB:IV:1.-6]
    A: . .'hhh Oh well it's *me* too Portia, hh (31)
                        yihknow I'm no bottle a' milk,
                            (0.6)
•   P: Oh:: well *yer* easy tuh get along with, but *I*
                        know he's that way.

[SBL:2.1.8.-8]
    B: I was wondering if I'd ruined *yer– week-* (32)
                        end by uh
                        [
•   A: No. No. Hm-mh. No, I just loved to
                      have–...

Subsequent to compliments, second assessments are regularly neither upgraded agreements nor contrastive opposites.

Agreements

Recipients of praise sometimes agree with the prior praise-assessment. When agreements are performed in this environment, they have a characteristic form. They are second assessments which are systematically altered relative to the prior assessments, containing scaled-down, or more moderate praise terms than the priors.

In the following sequences, praise profferer (P), incorporates strong-positive evaluative terms; praise recipient (R), responds with scaled-down agreements containing more moderate-positive terms.

[AP:fn]
    B: I've been offered a full scholarship at Berke- (33)
                      ley and at UCLA
  (P) ↑ G: That's fantastic
• (R) ↓ B: Isn't that good

[SBL:2.2.4.-3]
  (P) ↑ A: Oh it was just beautiful.   (8a)
• (R) ↓ B: Well *thank* you uh I thought it was quite nice,

[JB:II.I.-4]

D: I'm the boys Dean out there, so I gotta new   (34)
jo:b 'n=

C: =Yeah?

D: So it's a pretty good setup yihknow,

(P) ↑C: W'l my God it sounds *mar*velou s Don,
                                             [

●(R) ↓D: Yeah *it* is, it's
a– it's a good deal,

Scaled-down agreements exhibit features of both agreements and disagreements.

Their format is that of agreement turns: They frequently have initially positioned agreement tokens (Example 34) or appreciations (Example 8a). Although scaled down relative to the priors, they are, nonetheless, similarly classed, that is, likewise positive evaluations. As such, they may be treated by coparticipants as agreements with prior compliments. In the following fragments, praise profferers respond to praise recipients' scale-downs with subsequent agreements:

[SBL:2.2.4.-3]

A: Oh it was just *beau*tiful.   (8b)

↓ B: Well *thank* you Uh I thought it was quite
nice, A nd uh
                            [

● A: Mm hm.

[KC4:10]

F: That's beautiful   (35)

↓ K: Is'n it pretty

● F: Yea::h

[KC4:35]

F: That is beautiful   (2b)
                         [

↓·K: 'n that nice

● R: Yah. It really is

Although scale-downs are formated within agreement turns, they may display some sequential features of disagreements. In crediting activities, the respective parties, (P) and (R), have systematically discrepant positions.

Activities in which praise is proffered, including compliments, appreciations, congratulations, and so on, overwhelmingly contain strong-positive evaluative terms. That is, crediting actions are preferentially performed with strong-positive descriptors.[12]

Recipients of praise are subject to self-praise avoidance, or modesty constraints.[13] Praising self with strong-positive descriptors has a violative status.

Within praise sequences, the respective parties have different collections of descriptors that they preferentially draw from: profferer selecting strong-positive terms and recipient moderate-positive. A sensitivity to that discrepancy may be displayed by the coparticipants. To avoid affirming the prior evaluative terms as his own, a speaker replaces the prior terms with ones he endorses.

Praise sequences, then, may contain the party variants in alternation. A profferer's strong-positive term (↑) may be replaced by recipient's moderate-positive term (↓) which may then be replaced in profferer's praise reaffirmation with a strong-positive term (↑).

[AP:fn]

B:	I've been offered a full scholarship at Berke-	(33a)
	ley and at UCLA	
↑ G:	That's fantastic	
↓ B:	Isn't that good	
↑ G:	That's marvelous	

[GJ:fn]

The referent is L's new bride

↑ A:	She's a fox!	(7a)
↓ L:	Yeh, she's a pretty girl.	
↑ A:	Oh, she's *gor*geous!	

[NB:VII.-2]

The referent is M's friend.

↑ E:	That Pat. Isn't she a doll::	(36)
↓ M:	Yeh isn't she pretty,	
↑ E:	*Oh* she's a beautiful girl.	
↓ M:	Yeh I think she's a pretty girl.	

Scaled-down agreements, then, exhibit features of both agreements and disagreements. On the one hand they are formed as agreements, namely, second praises with more moderate terms. On the other hand, the replacements of the evaluation terms constitute discrepancies which may engender successive reassertions of the parties' respective positions.

Productions of scaled-down agreements seem to be subject to the following restriction: They do not normatively occur subsequent to compliments which *directly* praise coparticipant.[14] Compliments which may engender scaled-down agreements contain reference terms which locate objects, persons, activities, and so on, other than coparticipant directly ("you"), namely, referents through which coparticipants are accorded credit.

In general, scaled-down agreements occur subsequent to compliments containing reference formulations consisting of other-than-you terms, for example, "it," "that," "she," "he." The scaled-down agreements retain the other-than-me referents:

[AP:fn]

B:	I've been offered a full scholarship at	(33b)
	Berkeley and at UCLA	
G:	That's fantastic	
B:	Isn't that good	

[SBL:2.2.4.-3]
The referent is a performance for which B is responsible.

| A: | Oh it was just *beau*tiful. | (8c) |
| B: | Well *thank* you uh I thought it was quite nice, | |

[KC4:10]
The referent is a blanket that K is weaving.

| F: | That's beautiful | (35a) |
| K: | Is'n it pretty | |

[GJ:fn]
The referent is L's new bride.

| A: | She's a fox! | (7b) |
| L: | Yeh, she's a pretty girl. | |

[NB:VII.-2]
The referent is M's friend.

| E: | That Pat. Isn't she a doll:: | (36a) |
| M: | Yeh isn't she pretty, | |

Members of compliment response classes, then, are selected in part relative to the directness with which the recipients are praised. The more indirectly recipients are credited, that is, with compliments locating referents which are isolable as external to recipients, the more likely agreements are to occur. The agreements, however, are scaled down, the scale-down reflecting the constraints imposed by indirect praise of recipient.

Disagreements

Recipients of compliments frequently disagree with prior compliments. They may disagree by proposing that the creditings within the prior compliments are overdone, exaggerated, etc., and counterpropose that lesser amounts of credit are justified:

[JG:3C:6]
The referent is an athletic award R has received.

	C:	Well we'll haftuh *frame* that.	(37)
●	R:	Yee– *Uh*ghh it's not worth fra(hh)mi(h)ng,	
	C:	W'*sure* it is.	
		(1.0)	
	R:	*Well?*	
	C:	You'll have a whole *wall* of framings.	
●	R:	Tch! No, it's not really impo:rtnt,	
	C:	Well I think it's *very* important=En I'm *very* pleased.	

[SBL:2.6.-7]

	B:	*By* the way I *loved* yer Christmas card,	(38)
		.	
		.	
		.	
●	A:	I hadda hard time, but I didn't think they were too good, . . .	

[NB:5]

	A:	. .you've lost suh much weight	(39)
●	P:	Uhh hmhh uhh hmhh well, not *that* much	
		[	
	A:	*Aaghh Haghh Haghh!*	

[BS:2.1.192]

	T:	AH:: you saved *me* some!	(40)
●	L:	I(hh)t's not mu(hh)ch– ((sniff))=	
	T:	=Oh yer so nice=	
●	L:	=–tuh sa(hh)ve ((sniff))	
	T:	Yer so nice.	

[JS:II:9]
```
    L:                 You   brou:ght.  –like   a   ton   of   things.  (41)
                       (          )
                       [
●   E:                 Just a few little (thi::ngs,)
```

In proposing diminutions of credit, recipients generally do not altogether negate or deny prior assertions but rather downgrade the prior
terms.

[NB:5] "..not *that* much"   (39a)

[BS:2.1.192] "I(hh)t's not mu(hh)ch– . . . –tuh sa(hh)ve . . ." (40a)

[JS:II:9] "*Just* a few little (thi::ngs,)   (41a)

Disagreements as seconds to compliments are frequently marked as *qualifications* of the prior compliments rather than directly contrastive coun-
terassertions. Disagreement markers used with such qualifications include
"though," "yet," and "but."

[AP:FN]
```
    A:                 Good shot                                          (42)
●   B:                 Not very solid though
```

[JS:II:152]
```
    L:                 (Lookit how pretty that looks.)                    (43)
    J:                 Yeah.
    A:                 I don'know.

    B:                 (        ).
    E:                 Oh that does look pretty with the (    )
                                        [
●   M:                                  It isn't a very good
                       (    ) though.
```

[MC:I.-37]
```
    L:                 –and yer– ––logical reasoning. –––is taking  (44)
                       the upper hand as you go along.=
    W:                 =Oh yah.
    L:                 Yeh–you're not frustrated in six different
                       ways.
    W:                 No, No,
```

L: And this all sho:ws. –in everything yuh say 'n
                do ez yih go along.
●   W: Yet I've got quite a distance tuh go yet.

[KC4:38]
R: (   ) beautiful colors (   ) such a (nice) rich   (45)
                color.

                           .

                           .

                           .

●   K: But *real* tartons are much more subdued in
                their coloring than these vegetable dyes . . .

[BH:1-A:23]
K: Those tacos were good!   (46)
B: You liked them . . .
K: I loved 'em, yes.
●   B: I'm glad, but uh, next time we have 'em we'll,
                the uh, the tortillas a little bit more crispy . . .

Although these compliment responses are not contrastive opposites
but are rather diminutions and qualifications of prior praises, they
nonetheless are treated as disagreements. Subsequent to such disagreements, praise profferers may challenge or disagree with the diminutions
and qualifications and reassert praise:

[AP:FN]
A: Good shot   (42a)
B: Not very solid (though)
●   A: Ya' get any more solid, you'll be terrific

[JS:II:9]
L: You *brou:ght*.–like a *ton* of things. (   ) (41b)
                                                   [
E: *Just* a
                few little (thi::ngs,)
●   J: *Oh* (are you kidding?) (God   ) (Filled up
                the   ).

[SBL:3.6.-7]
B: *By* the way I *loved* yer Christmas card,   (38a)

                           .

                           .

                           .

A:	I hadda hard time, but I didn't think they were too good, but– – –
A:	-finally,
	[[
• B:	(Those) were *lovely*. *I* thought they were *love*ly. [
A:	Uh huh,
	thanks,=
A:	=–finally had tuh settle on something." cause I–
• B:	Well *I* thought uh ( ) choice was *beau*tiful.

To reiterate, disagreements as seconds to compliments display features which are similar to agreements as compliment responses. A large set of both agreements and disagreements are scale-downs of the prior praise accorded to recipients. Negotiations which occur within these compliment sequences follow predictable directions: Recipients downgrade prior praise, and profferers upgrade the prior downgrades.

Praise downgrades represent one type of solution to the incompatible preferences operating on compliment responses—that of "compromise." With downgrades, the referent of the prior is preserved, but the praise is neither totally agreed with (i.e., it is responsive to self-praise avoidance) nor totally disagreed with (i.e., it is also responsive to acceptance/ agreement preferences).

Agreement and disagreement downgrades are responses which partially satisfy each of the conflicting preferences.

Referent Shifts

A second solution type of compliment responses works on the principle of referent shifts. In a compliment (A_1) a recipient is praised either directly or indirectly; in this type of response, the recipient performs a subsequent praise (A_2) which has other-than-self as referent.

A_1: A praises B.
A_2: B praises other-than-self.

Two kinds of referent shifts, differentiated with respect to constructional and sequential features, are discussed below.

Reassignment of Praise.

In responding to a compliment, a recipient may reassign the praise, shifting the credit from himself to an other-than-self referent, for example, an object. The following sequence contains one such typical credit shift:

[WC:YCC.-4]

| R: | You're a good rower, Honey. | (47) |
| J: | These are very easy to row. Very light. | |

In R's compliment, J is praised as "a good rower." In J's second to the compliment, the type of boat is praised as "very easy to row. Very light." In response to the compliment, J forms an assessment in which the referent being praised is shifted from himself to other-than-himself, namely, the boat.

When the placement of credit is negotiated within compliment sequences, the amount of credit, per se, is not generally simultaneously negotiated. Routinely, if a second has a shift in the agent being credited, it does not have downgraded evaluational terms. Descriptors in seconds are topically selected relative to the shifts and usually are at least as strong as the prior descriptors.

[WS:YMC.-4]

| R: | You're a good rower, Honey. | (47a) |
| J: | These are very easy to row. Very light. | |

The praise within the compliment is accomplished with the phrase, "a good rower, Honey." In the compliment response, the praise terms, "very easy" and "very light," are co-selected for the type of boat. Whereas "easy" and "light" are positive descriptors, they are nonetheless upgraded with the intensifier "very."

Negotiations over the placement of credit are structured relative to the sets of constraints operant on the respective parties. Profferers of credit accord credit to coparticipants. Recipients of credit shift credit away from themselves. These positions are particularly visible in the following materials.

In (2c) below, F credits K by focusing on K *as the weaver* of the blanket which is being admired:

[KC4:31]

| F: | . . What ayou making? | (2c) |
| K: | It's a blanket | |

```
 •   F:              Did yu weave that yourself
                                    [
     K:                              I wove this myself
     D:              She wove all of this herself
                                  [
 •   F:                           Ya kidding
```

Later in the sequence, F admires the blanket with a positive assessment. K responds to the positive assessment first with a scaled down agreement, and then in her next turn with credit shift (←) away from herself as weaver:

[KC4:35]
```
     F:              That is beautiful                                (2d)
                          [
     K:                  'N that nice
     R:              Yah. It really is
 ← K:              It wove itself. Once it was set up=
```

A shift in focus from recipient, within the compliment, to "it" or other-than-self, within the response, may function like a disagreement. The profferer's credit of the recipient and the recipient's focusing of the credit away from self to "it" may be oriented to as a discrepant position, with the reinstitution of respective positions in alternation across a series of turns. In the following sequences, (→) marks turns in which coparticipants are credited; (←) marks turns in which credit is focused away from self.

[BC:IV:27]
```
 → B:              . . I love the way you do that commercial. ehh!  (48)
     A:              Muhhh!
 → B:              hhhh! It's original ehhh!
     A:              Well, you know, It's uh:::v- uh::: o–oddly
                    enough, have yuh tried the stuff?
     B:              No I have never tried it. I– I mean to.
                                                 [
 ← A:                                            For shame. It is
                    beautiful bread.
     B:              hhh you know, eh I– it– it's on a prob'ly onna
                    saturation campaign so they– it's on all day.
     A:              Mh hm,
 → B:              An', after yuh hear it o:ver an' over an' over
                    again, it's a pleasure when you do it. ehh! heh
```

A: Well the thing is, I figure thet if *I* wouldn'
wanna hear it over again the same way I heard
it before, why should *you*.

B: hhh! heh ri(hh)ght.

←A: Y'know Yuh– Y'know the guy who was really
great about that was a comedian named Joe
Cook.

[SBL:I.1.12.-35]

←A: So, they'll be nice to have in the house there, (49)

B: Mm hm,
   [

A: I won't– I won't worry about things.
           [

B: No,

→B: Uh and I think it's– and Bea, you know, well I
think it's awfully nice of you to r–rent to a
family with children.

←A: Well, that was uh *built* for that, it's in a– too
good a *school* area.

B: *Yeah.*

A: You know, That's what I intended.
   [

→B: Yeah.   Well
some– uh so many people, though, uh, you
know, they're just won't– *do* this.

←A: They have to go *some*place.

B: Well I know it.

A: Un huh,

B: I know, and I feel this.

[IS1:11]

→B: . . You're very intell'gent *person* by the way. (50)
You're bout the most intell'gent 'n– thet I've
talked to and I've talked to *many* over here.

A: Well,

→B: –Thet seem to *know* uh, y'know, a little–, its
nice to hear somebody ehhh hehh y'know
hehh–

←A: Well it's important stuff you gotta really do
your own research, . . .

Credit shifts as a solution type are responsive to the two sets of constraints discussed earlier. The focusing of praise away from self in the compliment response displays a sensitivity to self-praise avoidance. The compliment response consisting of a second praise (albeit refocused) is partially supportive of, that is, a partial warrant for or legitimization of, the prior praise.

Returns

A second kind of referent shift are those within return compliments.

Recall that a general procedure used in second assessment agreements is that of referent retention. A second speaker refers to the same referent as has the prior speaker within an assessment which stands in agreement with the prior assessment. Referent retention is one kind of interturn linking system for topical, sequential units.

Within returns, a slightly different linking system is employed: Rather than retaining *same* referent, a second speaker preserves the *relationship* of referent to speaker across the turns. That is, if the referent of prior speaker's talk is his coparticipant, namely, "you," a next speaker may refer to his coparticipant, namely, "you."

The action sequence for return compliments is:

A_1:   A compliments B.
A_2:   B compliments A.

A recipient of a compliment may proffer a return compliment—a compliment which is "similar" to the prior compliment. Returns use an agreement construct. In contrast to the prior credit shifts (from "you" to "it") that are typically viewed as disagreements (i.e., as recipients' creditations of "it not me"), returns are constructed as agreements (i.e., "and you too").

[MC]
    C: Ya' sound (justiz) real nice   (51)
• D: Yeah you soun' real good too

[NB:I.1.-2]
    E: Yer *loo*kin good,   (52)
• G: *Great. So'r you.*

[JG.-7]
B: Well anyway nice talking to you (   )   (53)
                                                    [
●   A: Nice talkin
                     to you honey . . .

[NB:VII.-4]
A: . . Ih w'z jis'--de*li*ghtful tuh come down   (54)
                     there that day, 'n meet the- -crowd, 'n,
                                              [[
●   M: Well,-   I,   -jis'
                     w'z so tickled thetche di:d,

[NB:VII.-13]
A: . . en, gee I sure hadda nice   (55)
                                       [
M: Yeh-
A: time the other day ih w'z=
                        [
●   M: Oh:well:I-=
A: beautiful.
●   M: =-jist loved havin' you come up Agnes . . .

Compliment returns, like other agreement constructs, provide possible
completion points for sequences. Return compliments regularly terminate
praise sequences.

As a solution type, returns offer a procedure through which a kind of
agreement is performed which simultaneously satisfies the constraint of
self-praise avoidance.

CONCLUSION

The productions of compliment responses are sensitive to the co-
operation of multiple constraint systems. One preference system is that of
supportive Action$_2$s, that is, responses which legitimize, ratify, affirm,
and so on, prior compliments. A second constraint system is that of
self-praise avoidance.

With reference to the prior compliments, compliment responses fall
into two broad groups: evaluation shifts and referent shifts.

Evaluation shifts take the form of praise downgrades, where recipients praise the same referents as are praised in the priors, incorporating
evaluative descriptors which are less positive than the prior. Referent

shifts include compliment responses in which recipients of praise proffer subsequent praises of other-than-self referents.

The two kinds of shifts reflect the co-operation of supportive seconds and self-praise avoidance. In praise sequences, praise may be scaled down (↓) and/or refocused away from recipient (←).

[KC4:35]

F:	That is beautiful	(2e)
	[	
↓ K:	'N that nice	
R:	Yah. It really is	
←K:	It wove itself. Once it was set up=	

Although not cleanly differentiated, the various classes of compliment responses tend to collect in particular sequential environments.

Returns are frequent in openings and closings of interactions, for example, in an opening:

[NB:I.1.-2]

E:	Yer *loo*kin good,	(52a)
● G:	*Great.* So'r *you.*	

in a closing:

[JG.-7]

B:	Well anyway nice talking to you ( )	(53a)
● A:	Nice talkin to	
	you honey . . .	

Returns are a kind of reciprocity response. The producing of returns is in part dependent upon the availability to second parties of complement praiseworthy referents to those that occur in first compliments.[15]

Appreciations are prevalent as responses to compliments when the parties are asymmetrically related to the referents of the compliments. In the following excerpts, second parties do not have available complement referents to the referents praised by first parties. They proffer appreciations as seconds. In (2e) and (54a) below, the referent of F's compliments is a blanket K is weaving.

[KC4:33]

F:	That's beautiful It really is	(2f)
	[	
R:	Yah	
● K:	Thank you	

[KC4:37]
F: . . beautiful though, really beautiful   (54a)
● K: Thank you

In (4a) and (1a) below, the referent of A's compliments is a performance for which B was responsible.

[SBL:2.2.4.-3]
A: Well I–I wannid to say I enjoyed your class so   (4a)
                        this morning, and *too*.
● B: Well, thank you

[SBL:2.2.4.-3]
A: Why   it's   the   loveliest   record   I   ever   (1b)
                        heard. And the organ–
                              [
● B: Well *thank* you.

In (38b) below, the referent of B's compliment is a Christmas card A sent her. B did not send A one.

[SBL:3.6.-7]
B: *By* the way I *loved* yer Christmas card,   (38b)
● A: Oh:: Thank y–
                              [
B: *Thank* you *so* much,

Praise downgrades are prevalent subsequent to compliments with other-than-you references incorporated. Appreciation tokens show a priority positioning over agreements and disagreements:

[SBL:2.2.4.-3]
A: Oh it was just *beau*tiful.   (8d)
● B: Well *thank* you Uh I thought it was quite nice,

[SBL:3.6.-7]
B: *By* the way I *loved* yer Christmas card,   (38c)
● A: *Oh:: thank y–*
                              [
                              .

                              .

                              . .

B: *Yers* was jus' (   ).
            (1.0)
 ● A: Oh::: Thank you.
                        [
 B: -(   ).
 A: I hadda hard time, but I didn't think
             they were too good, but– – – –finally,
                                        [
 B: (Those) were
             *love*ly. *I* thought they=
                           [
 ● A: Uh huh, Thanks,
 B: =were lovely.
 ● A: –finally hadtuh settle on *some*thing . . .

NOTES

[1] The *Los Angeles Times*, 28 Dec. 1975, Part VIII, p. 7.

[2] The structuring of the description of *her* behavior as *his* problem is a design which is well fitted to the format of such letters as "Dear Abby" and "Dear Ann Landers." A warrant for writing such letters often involves the posing of a problem that the letter-writer has, a problem with, as yet, no adequate solution. The printed responses, in such cases, typically include proffered solutions.

[3] It has been brought to my attention that therapy-oriented groups have developed "exercises" in which participants practice accepting compliments and agreeing with them. One such group are those who practice co-counseling.

[4] There are a host of sequential features which preferred and dispreferred seconds display. One feature of preferred seconds is their occurrence in initial positions of turns. In compliment responses, when acceptances and appreciations appear, they typically occur as first items within turns. For a more complete discussion of some features of preferred and dispreferred seconds, see Pomerantz (1975, Chap. III).

[5] This piece of work on multiple preferences is an extension of previous work on the interaction of preference systems. In particular, see Sacks and Schegloff (1978), and Pomerantz (1975, Chap. V).

[6] The kind of organization which is referred to by "action chains" is not unlike that of "adjacency pairs" in many of its features. See Schegloff and Sacks (1973) for a description of features of the organization of adjacency pairs. An essential difference between adjacency-pair and action-chain organization, in the opinion of this author, lies in the following:

> A basic rule of adjacency pair operation is: given the recognizable production of a first pair part, on its first possible completion its speaker *should* stop and a next speaker *should* start and produce a second pair part from the pair type the first is recognizably a member of [Schegloff & Sacks, 1973, p. 296; emphasis added].

That is, if a recognizable first pair-part is produced, then upon that production its second pair-part is conditionally relevant.

With "action chains," what is being proposed is that an Action$_2$, or "second pair-part" is not a *should* but a *may* for recipient, that is, an option among several specifiable options. In part, it is in the performing of the second that a prior becomes treated (formulated) as one or another first action which is linked with that given second. Although some number of appropriate Action$_2$s may be available subsequent to a given prior, initial evidence suggests that those alternative options are themselves preferentially ordered relative to each other.

[7] Pomerantz (1975, Chap. V).

[8] See note 4.

[9] Goffman (1971, pp. 63–64 and Chap. 3).

[10] There are a range of ways of *showing* appreciation. For example, upon receiving a gift, appreciation may be shown by displaying the gift, admiring the gift with strongly positive assessments, and so on. That is, in addition to *the giving* being an object for appreciation, *what* is given may also serve as a referent for appreciations. Subsequent to compliments, appreciations are routinely done with appreciation tokens and not with strongly positive assessments of same referent as is located in the prior.

[11] For a more detailed discussion of some sequential features of "optimals," see Pomerantz (1975, Chap. V).

[12] Examples of creditings performed with strong-positive descriptors include:

[BC:IV.27]

B:	I *love* the way you do that commercial. ehhh!	(56)

[SBL:2.2.4.-4]

The referent is a record for which the recipient is respon- (57)
sible.

A: . . Oh it was wonderful, I would *LOVE* tuh *have* one.

[BC:IV.-9]

B:	And I'll miss you very very much,	(58)

[AP:fn]

The referent is a scholarship recipient has been offered.

G: That's fantastic (33c)

[13] "Modesty" is an achievement subsequent to compliments, with, for example, laugh tokens and incompletions.

[NB:VII.4]

	E:	˙hhh Marjie I–I marvel atche really. Eh you fascinate me,	(59)
●	M:	hh ho ho hh	
		[	
	E:	I've never seen a gal: like you.	
		[	
●	M:	E(h)edna, uh!	
		[	
	E:	I *mean* it.	
●	M:	((falsetto)) No, no no.	

[SBL:1.10.11]

	B:	Well, they're lucky to have *you*.	(60)
●	A:	Well, I don't kno(hh)w heh . . .	

[BC:IV:-27]

B:	I *love* the way you do that commercial, ehhh!	(48a)
A:	Mhhh!	
B:	hhhh! It's original ehhh!	
• A:	Well, you know, It's uh:::v–uh::: . . .	

[14] A sample of compliments in which coparticipants are directly praised (with "you" as references) is included below:

[WS:YMC.-4]

R:	You're a good rower, Honey.	(47b)

[IS1:11]

B:	. . You're very intell'gent *person* by the way. You're about the most intell'gent 'n– thet I've talked to and I've talked to *many* over here.	(50a)

[NB:VII.-4]

E:	˙hhh *Marjie* I–I marvel at*che* really. Eh *you* fascinate me,	(59a)
M:	hh ho ho hh	
	[	
E:	I've never seen a gal: *like* you.	

[BC:IV:-27]

B:	I *love* the way you do that commercial. ehhh!	(48b)

[BC:IV.-69]

B:	And I'll miss you very much,	(61)

[GTS:1.66]

L:	I like you now.	(62)

[15] There are instances in which returns are modified and adjusted to asymmetric circumstances.

The following datum is taken from a two-way call in a radio show. The moderator (A) will be temporarily on leave in order to go into the hospital. The caller (B) initiates the following compliment sequence:

[BC:IV.-69]

B:	And, I'll miss you very very much	(61a)
	((pause))	
A:	*Thank* you.	
A:	*I'm* gonna miss it *here too* which is kinda strange,	
B:	N:no it isn't,	
A:	A man–	
B:	(Because you know) how much we all *like* you.	
	[[	
A:	I think a man is very lucky,	
A:	I think a man is very lucky when he has a job thet he *mi*sses when 'e isn't there.	

A's initial compliment response is an appreciation ("*Thank* you."). The appreciation is positioned in next turn to compliment. Next turn to compliment is an environment in which returns alternatively occur. That is, the "thank you" is positioned in a place where a return reciprocal compliment, for example, "I'll miss you too" typically would occur if it were to be proffered. The parties, however, are not symmetrically related: Whereas a caller "knows" a moderator by name, personality, and so on, the moderator frequently finds himself talking to an anonymous caller. In such circumstances, returns, which are subject to consistency constraints, are generally unavailable as seconds.

Even though a "thank you" may suffice as A's second to B's compliment, A continues his turn with a return which is adjusted to their asymmetric circumstances. In the first compliment, B is the referent: "And I'll miss *you* very very much"; in the return there is a referent replacement: "*I'm* gonna miss it here too . . ."

The fact that returns tend to be performed whenever they can be, and that adjustments are made so as to make them performable when they might otherwise be unavailable, is consistent with the previous observation that they simultaneously satisfy two constraint systems which are not simultaneously satisfied within other classes of responses discussed.

chapter 4

On the Achievement
of a Series
# of Stories

ALAN L. RYAVE

A rather commonplace conversational activity is telling stories and listening to stories.[1] On occasion a story appears as an isolated instance surrounded by a variety of possible conversational structures, but more frequently it seems to be that stories are manifested in clusters of two or more.

In the data principally to be focused upon here and in each case presented, there occurs a cluster of two stories and related story commentary, told at separate times by two conversational participants. For example, in the first instance presented below, Peter tells a story about a dangerously close call he experiences at a fairgrounds, and then Gordon follows with a story dealing with the possible prevention of trouble in amusement park rides in Long Beach. And, observe in the second instance, A presents a story dealing with the fact that an accident was witnessed which evidently was not subsequently reported on by the media, whereupon, B tells a story of a witnessed event that received the same fate. These instances, and two others, are presented immediately below, and the reader is encouraged to examine them carefully before

113

proceeding to the ensuing analysis. In my analysis, particular attention
will be given to Example (1).

Example 1

HAL:	They're– uh–they::'re uhm, they're easy.
PETER:	Boy, don't go at the fairgrounds though. ((whistles "wow"))
STAN:	Oh(hh)o Go(hh)d' OO'
HAL:	Why.
PETER:	C'z uh, (2.0) have one a' them things, they break loose up there.
GORDON:	Oh wuhnyuh buildin that yeah I know about that. —— They're prob'bly– there's cables wasn' uh strong enough tuh, —— pull'm *back*.
PETER:	Uh–no those big cable cars. Y'nuh the ones up on the, track.
GORDON:	Mm.
STAN:	Wih A one Boat *yuh::: uhlon dohlenko*, —— *etche*ruh *wooooops*.
	(1.7)
HAL:	I wouldn' ride on them, (cars.)
	[
STAN:	Gah' No *me*.
	(1.7)
GORDON:	Aw me I'd ride onna *bumper* car.
PETER:	An ah know who almos' got hit bah one a' them things.
STAN:	*You?*
	[[
HAL:	(You?)
	( )
(STAN):	*Go::d.*
GORDON:	Mm hm
GORDON:	Not me.
PETER:	((with mouth full)) If I didn't stop bout, ——
GORDON:	((with mouth full)) Eh w'z this——— ((chewing))
(GORDON):	( )
	[
PETER:	The cable car jus' went past me'n:: dropped. —dat, close to me.
HAL:	Jeez.
	[[

```
GORDON:        (                    ).
PETER:         That's how far ah was 'way f'm that cable
               car.                              [
STAN:          ((Whispered))                       Go::d.
HAL:           Wow.
STAN:          (Yeah.)
PETER:         I woulda been pinned under it.
                   (4.0)
GORDON:        They should check those things out–When
               they rent'm they should check'm out.
                              [
(      ):                   (           )
STAN:          Yea::h.
                   (3.0)
HAL:           W'sometimez they don't–––
                   (1.7)
GORDON:        Th–they should–they should
                              [
HAL:                              –check'm.
                   (5.0)
GORDON:        If they're gonna rent'm (through the day),
               the:n, they should sheck'm out. (2.0) or the
               boss should–sorra, "Got this thing checked
               up?" "No," "What's duh mar:: wih you." ––
               "Y' be'r check it out." (4.0) Cuz down here in
               Long Beach idjuh––– anh–an bumped inna
               the bass'n I say "Hey. (one a'yuh rides goin
               out over here"– "Well which izzit.") ––
               "Yerruh:: merry g'round ennuh::: dee– deh
               d'bump'm cars."–"What? I'll go to um
               now." Boy did he go. ('E really told'm
               though)
                   (3.0)
PETER:         One time I wiz pinned in the bump'r car one
               time.
GORDON:        Boy he check dem out 'e finally tol'm
               you guys better check the equipment out.
               hh an' now.
                   [
STAN:             En hyou know a' jing go ups go down
                              [
GORDON:                           (check'm out)
STAN:          eh duh –– de waduh
                              [
```

GORDON: Better check'm out.
GORDON: (He) did:d too
                                    (2.0)

Example 2

A: Say did you see anything in the paper last
              night or hear anything on the local radio, Ruth
              Henderson and I drove down to Ventura yes-
              terday.
B: Mh hm
A: And on the way home we saw the:: most
              gosh-awful wreck.
B: Oh::::
A: —we have ev— I've ever seen. I've never seen
              a car smashed into sm— such a small space.
B: Oh::::
A: It was smashed from the front and the back
              both it must've been in— caught in between
              two cars.
B: Mh hm uh huh
              [[
A: Must've run into a car and then another car
              smashed into it and there were people laid out
              and covered over on the pavement.
B: Mh
A: We were s—parked there for quite a while but I
              was going to listen to the r—news and haven't
              done it.
B: No, I haven't had my radio on, either.
A: Well I had my television on, but I was listen-
              ing to uh the blast-off, you know.
B: Mh hm.
A: The uh ah— astronauts.
              [[
B: Yeah   Yeah
A: And I—I didn't ever get any *local* news.
B: Un huh
A: And I wondered.
B: Uh huh,
B: No, I haven't had it on, and I don't uh get the
              paper, and uhm

A: It wasn't in the paper last night, I looked.

B: Uh huh.

B: Probably didn't make it.

A: No, no you see this was about three o'clock in the afternoon.

B: Uh huh
   [[

A: Paper was already off the press.

B: Uh huh

A: Boy, it was a bad one, though.

B: Well that's too bad.

A: Kinda (freak)–
     [

B: You know, I looked and looked in the paper– I think I told you f– for that uh f–fall over at the Bowl that night. And I never saw a thing about it, and I looked in the next couple of evenings.
   [

A: Mh hm
     (1.0)

B: Never saw a th– a mention of it

A: I did't see that, either.

B: Uh huh.

B: Maybe they kept it out.

A: Mh hm, I expect.

B: Uh huh, deli berately.
     [

A: Well I'll see you at– at–

B: Tomorrow night
    [

A: –at six at– hehhehh

Example 3

STAN: En hyou know a' jing go ups go down eh
     [

GORDON: (check'm out,)

STAN: duh –– de waduh
    [

GORDON: Better check'm out.

GORDON: (He) did:d too
    (2.0)

STAN: Hal you know thing go up go– down water,
                                                            [
HAL: Yeah
               the roller coaster?
STAN: Yeh one – rollie coaster broke loose eneh
               down it landed –– *BANG* uv went– ow– down
               the ocean.
HAL: ((softly)) Yeah.
                    (4.5)
STAN: S'mbody w'*killed too*
                    (1.7)
PETER: Yeh I w'z–
                    [
GORDON: By people eh–actin smart'n gen up
               there'n actin like a fool.
PETER: No,
GORDON: (Stannin up go– Stannin– Hangin' from the
                                                [
PETER: See,
GORDON: thing.)
                    (2.7)
PETER: What *he* means, (2.7) the *track* uh let loose.
                    (2.0)
STAN: Broke loose
GORDON: =*Oh::.*
PETER: See 'n when– hh
GORDON: Well when *I* w'z–
                    [
PETER: It w'z goin' up the hill 'n they
                                                      [

PETER: couldn't see the other side
STAN: (   )
                    (1.0)
STAN: Mh–h–h ev tooeh:: ubm– uv (   )
                                              [
(   ):   (   )
STAN: –summaw eh crack.
GORDON: But now;
               [[
PETER: Yeh. It wen' off the track. (Straight off.)
                                           [
GORDON: But now deh got'm

	fixed now, they got'm
	[
STAN:	Go *BANGO!*
	Fall, (dem *off*nen.) ***Uhh HH'***
	[
GORDON:	They gotta heavy
	cable
	[
STAN:	Uhh'
GORDON:	on (the top) so deh (closed a' track) *down.*
HAL:	If you know howtuh swim you c'd su:re come
	*ou*tta that,
GORDON:	( )
	[[
STAN:	'N:: y::ou djoo– yih junkeh all *ki::ll!.*
	(3.5)
PETER:	They wen' on the–
	[[
HAL:	Becuz the one in:: Santa Monica did that,––
(GORDON):	(Uh::?)–
HAL:	–a:nd
	[
BILLY:	(Gna:::h),
HAL:	There w'z a guy that w'z a sailor 'et w'z *on*nit.
	––Took 'iz girl for a ride on the rollee coaster
	en the– thing jumped the track went– –– an'
	floated in the top a'd'water 'n 'e hadtuh–
	swim for 1– –– sho:re.
	(2.0)

Example 4

C:	Yes, I do, today. And, uh I also think that if a girl does get her degree, that it doesn't really matter too much, she is labeled differently and she ya know, like I know one lady engineer who's a *fantastic* engineer and she told me that in every meeting she sat in on, all the men engineers automatically expected her to take notes. And on her application, and
R:	Unnhah
C:	when she was interviewed she was asked if

R: she could type. And, she said that they never asked any of the *men* if *they* could type.

R: Unnhah.

C: Ya know, it's just the role that–that women are, ya know, given automatically.

R: I've made mistakes like that. Ah, an' I–I know of a particular case in point. A very critical group of a committee, where there happens to be only one woman–– it's a faculty committee––and in the first meeting, the *senior* personnel management faculty member, who, if *anyone* should know better

C: ((laughs))

R: without even thinking, said, "could you take notes?" Ya know, an' it's

C: What was her response?

R: Well, after the a deadly silence and sharp daggers,

C: Far out! ((laughs))

R: The ah she said, "If you would like." But tha, but the message it got across. Ya know that guy, nor–nor, and I–I could see myself making the same mistake, because (–) but, I don't, ya know.

I wish to focus my interests and analyses on the interactional relationships of these clustered stories.[2]

THE SERIES-OF-STORIES PROBLEM

By "cluster" I mean to point out that the stories referred to occur in close proximity to one another. However, it takes only a cursory investigation of these clustered stories to conclude, as a primary observation, that the sorts of relationships that exist between the two stories extend well beyond the simple matter of sequential adjacency. The study of the various orders of relatedness operating between clustered stories presents a fascinating research topic, where often the nature of the relatedness to be discovered, described, and appreciated functions to render our everyday social intuitions subverted.[3]

Justification for this claim is available by taking note of some of the elements of relatedness operating between the clustered stories. First, in examining Example (1), it can be readily observed that each story displays a potentially related topical orientation, namely, to amusement park rides, also, suggesting that each event being related occurs in a similar setting. More refined, the topical orientation of each story focuses, in some manner, on the faulty operation of these amusement park rides, and not, for example, how much fun they are, which ones are too expensive, and so on. Second, the two stories seem to be further related in that each storyteller is somehow implicated as a principal character in the story each is reporting. Again, all character portrayal is built in and around the issue of the operation of amusement park rides. And, each story has a course-of-action depicted that either leads up to or out of the faulty operation of amusement park rides. Finally, it can be observed that each storyteller constructs and employs his story in such a manner as to make a moral point or illustrate a maxim, at which point the storytellers do not leave this matter to be understood from the specifics of the story, but instead formulate the moral point independently of the actual recounting or relating of the story. Again, this potential order of relatedness can be further delimited by noting that each moral point is so constructed as to relate to the issue of faulty amusement park rides. This mode of observation can readily be performed on each instance, bringing forth similar results. The reader is encouraged to do so as a means of further acquainting himself with the data and phenomenon to be addressed in this paper.

Although these observations may suffice as an initial down payment supporting the claim that the stories display more in common than simple proximity, they in no way present a conclusive or convincing exposition, nor are they intended to be an exhaustive analysis of the potential modes of relatedness. They are, however, suggestive of the following supposition: The relations displayed between the two stories are not capricious and happenstance, but are instead the products of the conversational participants' attention and careful management. When the proximate stories obtain this status I wish to speak analytically of them as a *series of stories*, as opposed to the earlier invoked concept of "cluster."

The notion of a series of stories can be further articulated by considering the following possibly implied analytical problem. It would seem that in order for stories to obtain this series-of-stories status, conversational participants would need to listen to and analyze an in-progress story in such a manner as to permit them, upon the completion of the present storyteller's story, to construct their own story utilizing the results of their prior analytic attention, in such a way as to assure that their succeeding story is seen as a successive story with definite, observable relationships to the previous story. An implication of these considerations is that the occurrence of a series of stories, as a conversational phenomenon, is not a preordained, pregiven matter; it is not guaranteed independent of the occasions on which the stories are told, but resides in the succeeding storyteller's situated *achievement*. A problem arises from such an orientation: How do conversational participants go about orienting to a present story, in such a way as to transform the results of that orientation into the work of constructing their own succeeding story, so as to assure the constitution of a series of stories?

Having stated this preliminary but primary problem, we can turn our attention to a more detailed consideration of the particular data under investigation and attempt to articulate the necessary analyses.

REFINING THE PROBLEM

Implied in the above formulated problem is a direct recommendation as to how to begin searching for a solution. That being the case, since the resources for Gordon's succeeding story are presumably to be found in Peter's preceding story, the recommendation then should be for the researcher to begin by carefully examining and comparing the contents of the two sequentially adjacent stories. However, closer inspection of Example (1) provides an observation which belies this recommendation. Avoiding any extraction or isolation of the two stories from the surrounding related story commentary reveals that the origin of Gordon's succeeding story is more directly traceable to one of his own prior utterances that immediately follows Peter's story—"They should check those things out–When they rent'm they should check'm out"—than to Peter's story itself, as was suggested in the formulation of the problem above. The import of this observation is rather obvious in the context of the previous discussion, which attempted to establish reasonable grounds for proposing that the generative sources of Gordon's succeeding story were Peter's preceding story. Further, as in the previously discussed case of constructing a succeeding story from a prior one, when I speak of a story being *derived* from an utterance, I am pointing to not just a technical matter, but a phenomenon oriented to by the conversational participants. That is to say, Gordon, the storyteller, incorporates resources from the preceding utterance in such a way as to construct his story so as to show it as occasioned by the utterance, and thereby displays the story as observably motivated by a preceding utterance, where such a particular mode of storytelling is a consequence of the participant's situated achievement. Before I attend to the implications of this observation for our initial problem, I would like to provide substantiating comments with respect to the observation.

It is not unusual to find instances of storytelling in conversation where a story is being told in such a manner that it can be objectively seen as being occasioned by and derived from some preceding, or succeeding, utterance. For example, this phenomenon can be observed to occur on those occasions where an utterance takes the form of a maxim, proverb, rule, assertion, major point, for example, and where a sequentially related story is observably organized vis-à-vis the particular utterance so as to objectively display an illustration, proof, explication, demonstration of the utterance. In such cases the storyteller's talk is constructed such that the observable purpose of their telling a story is to illustrate, substantiate, prove some asserted state of affairs. For a story, then, to obtain this status of being observably derived from and occasioned by a preceding utterance, it cannot be produced in just any manner, but rather has to be fashioned with an attention to the state of affairs being proclaimed in the utterance.

Appreciation of the kind of "attention" such a story production requires can be obtained by offering the following observation concerning Gordon's story. Gordon's story is worked in such a fashion that we find as the *developing conclusion* of the story an utterance—"Boy he check dem out 'e finally tol'm 'you guys better check the equipment out. hh' *now*"— that markedly resembles his preceding proposed instanceable utterance—"They should check those things out–When they rent 'm they should check 'm out." What I am pointing to here is not some concluding utterance which is tacked onto the story as an afterthought or some sort of story-related commentary, but instead we have a depiction of a series of events which are progressively organized and realized so as to properly and reasonably culminate with the presentation of his preceding utterance as an integral part of the story. Note, for example, how the story is displayed with a developing course of action which supplies the relevance and appropriateness for executing the very course of action as indicated in his preceding instanceable utterance—an utterance which asserts a rule for proper behavior.

The import of these observations is to recommend a reconsideration of the general appropriateness of the previously stated series-of-stories problem. Recall that the problem was directed at reconstructing a process that spewed out a particular product (a series of stories), where the sense of that product was founded on and defined in terms of sequentially adjacent stories possessing common elements, and where it was presumed that the succeeding story was somehow derived from the first. The descriptive adequacy of this formulation has been confounded. Can the data be re-examined for new resources that might salvage our efforts? How do we get what clearly looks like a series-of-stories product, when Gordon's succeeding story is constructed with attention to his own pre-

ceding utterance, rather than the preceding story, which it is presumably
linked to and motivated by?

As a means of sustaining the sense of a series of stories as a prob-
lematical phenomenon with respect to Example (1), I offer the following
observation: A feature of Gordon's utterance—"They should check those
things out–When they rent'm they should check'm out."—is the fact that,
at the time of its production, it is exclusively tied to the preceding talk. By
"exclusively tied" I mean to note that the utterance is produced as a
response to Peter's story, and when produced exhibits no prospective
expectations for more to be said on Gordon's part, including a succeeding
story. That is, if Gordon produced no further talk pertinent to the matter
raised by this utterance, then such an "absence" would not be observable. Such being the case then, that more talk is forthcoming, talk which
in fact instances the utterance in terms of a succeeding story, suggests
the possibility that the source and relevance of this talk is somehow
embedded in the preceding talk.

This observation seems to commend the following possible refine-
ment of our initial problem. Are there certain qualities that Gordon's
utterance exhibits with respect to the preceding conversational materials
which, when subjected to a developing conclusion methodology for constructing an instanced succeeding story, yields a series-of-stories relationship with the prior story? Although the research problem is presently
formulated in terms of a specific instance of data, it will become clear that
my interest is with developing a description of a general procedure for
achieving the series-of-stories phenomenon.

SOLUTION OF THE PROBLEM: THE SIGNIFICANCE AND
RECOUNTING ASPECTS OF STORYTELLING AND THE
ACHIEVEMENT OF SERIES OF STORIES

A major conceptual apparatus that can be profitably introduced in
order to articulate further and solve the problems developed in the previous section involves the noting of two separate, but deeply related,
aspects of organization that many stories in conversation seem to possess. I will refer to these two modes as the *significance aspect* and the
recounting aspect of story organization.

In offering the discrimination between the significance and recounting aspects of story organization, I wish to note a regularity such that,
within the confines of a story, storytellers not only involve themselves in
the relating or recounting of some event, but are also frequently attentive
to and concerned with expressing in so many words the import, rele-

vance, significance of that recounting, and/or indicating just how the import and significance of some assertion(s) can be appreciated and evidenced in and through the recounting of some event. The "and/or" is not an incidental appendage, but is used to invoke the sense in which these two aspects of story organization are intimately interrelated functions which inform on and elaborate one another.

And, as a general practice, it seems that the recounting portion of a story is notable for its particular delineation of some event, usually requiring a number of utterances tied together by some developing course of action; whereas, the significance aspect takes the form of an idealized, abstract form of an assertion, accomplishable within an utterance.

In Peter's story, for example, both of these aspects of story organization and their functions are exemplified. There is a recounting of a particular event that once occurred at a fairground, which is prefaced by a generalized statement admonishing and warning the other participants about visiting such places. The generalized admonition seems to occasion the relevance and propriety of introducing the particular recounting, which deals with a dangerous event at a fairground. The recounting, in and through its presentation, serves as a source of evidence and support for producing the admonition in the first place. It was observed, in the previous section, that Gordon's initial assertion was followed by a recounting that was informed by and informed this assertion; and where it was noted that this reflexive relationship operative between the two was the result of the storyteller's constant work and supervision of his own talk. In fact, I wish to propose that Gordon's initial utterance not only operates as a significance statement to his own succeeding recounting, but when produced has this same relationship to Peter's preceding recounting. And, this is the crux of the matter. That is, contained within this observation is a solution to our problem, and with it we will be able to chart some of the interactional work a succeeding storyteller can engage in in order to achieve a series of stories. I will begin to develop this proposal by first taking up my claim that Gordon's intervening utterance, when produced, functions as a significance statement for Peter's preceding recounting.

In accord with the previously discussed features of these two modes of story organization, Gordon's utterance is fashioned in the form of a generalized statement, presented as a response to Peter's story as an entity in its own right, and not to, say, some segment or selected aspect of the overall recounting. This can certainly be contrasted to those utterances produced by Gordon, Hal, and Stan that appear within the confines of Peter's unfolding story, and are oriented to some developing concrete element of the recounting. Gordon's utterance, again, makes sense as a response to the story as a whole. Finally, the utterance exhibits a reflex-ive informing relationship to Peter's recounting in a fashion that can be seen as warranting the presentation of the recounting, and/or the presen-tation of the utterance as a warrantable moral conclusion for a potentially completed recounting. That is to say, Peter's recounting can be viewed as standing as a source of testimony occasioning the relevance and coher-ence of Gordon's assertion, and, at the same time, the assertion suggests the/a[4] significance or import of the recounting. This feature can further be appreciated by engaging either of the following two exercises. First, if one removes from a reading of the transcript Peter's opening significance statement, thereby leaving his following recounting and Gordon's ap-pended utterance, the sense of the remaining transcript as exhibiting a coherent and reasonable story (albeit collaboratively produced) is left intact. Second, the removal of Peter's significance statement and its replacement with Gordon's intervening utterance also does not seem to interrupt our intuitive sense of a coherent, flowing story, where the two orders of story organization inform on and elaborate one another, and, where the sense of Gordon's utterance being constructed with respect to Peter's recounting so as to see the latter as instancing the former, can be appreciated. In both exercises the sense of Peter's recounting and Gor-don's indication of the significance of that recounting are, in their own right, independent of Peter's indication of the significance, and reflexively informative of one another so as to constitute a reasonable and coherent story description. The notion that Gordon's utterance functions in a parallel manner to Peter's preceding significance statement vis-à-vis the attached recounting has some support.

An additional feature of these two modes of story organization seems to be indicated in the preceding section. Not only can a single recounting aspect of story organization have more than one significance aspect of story organization bound to it within the confines of a single story, each being structurally independent of the other, but these independent indica-tions of significance need not—and our data suggest, do not—have to resemble or reformulate one another.[5] Moreover, with respect to each instance of a significance- recounting relationship within the bounds of a single story, the feature of reflexivity could be applicable. That is, while each particular significance- recounting relationship in a single story may perhaps display different meanings, they, each in its own right, can exhibit a coherent and reasonable description. As our data also indicate, the same observation is operative in the case of a single significance statement being bounded by two structurally independent and meaning-fully different recountings. A potential source of sociological interest residing in this feature is the fact that what the meaning, relevance, import of some recounting or significance statement may be is not a pregiven or established matter intrinsic to a recounting or significance statement, but instead seems to be an issue that is a contingent, managed concern of the conversation in which it occurs.

My analytical interest with this final feature is not to determine which significance statement or recounting more adequately informs a recounting or indication of significance, but to inquire into the structural features that make possible such a practice in the first place, and to investigate the kinds of conversational activities and practices that are interactionally generative in and through such structures.

I am now in the position to propose that the characterization of Gordon's intervening utterance as orienting to Peter's story in terms of a significance statement, is useful in describing how it is that the same utterance, when subsequently subjected to a developing-conclusion methodology for building a story, yields a series-of-stories relationship. More important, a general procedure for achieving a series of stories can be indicated.

A general procedure employable by a succeeding storyteller for constructing a story that observably displays a series-of-stories relationship with a preceding story, is to organize the story in terms of a significance statement which also serves to formulate a preceding story. A corollary to this procedure is: If one hears a recounting as reflexively embedded in a significance statement, where that statement also formulates a preceding story, then one can properly hear that recounting as constituting a series-of-stories relationship with the previous story.[6] I wish to refer to this practice as the "same-significance procedure," and I will describe two variations to it.

One variation—Type 1—involves a succeeding storyteller utilizing the very same significance statement of a preceding story in order to construct his own recounting. That is to say, if a story is produced which contains reflexively related significance and recounting aspects of story organization, then one way a succeeding storyteller can achieve a series-of-stories relationship with *that* prior story is to construct a recounting that also is embedded reflexively in the significance statement of the prior story.[7]

Examples (2) and (4) of the earlier introduced data are examples of Type 1 of the same-significance procedure. In Example (2) the issue of the media failing to report a newsworthy event formulates each of the two recountings presented. Given all the multitudes of facets that B could possibly recount in terms of the witnessed event, its telling is done in terms of strict accordance with the formulated significance of A's preceding recounting. Thereby, achieving a clear connection and series-of-stories relationship with the preceding story. One of the consequences of utilizing the Type 1 procedure is that a succeeding storyteller can show, in and through his story, that and how they understand, support, sympathize, and agree with the preceding story.

When Type 1 of the same-significance procedure is being employed, there are means by which a speaker and hearer(s) can indicate that this procedure is being employed. For example, succeeding storytellers, on occasion, will begin their story by repeating the same or a similar significance statement from a previous story. By so doing, this aspect can enable a hearer to thereby locate a "previous story" as potentially one other than the last-story-to-have-been-produced. On the other hand, when a succeeding storyteller wishes to build a story using this procedure vis-à-vis some immediate last-story-to-have-been-produced, then his story can be constructed such that it would need not repeat or contain any significance aspect of story organization, but only a recounting reflexively embedded in the prior story's significance statement. This feature can be, in part, empirically sustained by noting that in instances of series of stories, it is a more common occurrence to find the first story in some series containing both a significance and recounting aspects of story organization, while succeeding stories, in some series, may lack any explicit indication of significance. Example (4) exemplifies this point. R launches into a prefatory remark that indicates that the ensuing recounting is to make the same point as formulated and illustrated in the preceding story—"I've made mistakes like that. Ah, an' I–I know of a particular case in point." Where the recounting can then be seen as another case of the consequences of labeling females, as formulated by C in the initial story.

As already observed in my discussion of Example (1), Gordon does not strictly use the above described same-significance procedure (Type 1), in that he does not construct his recounting in terms of the significance employed in Peter's preceding story. However, the basic feature of the same-significance procedure can still be appreciated in the data by recalling that Gordon's intervening utterance functions as a significance aspect of story organization with respect to both Peter's preceding recounting and his own succeeding recounting. The utterance, then, is the same significance source, for which two independent and adjacent recountings stand as reasonable and sensible instances. I am arguing that Gordon achieves a series-of-stories relationship, first by building an utterance which independently and exclusively orients to the preceding recounting in terms of a significance aspect of story organization, and, second, following that utterance by initiating a recounting which comes to relate reflexively to it as a significance aspect of story organization. It is in this sense that the same significance statement characterizes each of the adjacent recountings, and we can speak of it as a variation to the same-significance procedure (Type 2).

The Type 2 procedure can also be observed in Example (3). Hal produces an utterance—"If you know howtuh swim you c'd su:re come *ou*tta that,"—that when initially produced reformulates Stan's preceding story, and subsequently is followed by a recounting that clearly illustrates and proves the point being made. As in Gordon's story, Hal uses the developing-conclusion methodology in building a recounting in terms of this statement. An implication of Hal's story, in both its significance and recounting aspects, is to alter the meaning and significance of Stan's story. No longer is Stan's story strictly about people killed as a result of an unavoidable catastrophe, but instead killed as a result of their inability to swim for the shore. Both adjacent recountings come to be formulated by Hal's utterance. That and how the Type 2 same-significance procedure alters the meaning of preceding talk will be taken up in the final section of this report.

CONCLUDING REMARKS

Why would a succeeding storyteller go about introducing his own significance aspect of story organization, employing it to achieve a sense of series of stories, when he could have achieved the phenomenon by utilizing the Type 1 procedure, that is, by using the significance aspect of story organization introduced by the previous storyteller? Relatedly, if the Type 1 procedure does support, sympathize, and agree with the preceding story, then what does the Type 2 procedure accomplish?

Recalling the initial formulation of the series-of-stories problem, it can be appreciated that certain interactional strengths obtain in the structural position of the first story of a to-be-constituted series of stories. It is the first storyteller who not only provides a maiden recounting (with all its implications of topic, setting, character organization, detail, etc.), but also has first crack at indicating the significance or relevance of that recounting. Any potential succeeding storyteller desiring to create, for whatever reason, a series of stories with a first story, must somehow in the process of constructing his story, orient to and incorporate resources of the prior story. For a succeeding storyteller to ignore these resources is to forgo the possibility of producing a next story, that in a coordinated manner establishes a series-of-stories relationship.

Under these auspices, I wish to argue that Gordon's and Hal's (Examples [1] and [3], respectively) intervening utterances, in functioning as alternative significance statements with respect to Peter and Stan's recountings, do the interactional work of reordering the strengths and constraints inherent in Peter and Stan's designs and interests. Gordon and Hal's reflexively related alternative significance statements provide new materials for connecting two stories in a manner that might not at all be apparent, or interactionally feasible, given merely the significance and recounting aspects of the initial story organization to work with. It supplies the listener with a new sense of what the preceding story is actually about.

It is, then, Gordon and Hal's intervening utterance and not Peter or Stan's opening significance statement that connects and operates as a mutually informing significance statement for the two sequentially adjacent recountings. By presenting his own succeeding recounting, for example, Gordon is able to supply additional articulation and support for his understanding of the relevance of Peter's recounting. Recall that I observed how carefully Gordon constructs his own succeeding recounting in terms of his preceding utterance. Once the succeeding recounting is produced, then Gordon's significance statement, as opposed to Peter's, becomes the only one of the two which meaningfully interrelates with the two independent recountings.

The reordering work of Gordon's intervening utterance is directed at altering and undermining the implications of Peter's significance aspect of his story organization and not so much the specifics of the recounting aspect of story organization. Note that the recounting aspect is left intact, there is no formulated challenge to the credibility or accuracy of the recounting. And, to be sure, one way to alter the informing properties of another's story is to, in some manner, question, challenge, correct the details and particulars of the recounting. Instead, the issue as to what the recounting might come to mean is taken to task: That is, Peter's recounting is not about the dangers inherent in the fairgrounds, as he indicated, but concerns possible faulty operations whose blame can be located and rectified.

I have now provided the materials, in the course of this chapter, for proposing that we have a segment of data for which the following theoretically suggestive characterization can be offered. The meaning and relevance of a description, as exhibited in the form of a story, is not a pregiven matter to be analytically determined solely by inspecting the particulars of some recounting, but is itself best conceived as a social activity that is interactionally negotiated and managed in and through the emerging particulars of a situation. The preceding analysis can be appreciated as charting some of the features of this interactional work. What Peter's story is actually about is not a static fact, but is a participants' phenomenon open to emergent realization, as demonstrated by the specific interactional work that Gordon's story performs. And, this observation could well have served as a starting point for this research report. In this sense it can be said that Gordon achieves a series of stories in and through the transformation of the previous story.

NOTES

[1] The study of storytelling in conversation, as a topic of research, was established by Harvey Sacks. For a number of uniformities and regularities uncovered in his researches, see Harvey Sacks (1970). The basic thrust of the present report is deeply indebted to features of this work, although I accept full responsibility for uses made of the materials.

A couple of additional clarifying remarks: First, by the notion of "story," I mean, for now, the telling of some event in more than one utterance. Second, when I speak of the "telling of a story in conversation," I have in mind not only the utterances of the storyteller, but also the comments made in the course of a story presentation by those who are the recipients of the story. The fact that this sort of work goes on can affect the in-progress unfolding of some relating of an event, and consequently the very sense that a series of utterances might obtain. This is a distinguishing characteristic of stories told in conversation as opposed to, for example, stories told in performance situations. This not only differentiates our concerns and interests in storytelling from students of, for example, folklore, who show an abiding interest in this phenomenon, but it affirms the sense in which storytelling in conversation is an interactionally collaborative achievement.

[2] Examples (1) and (3) are part of a larger corpus of tape-recorded conversations made at a Los Angeles County Board and Care Home for the mentally retarded. Some comments may be in order with respect to these two instances. It may be of interest to note that although the participants can be readily labeled as mentally retarded, this category in no way is utilized—either as an analytical resource or as a topic of investigation—to inform the following analyses. If the reader chooses to invoke the category, then he may come to appreciate the sense in which the ensuing analyses indicate and describe competent, creative, ingenious social behavior on the part of a population who are ordinarily conceived of and defined in terms of defective, incompetent social behavior. This potentially available feature of our research is, in part, the result of recognizing that the participants are talking to one another, and subsequently treating that simple observation as a fundamental problem in its own right.

Example (2) was supplied by Harvey Sacks, and consists of a telephone conversation between two adult females. Example (4) is from a collection of student-made tapes and transcriptions. The conversational participants are two adult females and one adult male.

Any interested reader can obtain additional instances of the conversational phenomenon addressed in this paper by writing to the author.

[3] The present line of discussion should not be construed as undercutting the fundamental importance of proximity to the general phenomenon we are presently attempting to appreciate; rather, we are only interested in marking its insufficiencies for understanding and explaining the developing issue of related stories in conversation. In fact, participants rely on, and orient to, the issue of proximity for displaying these other orders of relatedness presently hinted at. For example, on occasion, a prospective storyteller is unable, for whatever reason, to adequately present a succeeding story in the sequential place he deems relevant. When this occurs, there are special conversational devices available for indicating the slot in which the story should have appeared, and should accordingly be heard as appropriate and relevant. Thus, in the same conversation from which Examples (1) and (3)

are extracted, Peter attempts to start up a story, following Gordon's, with the utterance, "One time I wiz pinned *in* the bump'r car one time." Being interrupted, when the opportunity afforded him to start up again he began his story again, but in a slightly different manner, " 'N like I w'z goan say about bumping cars,––." With a preface like " 'N like I w'z goan say . . . ," Peter is able to link the present unfolding story with his prior effort, and thereby indicating to the recipients the story's proper relationship to the proximity of the previous and appropriate story and its context.

⁴ A note to clarify our usage of "the/a." From the analyst's viewpoint the choice is "a" in that one of the points to be developed shortly about storytelling in conversation is that multitudes of sensible, reasonable significance statements can be attached to any recounting. Furthermore from the analyst's point of view, interesting grounds seem to be lacking for assessing the validity, correctness, soundness, and so on, of any one significance statement over another. Rather, the analytic interest is invested in searching out the structure of activity, in its own right.

However, from the participants' vantage, this attitude might not always be shared. Quite the contrary—often they do possess an interesting basis for asserting, negotiating and knowing that one characterization or formulation holds sway over another. Not all are reasonable. Thus, the possibility and viability of invoking one over the other, thereby providing the basis for our use of "the." This is not to claim that from the participants' point of view "a" cannot be invoked. It sometimes is.

We utilize both "the/a" in our present stage of discussion, because the level of formulation is yet to be clarified, that is, is a significance statement to be examined from the analysts' or participants' vantage.

⁵ There is a sense in which Peter and Gordon's significance statements stand as alternatives to Peter's recounting. It can be observed that Peter's significance statement, which prefaces his impending recounting, takes the form of a "warning." It uses a conventional frame for doing "warnings"—Don't do X (that is, don't go to the fairgrounds). Where his succeeding recounting stands as an evidential instance of a dangerous thing that can happen to you if you choose to do X. In contrast, Gordon's appended significance statement locates specific blame and explanation for the fairground's catastrophe, thereby providing potential resolution to the troubles, dangers inherent in Peter's story. That is, the danger as developed by Peter in and through his story, is presented as embedded in the setting, whereas, Gordon, by assessing specific blame, shifts the attention from the setting to certain individuals; the danger is not irremedial. If "they" would check out those things, then presumably the sort of danger incurred by Peter could be avoided. And, along with it, the propriety of Peter's warning. The fact that Gordon's intervening utterance can be conceived as an alternative significance formulation is a matter that shall eventually take on additional import.

⁶ One import of this hearer's maxim is that a previous story does not have to be an immediately preceding one in order for the series-of-stories phenomenon to be obtained. That this is the case can be appreciated by the way in which this maxim is invoked by lawyers in locating and determining a precedent for some story they are presently involved in constructing. For further articulation of this point see Moerman (1973). There are numerous other analytical disciplines that require practitioners to know and work with the intricacies of this procedure, for example, history, psychological counseling and therapy, analytical interpretation of open-ended interviews, and medicine.

⁷ When the same significance device is employed, it is not uncommon to obtain two related stories whose story elements (e.g., characters, setting, time, and topic) do not display any sense of strict commonality. Therefore, the analytical procedure of searching for common story elements (as pursued in the opening part of this paper), as a means of substantiating their status as a series of stories, will not necessarily yield valid results.

chapter 5

The Recommencement of a Meeting as a Member's Accomplishment

M. A. ATKINSON, E. C. CUFF, AND J. R. E. LEE

In this chapter we intend to describe and suggest a tentative analysis of some of the ways in which persons might talk in a meeting, so as to achieve and sustain the meeting as a social setting. We believe that social organizations such as meetings and debates, are constituted in an ongoing manner out of the talk in which those present do their business. This analysis of talk extracted from a meeting is, therefore, directed towards producing an understanding of how people routinely solve the kind of organizational problem involved in achieving a meeting and perhaps in achieving other forms of organization where similar problems are encountered.

In saying this we are not suggesting that talk in meetings has some essential characteristics that necessarily differentiate it from other types of multiparty talk. Experience in analyzing numerous examples of multiparty talk has suggested that any particular organizational device that provides for ordered talk and conversation might occur in an almost limitless variety of settings. Nor are we suggesting that meetings have essential characteristics that can always be found to exist wherever a meeting is present. We recognize the wide variety of phenomena that might be seen as "meetings."

What we are suggesting is that certain examples of multiparty talk extracted from meetings, whether formal or otherwise, can be viewed or analyzed for the manner in which they might reveal machinery oriented to the solution of the sort of interactional or organizational problems that we might expect to be encountered at meetings.

To this end we shall analyze the following data in order to demonstrate and to describe the nature of the recommencement of a meeting as a member's achievement. More specifically, in Part I, we will examine how an item can be heard as a possible attention-getting summons-to-a-meeting; in Part II, we will attempt to show how subsequent talk might reflexively serve to confirm a hearing such as "the recommencement of a meeting"; in Part III, we will seek to show how the hearing of the talk in this way occasions and is occasioned by members' collaboratively orienting to certain features, the preservation of which might be seen to have some import in achieving and sustaining a meeting, as an orderly form of social organization.

PART I

Our analysis draws upon the following excerpt of data which is taken from our transcriptions of a series of tape-recorded meetings of a local radio station. The excerpt is taken from the recommencement of one of these meetings, following a coffee break.

The Data

	((general background noise))	1
C:[1]	Right–e:r–	2
	((general background noise))	3
	((pause ca. 4.00)) ((general background noise))	4
C:	–Are we ready to go again now?	5
	((general background noise))	6
	((pause ca. 3.00)) ((general background noise))	7
R:[1]	Yes	8
	((general background noise))	9
C:	Good, Ray's ready – e:r can I just mention um. . just–	10
	just mention one more thing before I go round the table	11
	and then I really have got a batch of (other points).	12
	Ray has – ((background noise ceases))	13

c: –just reminded me might as well bring this one up as well 14
c: just to mention it . . .   15

The data commence with "general background noise" in which parties to a meeting are having a coffee break. The "noise" is made up of a
number of separate and discrete conversations, in which groups of people
discuss various topics, which may be heard above the chinking and
clattering of crockery, and the sounds made by people moving around the
room. We can presume that the parties are aware that the meeting will
recommence because they were so informed by the chairman prior to the
coffee break. The description "background noise" represents an interesting idea with which to commence our analysis. Clearly the sounds which
we have so labeled do not announce themselves as background noise.
Those who are engaged in the conversations do not consider themselves
as participating in background noise. What we are suggesting is that those
present, we, ourselves, and the reader, can call it "background noise,"
by focusing upon c's utterance and viewing it in the ways that we have
chosen to do so in the course of this paper. The description is made
possible by intuitive reflection upon the talk and by our orientation, as
members of a culture, to the features of meetings. While it could well be
the case that some or all of the parties engaged in producing "background
noise" could be orienting to the purposes of the meeting and, perhaps
could be discussing the business of the meeting, they could not reasonably be seen to be doing the business within the meeting. Their talk,
insofar as it is concerned with the meeting, is not recordable or usable as,
for example, the "discussion," the "decisions," or the "policymaking" of
the meeting. Should some members of the organization attempt to view
this kind of talk, as taking the organization's decisions or as having
established policy, then others *might* be able to see those decisions and
that policy as improperly constituted. They *might* be able to complain that
they had not been able to hear the debate or take their proper part in it.
They might be able to complain that they had not had their proper say and
that things were not in order.
    As members of the same culture as the parties to the gathering, we
ourselves are able to hear the talk of these parties as "background noise"
as a consequence of our own orientation to the recommencement of a
meeting. The tape recorder was switched on in order that the recommencement and subsequent talk in the course of the meeting could be
recorded. Our recording of their talk might thus be seen as a motivated act
in that we tape-recorded the recommencement of a meeting. We can thus
be seen as orienting to and utilizing routinely available methods to find
that the meeting is recommencing. For parties to the meeting, the talk and

events which occur as "general background noise" may be characterizable in a variety of ways: as gossip, as shoptalk, as passing the time—and
all can be viewed as appropriate behavior in coffee breaks. In whatever
manner the parties characterize such talk and events, they, like us, would
hardly characterize them as "talk in the course of a meeting." Insofar as
the parties are to engage, and be seen to engage, in "talk in a meeting"
engagement has to be achieved, made visible and recognizable. And for
us such engagement is both recognizable and producible as a co-oriented-
to phenomenon—a collaborative production.

In referring to meetings as collaborative productions, we wish to
draw attention to their complex nature as a form of social organization
involving the co-orientation of its parties to the business or topics at hand
in a manner that makes possible the orderly achievement of that business.
It is the case that meetings may produce decisions and policy that might
properly be referred to as a product of the meeting. Recognition of this
fact may be given by those attending insofar as they distinguish between
"official" talk and all the various asides or side engagements which
expectedly happen in the course of a meeting but which are not seen as
accomplishing the business of the meeting. Insofar as talk might be seen
as not properly oriented to "our discussions," "to our policies," or to
"the decisions that *we* have taken and the policies *we* have decided
upon," then such talk might be found as external, in a sense, to the course
of the meeting. Of course such talk might run the risk of bringing forth
sanctions upon the speaker concerned. This depends upon local convention, but it is not surprising that various organizational settings, often
including the "most" socialistic or "democratic," accept conventions
whereby participants may be sanctioned for failing to attend to the business of the meeting. Lack of attention and the holding of "counterconver-
sation" can often be seen as detracting from what needs to be and needs
to be seen to be a joint, co-oriented-to production.

Those present at a meeting must achieve this collaboration. In our
data, this achievement involves the concerted transition from a coffee
break in which meeting participants are engaged and the re-establishment
of a common focus of attention and talk.

Of course collaborative work is required to sustain any conversation.
Our task in this paper is to describe the methods members use to effect a
transition from one form of collaboration to another.

Our data continue with "Right–e:r–" (line 2). We take it as significant that we can hear and therefore transcribe "Right–e:r–" which can
be clearly heard against the "general background noise." Presumably
some or all persons present can also hear "Right–e:r–." It can thus serve

or be produced as an attention-attractor for some or all parties to the coffee break.

In saying this, we may draw attention to a distinction between an "attention-attractor" and a motivated "attention-getter as a summons-to-a-meeting."[2] An attention-attractor might consist of any utterance or movement, such as a cry of pain, shout of anger, sudden or violent gesture. To determine whether the attention-attractor is motivated, members must be able to analyze its intentionality and, hence, its possible interactional consequences for them. In either case, such structures might get attention and are, in this sense, attention-getters. But their facility in appropriately obtaining more than passing attention and in having that attention focused on some particular object, depends upon the hearers' findings about their motivational character.

To analyze the utterance part, "Right–e:r–," hearers might require an analysis of speaker, scene, and utterance. Their analysis almost certainly involves their discovery of an appropriate identification of the speaker which is required to find the relevance of the utterance for them. Knowing who the speaker is and in what capacity he is speaking, might be required in order to find whether the utterance is designed for them, and if it is, in what ways it is so designed. The discovery that it is so designed, hinges upon the hearer's achievement of a categorization of the speaker, in some way, that would provide for the relevance of their hearing and for their continuing to listen. For example, should they be able to find the category "chairman of this meeting" or as boss of the station as an appropriate way of categorizing the producer of the utterance, then this category might enable them to see the utterance as relevant to them with respect to motivation, given their own known membership category of "members of this meeting" or organization or gathering. A chairman of a meeting, however, may be categorizable in many other ways. Thus our data, "Right–e:r–," may represent talk which, though done by the chairman, can be seen in terms of other categories of relevance, such as "coconversationalist" or "conversationalist with another party or parties."

If a speaker is engaged in conversation with others (or talking to himself), some hearers may discover themselves to be overhearers or potential overhearers. Such a discovery might involve finding that the utterance concerned does not condition any relevant next action which demands an orientation to the speaker's completion. Moving away so as not to be seen to be an overhearer, represents an interesting possible relevant next action, which specifically does not involve the hearers' listening for completion. Such findings of overhearing are made possible for listeners by, for example, their hearing the speaker's utterance as conditionally relevant to a previous utterance, in a conversation to which they are not party, and in which they can find no intended or proper basis for their participation.

We would suggest that hearers may not find in "Right–e:r–" alone sufficient materials to determine whether or not they are intended recipients being addressed as comembers of a meeting, or being addressed in some other capacity, or whether they are overhearing. Certainly "Right–e:r–" does not of itself provide the materials that enable hearers to discover a summons to a meeting. Even the "omnirelevance" of a "meeting" and the fact that *this* is a break in a meeting do not necessitate its being interpreted that way. Members to a meeting might analyze such utterances as signals that the meeting is recommencing, thereby involving relevant rules of sense-assembly to produce this finding and, in so doing, see that their collaboration and their co-orientation to business is required. Though they may require more materials before they can make this finding, members, depending on the setting, might hear the banging of a gavel, the ringing of a bell, or even, the hitting of a teaspoon on an empty cup, as attention-getting devices, signaling the commencement of a meeting. Nevertheless, even such "automatic" signals require a member's analysis, invoking relevant rules of sense-assembly to decide upon their character and thus, like "Right–e:r–," they are not self-defining.

Should members analyze "Right–e:r–" or such signals as banging a gavel, as having been performed by the chairman of the meeting or the boss of the organization, then they might have sufficient resources to understand that they are being summoned to the meeting. On the other hand, should "Right–e:r–" have been uttered by someone other than the chairman (or someone who could not be found as capable of acting for the chairman), then it might fail to provide for the utterance as such a summons. Though such an utterance might attract and thereby get attention, it might be difficult for it to sustain the attention of the hearer with the notion of "meeting" which could provide for the relevance of further talk by the speaker. That is it might not be seen as an attention-getting preface to a restart. Thus, anyone who is not the chairman might be seen as joking, being facetious, for example, if he is seen as trying to recommence the meeting.

Regardless of whether those present at the meeting provide for the relevance of such an utterance as "Right–e:r–" as prefacing the recommencement of a meeting or as a joke or whatever, their finding is a consequence of their analysis as members, wherein some activities are seen as properly bound to the particular categories of some persons. It is their proper knowledge of the world that enables members of a culture and members of organizations to make such findings. Should the speaker of "Right–e:r–" be other than the chairman or chairman-surrogate, then those present would not re-organize their local knowledge of the world in an attempt to make him into the chairman; they might on the other hand see him as doing inappropriate work. The hearer, by making such an analysis, simultaneously finds an appropriate category for himself; by making such a finding he is able to see the capacity in which he is being addressed or whether, indeed, he is being addressed at all. In this way, the "membershipping" of speaker and of hearer, together with a reading of the action performed by speaker, is seen as mutually constitutive. When people at a meeting make such findings as "chairman" for speaker, "summons-to-a-meeting" for utterance, and "comember of meeting" for hearer, they do not make each finding separately; they do not latch on to just one of these findings as the "crucial" one. By saying that such findings are mutually constitutive, we mean that these categories and actions are *co*-selected; that accounting practices involve a search for a principle of co-selectivity which can account for and make sense of, the world in a proper, known, methodical, ordinary, taken-for-granted and unproblematic manner. The use of category-boundedness to produce such findings facilitates the ability to read off, to make coselections of appropriate category pairings, in that "chairman of a meeting" might suggest as appropriate "comember of a meeting," just as "father" might produce the finding "son" or "daughter" as the second part of the pair.[3]

We have said that participants recognize some others as inappropriate persons to start the meeting and that this recognition is made possible by their local knowledge of the world. It is difficult, if not impossible, to see some persons as having any right to start meetings. They are not viewable as candidate occupants of the categories which would make such activities appropriate. Thus, anyone who is seen as occupying categories which preclude his having the rights and obligations of starter might be seen as "just joking." A junior-status technician, or secretary, for example, could be found to be joking because it might be seen as inconceivable that he should even think himself as a potential starter of a meeting. He could of course be found to be incompetent and ignorant, a finding which might be used by any of those present to justify his having a position of low status. On the other hand, should a person of higher status, but whose rights and obligations visibly preclude his starting a meeting, attempt to start a meeting, then a different series of inferences might be possible. Such a member might be found "presumptuous" and possibly even, "a climber." Where some doubt might exist as to one's right to start a meeting, then members may seek to determine how one's "credentials" are seen by others. In these ways, members tacitly recognize prestige and power hierarchies and use such hierarchies to make practical findings which enable them to order events and activities. On the other hand, it might be seen from this last example that though continually usable, anyone's organized local knowledge of the world is always revisable and, when revised, may still be used to order everyday events and activities. A person present might have occasion to revise his knowledge of the distribution of power and prestige if, for example, others accept someone whom he had thought to be an "inappropriate starter" to a meeting. In this way, social change might be both recognized and achieved as part of the ongoing activities of members in organizational life.

Members then have the capacity to use categories such as "starter to a meeting" and "appropriate starter to a meeting." The category "appropriate starter to a meeting" may be used as an aid in the discovery that a start had been made. This makes possible the discovery that the "appropriate starter" was "the starter to the meeting." On the other hand, a meeting may be found to have been started by an "inappropriate starter," and here the finding "the meeting has started" is itself a resource to make the finding an "inappropriate starter." Such starts may provide members with the resources for news, stories, "tellables," that is, something unusual or odd has happened. If members make the finding that the speaker is "just joking" because he has not the authority to start the meeting, this finding does not preclude the achievement of a recommencement. The distribution of authority for startings and recommencements is one thing, but starting and recommencing *might* be something else.[4]

"Right–e:r–" of itself might have provided no firm basis whereby members could see themselves as included or excluded from participation in the speaker's talk. They require a method of seeing if the speaker *is* acting as chairman. If he is so acting, they can see that the speaker is viewable as chairman and, as such, as someone having rights to sanction "improper" behavior, rights to talk on behalf of a meeting, and, of course, rights to call the meeting to attention. We suggest that parties present might hear "Right–e:r–" as not specifying any particular addressee, as for example in "Right–e:r–Jim" and thus they might find no basis for excluding themselves from the category of possible addresses who should hold themselves in readiness for subsequent interaction. It is not only interpretable as nonspecifying but also as possibly an incompleted utterance. Its incompletion might be indicated by "e:r" being heard as a floor holder helping to render "right" as an incomplete utterance. Also its possible incompleteness might be signaled, in that it can be heard as indicating some conditionally relevant next action for hearers, though of itself, it does not provide that next action or specify its nature. "Right–e:r–" might then be heard as the first part of an utterance still to be completed. It might thus be heard as a motivated attention-getter, though not yet specified, in that it could possibly be unclear to those present as to whether it is an attention-getter, acting as a summons-to-a-meeting or, perhaps, an attention-getter for some hearers for some other purpose.

In the meeting from which our data is taken, some or all of those present might have "known," on hearing "Right–e:r–" alone, that the meeting was recommencing. Should they have "known," the following data present confirming materials. Should they have been "mistaken," the following data present materials enabling them to revise their initial hearing and find it "mistaken." The talk subsequent to "Right–e:r–" may demonstrate how additional and unfolding materials serve to confirm or *maintain* an initial hearing.

PART II

Given that the "–e:r–" is heard as a floor holder, then the 4-second pause which follows could signify a motivated pause, made in order to allow participants to see the relevance for them of this and future talk. The speaker could be heard in this way as pausing not in order that he might find appropriate words, or to think about what he requires to say. Instead he can be heard as orienting to the need for silence and order by allowing time for those present to close their current interactions. Such pauses could be viewed as "pregnant pauses" in that they may be heard as the speaker waiting for appropriate next action from hearers.

Of course, insofar as hearers have analyzed the speaker as chairman/starter-of-the-meeting, then they may analyze the 4-second pause as "the chairman waiting," and may therefore analyze the talk and actions of nonhearers or nonattenders as "holding up the meeting."

The same speaker continues with "Are we ready to go again now?" (line 5). The use of the "we" might enable the company to orient to an organization, to the fact that an organization is being referred to or being called into being. The use of the "we" would not of itself, however, enable the hearers to find that it is the "we" of the meeting and that the chairman is speaking in his capacity as chairman. It may be noted, however, that during the course of a meeting, the attenders are able to refer to themselves reflexively as a group. Indeed, during the course of a meeting, competent membership involves the ability of those party to the meeting to see the sense of themselves as "we" in unproblematic and taken-for-granted, mundane ways. As each and every use of "we" clearly does not refer to the meeting as a state of organization—"we" may refer to any subgroup within the meeting, or any group found relevant to the business of the meeting—participants must therefore have methods available which enable them to "repair" the sense of "we" whenever it may occur whether prior to or in the course of the meeting. Thus we need to be able to describe the selection work which such parties must do in order to locate an organizational sense of "we," where the "we" might otherwise be found to be ambiguous.

Our suggestion is that the production of coselectors may be seen as relevant in aiding the parties to find an appropriate sense of "we."

In our data, "Are *we* ready to go *again* now?" (line 5, emphasis added), such co-selection might be seen to be employed. This utterance continuation might enable the hearer to find a selector which illuminates a sense of "we." "Again" might be referred to as a candidate selector in that it might enable the hearer to find as relevant a grouping or a state of talk which existed previously, which may not be said to exist currently, but can, at the same time, be seen to be continued when a recommencement of the meeting takes place. Thus the hearer's search to repair "we" might be directed towards an activity or state of organization that is capable of going on *again*, where it may be presumed that a currently ongoing activity may not. Our previously suggested possible finding which determined that the speaker might be heard to be speaking in his capacity as chairman, might thus be a relevant finding for the hearer, given that it is possible for the hearer to refer back to a state of organization, in which the speaker is known by members present to have acted in that capacity. In this way, further materials are made available, allowing hearers either to confirm or to discover the sense of the preceding talk.

Thus, hearers may *retrospectively* discover the nature of "Right–e:r–" by finding it relevant to them in a manner similar to the way in which hearers might subsequently hear the first ring of a telephone.[5] The significance of "Right–e:r–" and the first ring of a telephone are discoverable by means of what later events provide as materials for analysis. The first ring is interpretable as such in relation to a later finding—a second, or third ring. Otherwise, without such later findings hearers might interpret a single ring to be a mechanical fault, an aborted call, a mishearing, and so on. Similarly, a summons to a meeting may be discoverable over time. To achieve an appropriate level of coparticipancy interactions might be required to engage in an analysis over time to discover that "Right–e:r–" was, in fact, not just a summons, but the first part of an attention-getter as a summons-to-a-meeting.

The retrospective discovery or confirmation of "Right–e:r–" as an

attention-getting preface-to-a-meeting might be further aided by participants' analysis of "now." They have appropriately to repair the sense of
"now" and can do so by discovering the activity to which it relates. They
might discover or confirm the activity by using "now" as a co-selector
with "we" and "again" where "meeting" could be seen as a form of
activity which might appropriately be done by "we . . . again *now*."

As it appears in our data, "now" might occasion for members a
reference to some appropriately timed activity. Such terms as "now"
might require analysis by hearers wherein their sense of proper time might
be used to discover this significance. In this way, "now" might be used as
the basis for discovering a topic or an activity that can be seen as
"properly done now." As in our data where an activity or topic is
unnamed, hearers might be able to use their local knowledge of proper
timing as the basis of discovering the topic or activity carried by "now."
Their ability to repair "now" in this manner allows them to treat "now"
as an activity constituter, carrier, or occasioner.

It is also the case that the discovery of a next activity which might
appropriately be done "now" might enable those present to discover the
time reference of now. For example, "now" could be used to refer to a
period of time in which the indicated activity need not be seen as instantly
relevant. Thus, a discussion between two work collaborators in which
one speaker says, "We've messed about for the past 5 years, *now* we
must start work," could be found as indicating that work might not be
relevant "this instant" as next activity.

In the data we have presented here, members might repair "now" by
finding that the meeting might recommence, and given their knowledge of
local customs and conventions, might therefore hear "now" by making
an appropriate selection from, for example, "immediately," "shortly,"
"some time," "in the future," "next year," and so on.

After the chairman's opening utterance—"Right–e:r– ((4-second
pause)) Are we ready to go again now?"—the data continues with Ray
saying "Yes" (line 8). There are many possible readings of Ray's utterance.

Ray's utterance could of course be seen as an answer to a question
posed by the chairman. That is, the chairman might be understood to have
asked a question which requires an answer. Indeed, the provision of an
answer by any party in a multiparty gathering, might raise questions as to
the right of that party to provide an answer and thereby to speak for the
gathering. Those present might be able to raise questions as to the right of
that party to provide an answer and thereby to speak for the gathering.
Those present might be able to raise questions as to Ray's right to talk and
to take that slot in the talk. His utterance may therefore be open to

analysis by members as to its motivation or reason and, in this way, his talk may be made accountable by others in the gather 1g.

Of course, Ray's reply could in fact be viewed by members as a response to a question which was directed to Ray alone. Ray might, conceivably, be in charge of taking the minutes of the meeting or of tape-recording the proceedings, for example, so that his attention and services might be a necessary prerequisite to the commencement of the meeting. Were this to be the case, then those present could use this local knowledge to see that recommencement is at hand and the talk with Ray could serve the function of summons-to-the-meeting. This possibility could hold if participants themselves could see Ray's involvement at this stage as crucial to the meeting's recommencement.

As we have said, many different versions of Ray's utterance could be given.[6] Ray could be seen as talking to somebody else, talking out of turn, impatiently suggesting that he alone is ready. Alternatively, Ray's "Yes" might indicate to other hearers that the preceding talk was possibly not, after all, an attention-getting summons-to-a-meeting and that it was, in fact, directed to Ray alone. Insofar as the chairman has been performing and has been heard as performing an attention-getting summons-to-a-meeting, both he and his hearers could possibly see Ray as "subverting" his intentions.

A precise or definitive reading of Ray's response is neither possible nor of any interest to us. The point we wish to make is that, regardless of what Ray "really means," his utterance can be seen to provide a resource for the chairman to continue to speak. When, in fact, the chairman does continue to speak with his utterance "Good. Ray's ready . . ." (line 10), he could be heard to be addressing a wider audience than Ray alone and, in this way, to be attesting to the noticeability of Ray's "Yes." Clearly, by using Ray's "Yes" as a reply, the chairman not only regains the speaker's slot, but he can also use the reply as a resource for continuing his talk. It is interesting to note that had Ray not said anything at all, the speaker's slot might still have remained with the chairman who, as discussed earlier, can use the responsive silences of participants as a resource. Similarly, should the chairman's whole utterance "Right–e:r– ((4-second pause)) Are we ready to go again?" have been unattended, it would have been repeatable in the way that an unheard or unattended-to summons may produce repeats.[7]

Possible readings of the chairman's utterance "Good. Ray's ready" are that he is jokingly signifying the inappropriateness of Ray's "Yes" or that, while he required the attention of all members of the meeting, he received only Ray's attention. It is possible to provide a sense in which the chairman's utterance can be heard as a joke in that he may be seen to have requested the attention of all and received only the attention of Ray. Thus he might be pointing out his own lack of success in securing a required effect; or he might be signifying in a "nonserious" manner Ray's own incompetence or jocularity in answering. Here his tone of voice might prove of significance. It is possible, however, to provide a sense in which the chairman's remark can be heard more "seriously." In that it might attest to the motivated character of the original "Right–e:r–" he may be seen as reinforcing his original call to attention with a rebuke even though it may be a gentle one.

Whatever the reading of Ray's "Yes" and whatever the reading of the chairman's use of it as a resource for his continuation, the fact that so many different readings of it are possible can illustrate not only the contingencies that are faced in recommencing a meeting, but also the contingent nature of social talk and activities wherever they occur. This fact also suggests that we would be mistaken to regard items of talk such as "Right–e:r– ((4-second pause)) Are we ready to go again now?" as necessarily succeeding in either achieving attention or in securing such attention in some specifiable time. The judgment as to whether attention has been given or appropriately given is a member's judgment.

By regarding the chairman's talk as summons-to-a-meeting, participants can provide for his further talk as being appropriate to getting-on-with-the-meeting. Ray's return of the speaker's slot to the chairman leaves to the chairman the task of talking appropriately in relation to his having constituted the meeting. If, at this point in the talk, the chairman had continued in a manner that could be seen as talking *to* Ray, rather than *about* Ray, then hearers might reanalyze his previous talk as having been, after all, something other than a summons-to-a-meeting.

In our data, we suggest that it is possible to see the ensuing talk "–e:r can I just mention um . . just–just mention one more thing before I go round the table and then I really have got a batch of other points." (lines 10–12) as relevant to them and as accomplishing the business of the meeting.

In this sense, the chairman may be seen to be competently relating the "now" of his previous utterance to the meeting at hand. That is, in formulating talk that may be seen as "meeting talk," he is providing the "now" with proper prospects. The "now" might thus be seen as a temporal marker which both signals and constitutes synchronously the "end" of the coffee break and the recommencement of the meeting.

PART III

As we stated at the beginning of this paper, our intention is to suggest tentatively some of the ways people might structure their talk in order to achieve and preserve meetings as social settings or orders of talk and activities. We are concerned with examining the talk which occurs at meetings to see how it might be produced in order to solve the organizational problems that sustaining the talk of meetings poses to those who participate. In this sense we hope to contribute towards the production of an ethnography of meetings. However, in another sense we have little interest in meetings as such, but are concerned with developing an understanding of the kind of structures which might expectedly be found in meetings, but which might also be found in other orders of multiparty talk, such as natural conversation, debates, and the like. We take it that the kind of talk practices that might be found typical of meetings, such as chairing or controlling talk, scheduling the topic or items of discussion into recordable episodes to reflect business, can and do occur, in all forms of multiparty talk. Certainly structures such as attention-getting prefaces to multiparty gatherings and rounds, are common in many species of talk.

Our interest in focusing upon meetings is that in at least some meetings an institutional framework is provided that attempts to preserve the order of organization, so that the talk structures are in some senses preplanned and speaker roles preallocated. While the talk that occurs can be viewed for the sense in which it has a local management system, in which speakers self-select and select others on an utterance-by-utterance basis, it is noticeable that some speakers such as the chairman might have overriding speaking rights and the duty to exercise a control function which makes him in a sense responsible for the order of the meeting.[8] It is also noticeable that speaker slots often revert to him and that he uses machinery ensuring the return of speaking rights so that he can decide and announce the order of business—"the what exactly we are talking about." The execution of the agenda and the movement from one "item" to another, as well as decisions as to relevance and appropriateness are often in his hands, subject, of course, to the particular conventions of the meeting.

This is to say that some organizational problems that meetings and other orders of talk might face, can be met by machinery which shapes the talk in predesigning ways, so that a common purpose can be and can be seen to be achieved. The point about some meetings, especially business meetings, is that they often decide, display, and execute a series of organizational tasks, involving a complex division of labor, and a series of intricately allocated rights, duties, and obligations. Persons present have to be and have to be seen to be, occupying their appropriate roles (and this includes listening and talking properly), so that those present can see the meeting to have been properly and seriously constituted, so that business may be seen to have been done in a proper and legitimate manner.

However, as with all multiparty talk engagements, conversationalists in meetings face the possible problem of fissure. The talk may break up into a series of discrete conversations so that a common order of talk may be destroyed or at least not achieved. Likewise an orientation to the talk by certain persons might lapse, so that their not listening may indicate their nonparticipation in the discussion. Often within the realm of natural conversation such things happen with no serious consequences or implications; conversations naturally fizzle out or change their nature just as ongoing developments occur without the need for plan or agenda. Often, too, it is the case in natural conversation, that topics or items of the talk are changed or merge into one another without preplan or agenda, parties to the conversation negotiating in order to make relevant talk on a fairly ad hoc basis. Sometimes they make or await the opportunity to say something that they have stored up, sometimes they discover what they have to say in relation to the previous utterance. However, natural conversations do not always have this open texture, as participants might themselves have tasks to fulfill in the talk which demand a common framework of discipline. It is at this point that we can draw some loose distinction between the kind of thing that happens at least in some meetings (particularly business meetings) and the kind of thing that often happens in forms of natural multiparty conversation.

In meetings, such as the one from which our data were extracted, participants use an institutional framework and a set of local common conventions to try to prevent the danger of fissure or lapsed talk. They also orient to the necessity of dealing with items or topics in appropriate places, so that the meeting's plan may be available to those who have a need to participate, and so that the events or items of business and the way they were dealt with might be recorded as having occurred as relatively discrete events in separate episodes. Again, of course, such *may* be the case in any natural conversation, but in the meeting from which our data were extracted, and in many meetings we have attended, most elaborate effort was invested in avoiding the dangers and in achieving a common basis of agreement, as to what the events and decisions were. Obviously, the whole basis of organizational discipline hinges upon the possibility of this common agreement.

The chairman of a meeting might then be expected to use his special speaking rights in order to avoid the dangers and to secure the natural plan or agenda, as a pathway to the achievement of the business of a meeting. It is most noticeable that should a speaker lapse in the course of his utterance or fail to select a next speaker, or should no natural self-selection occur, then the chairman might be expected to occupy the next slot in order to secure the continuation. After a passage of time a silence might come to be seen as the chairman's silence, and judgments as to his competence might be made, according to whether or how he is able to repair the lapse in the course of the meeting.

The techniques or machinery that a chairman might be involved in using, to ensure that speakers and hearers have their rights and have appropriate slots to talk in relation to their responsibilities are varied and involve him in using his preallocated rights and slots to talk in order to secure the satisfactory completion of episodes and activities. An interesting example, is presignaled in the data we have cited. The chairman refers to his need to "just mention one more thing before I go round the table." Going round the table in this instance, relates to his invitation to each and every member of the meeting and the organization, to raise any issue or issues that might be troubling them. To effect this "round" he uses the ecology of the gathering going from left to right to select next speaker. Thus, he is able to use the notion of a "round," with its natural passage from one speaker to the next, in order to select speakers to engage in the activity by simply calling their names. If the invitation to raise anything is declined, the slot naturally reverts to the chairman, who has all the resources to proffer the invitation to the next-in-line, by simply calling his or her name. If the invitation is accepted and the turn in the round taken up, then the possessor of that turn in the round has the right to continue raising appropriate issues until his head has been cleared. In the course of this occupancy others might also talk. However, at the close of such a turn the talk naturally reverts to the chairman, who may check that the holder of the turn has indeed finished, but who then is at liberty to pass on to the next in line, until going round the table is seen to have been completed.

The chairman thus has at his disposal a complicated speaker selection device, in which an utterance-by-utterance selection principle is transposed by the chairman's having established preallocated slots for himself, and by the way speaker slots are chained into a round forewarning future speakers about what they might appropriately do or say. By such a device the chairman might be seen to give each his "rightful say" in an organized and perhaps democratic manner, and to effect a scheduled episode recognizable to those present as a round, so that each could play an appropriate part, knowing what is happening and using that knowledge to contribute to an organized and commonly oriented-to event.

One way that we may describe the role of a chairman, is in terms of the way in which he may be said to work, in order to attempt to secure the preservation of certain features of the kind of meetings that we have described. Clearly, there are innumerable features, characteristics, phenomena, and so on, observable in any social setting, such as a meeting, and we would not expect either the chairman or the others present to orient to the preservation of all features as a way of attempting to keep the meeting in order. However, we would suggest that some features are oriented to by parties in their attempts to constitute and preserve the social setting. In any given setting, such oriented-to features are not always continuously present. Absence of these features *may* be noticed and *may* motivate those present to engage in repair work in an attempt to restore and sustain a given order of talk. Attenders of meetings may work to achieve and preserve these oriented-to features in their attempt to sustain an order of talk, but their success can never be guaranteed.[9]

We suggest that a chairman and others present at a meeting *may* orient to at least the following features in order to achieve and constitute a setting as a meeting. We also suggest that their talk can be inspected for the ways in which this orientation is displayed and secured.

1. Those present orient to meetings and to the course of events and activities in meetings as episodic.
2. Those present orient to the scheduling and controlling of these episodes and the talk within them.
3. Those present orient to meetings as having purposes which can be used to frame the business, and the episodic organization of the business.[10]

Through members' orienting to meetings as episodic, intervals in meetings, such as the coffee break in our data, may be said to involve their being temporarily scheduled "out of the meeting." Likewise, events seen as "prior to" meetings, insofar as they are so viewed, are also "out of the meeting" and can deliberately be formulated as such in the course of a meeting. These distinctions are so general and commonplace that it is difficult to conceive of meetings taking place and of being seen to take place without their being used and treated at the same time as mundane facts of life. In other words, participants orient to the "when" of an event's occurrence as being critical in establishing its recognizable character. Where talk cannot be seen as an episodic event within the frame of a meeting in which business is both oriented to and enacted, then it might be found as "out of the meeting" or, possibly, as irrelevant.

Such talk can be incorporated into and utilized in the course of a meeting, if those present make it both a scheduled and a controlled event so that it constitutes proper talk within the course of the meeting. This achievement requires those present to engage in seeing and to engage in making visible, such an event as addressing the purposes of the meeting. Talk so visible depends on its timed appearance.

In our data, it will be seen that the chairman says "Ray has just reminded me" (lines 13–14). In making this remark, he might be heard as giving meeting status to talk which has occurred "outside" the meeting. Its role as meeting talk depends, of course, on those present finding or having found, that the chairman is addressing them in his capacity as chairman. Given this finding, private talk can be transformed into "public property"; and it is even the case that such private talk could be used as a resource for scheduling the business.

This possible reading of "Ray has just reminded me" involves seeing such talk as a way of introducing a relevant item of business. It could be heard as the chairman praising Ray for drawing his attention to a salient point, as praising Ray for his vigilance in spotting something that the chairman might have overlooked or forgotten, as commending Ray for paying attention to what might be Ray's special responsibilities within the organization, and so on. Whatever reading is made of this item of the chairman's talk, it would obviously be inappropriate in the context and course of a meeting for the chairman to produce acknowledgment of *any* reminder which he might have received "out of the meeting." For example, if the chairman were to have said, "Ray has just reminded me to change my socks tonight," such a reminder might come off as funny, sarcastic, or just irrelevant. Remarks of this sort may be found to come off in these ways because they might not easily be found as oriented to the production of business and as appropriately organized episodically. Of course, any remark can be made in a meeting and, given sufficient work on the part of members, may possibly be found to make sense, to be accountable in terms of appropriate episodes of the business, which itself achieves the purposes of the meeting. For example, the chairman's use of Ray's reminder about changing his socks could demonstrate the lack of appropriate orientation on the part of Ray or, perhaps others, and thus possibly be made relevant.

It should be said that this reading of "Ray has just reminded me" is not of itself sufficient to illustrate the practices by which members achieve the co-orientation required to recommence meetings. It does, however, provide some understanding of how further materials are analyzable as appropriate to beginnings, and which are therefore usable by members as further demonstration that the meeting has, in fact, recommenced.

As we have suggested, the episodic nature of meetings, and therefore of talk within meetings, is an achievement consequent upon the mutual efforts of chairman and those present, in their scheduling and controlling of the talk constituting the business. The chairman's continuation, "might as well bring this one up as well just to mention it" (lines 14–15), is interpretable as introducing and scheduling an item of business. Given an orientation to scheduling and "agendaing," those present might see the "one" as a topic or item of business within the course of the meeting. The scheduling fits events and items such as this into a proper episode or place within the serial order of the business of the meeting. Attenders of meetings require to see how events are items of business, and also require to locate such items, to see how they are or can become, "the present topic of the meeting." Such topics or items of business do not arise and cannot be recognized in an haphazard fashion.[11]

If we consider "one more thing," members might see the speaker as invoking a list of "things" which has already been referred to and which he wishes to extend and to complete. Thus those present might be able to see this "thing" as "one more thing" similar to previous such items. Should they find such items to be items of business, then they could be instructed to find "one more thing" as a further item of business which is, in some sense, "the same" as previous items. They could also take instruction that it is the last such item before some other course of activity is made relevant. In our data, such an activity as, "going round the table" in indicated. In this way, the meeting might be instructed of a possible passage from one activity to another. Similarly, other passages are indicated by "then I really have got a batch of other points." In this way those present might be provided with materials that retrospectively–prospectively enable them to discover where they are, where they are going, and perhaps, where they have been, in the business of the meeting.

In relationship to our initial discussion of attention-getting summons-to-a-meeting devices, we now suggest that by such devices members might be enabled to co-orient to the production of some form of scheduling and control of business. The recognition of such a device signals the appropriateness of such a next activity. Given the summons-to-a-meeting, then some form of scheduling and control of talk and activities has been made conditionally relevant. For the meeting to continue and to be seen to continue, some detailed sense of what might constitute relevant talk and action is required. Appropriate materials for determining relevant talk are made available directly following this kind of summons and the fact of their being made available might serve as a further resource for confirming that, in fact, a summons-to-a-meeting has been given. This discovery achieves for members a continued orientation to scheduling and controlling talk and activities as an ongoing and recognizable feature of their subsequent interactions.

Thus if we look at our data, we find that the chairman says "e:r can I just mention um . . just– just mention one more thing before I go round the table and then I really have got a batch of other points " (lines 10–12). This talk presents members with materials which enable them to discover the sequence of activities which constitute the first business of the recommenced meeting. It enables hearers to analyze further the speaker's initial remarks as a summons-to-a-meeting because scheduling is a conditionally relevant next-course-of-action following a summons-to-a-meeting. Moreover, in that these materials display that a meeting is in course, they also provide for scheduling and control as relevant action throughout the course of the meeting. In this manner, both a summons-to-a-meeting and the conditionally relevant next action of initial scheduling, provide for a sustainable orientation by members to the scheduling and control of the business of the meeting throughout its course.

By orienting to these distinctive features of "meeting talk," the participants appropriately display methods for constituting that talk for what it is. They organize turns to talk, place the items of talk on an agenda, and, generally, accept "proper" control of talk in organizationally specific ways. We have already touched on one aspect of the general control of meeting talk, when we referred to the part played by the chairman, and a detailed analysis of speaker sequencing in meetings is the subject of a forthcoming publication.

Initial scheduling is also recognizable as such in that it may be seen to frame the business of the meeting as achieving known purposes and in terms of its capacity to orient those present to the episodic events of meetings in an orderly fashion.

Hopefully, we have fulfilled our intention of providing a description of some methods and machinery involved in achieving and sustaining meetings as a social setting. Throughout the paper, we have treated meetings as cultural events which members make happen, through those production and recognition practices which make visible a co-orientation to a course of action, which can be witnessed as exhibiting those distinctive features whereby members can sustain their sense of being in a meeting.

ACKNOWLEDGMENTS

We acknowledge with thanks the facilities made available to us by Didsbury College of Education, which has made possible the establishment of the Didsbury Conversation Analysis Workshop in which this paper is one of a series currently being produced.

We are indebted to many people. We especially wish to thank W. W. Sharrock for help and advice, for allowing us to use data that he has collected and for introducing us to ethnomethodology; also J. Schenkein, R. Turner, and Y. Stride for help and encouragement. We also wish to register our debt to the late Harvey Sacks for his friendship and for his personal advice and encouragement at the Manchester/Didsbury Symposium on Conversation Analysis held in April 1973, at Didsbury College of Education. We also wish to express our gratitude to Sacks for making available his great corpus of writings. We particularly wish to record our indebtedness to Christine Atkinson as an indispensable part of the Didsbury Conversation Analysis Workshop in her capacities as transcriptionist and typist. We also wish to thank other members of the workshop, David Francis and George Payne for their participation in ongoing data analysis sessions.

NOTES

[1] c = Chairman; R = Ray.

[2] See Schegloff (1968) for an analysis of some of the general features of summons and answers sequences.

[3] In this paragraph and, indeed, throughout this paper, we are greatly indebted to the work of Harvey Sacks, as anyone who knows his work will recognize. For his published work on membership analysis, see especially Gumperz and Hymes (1972).

[4] For this paragraph, we are indebted to Jim Schenkein. We are also indebted to him for his detailed criticisms of earlier drafts of this paper and for his many suggestions, many of which we have incorporated in this paper.

[5] Example given in a lecture by H. Garfinkel (1973).

[6] The inspection of conversational data often reveals for the analyst the problem that a variety of possible hearings would provide a sense for the item under consideration. This problem does not normally obtain for the members themselves in that while, of course, they may find items ambiguous, or even clear but subsequently revisable, the very fact that they can find "this is ambiguous" or "I got it wrong" reveals the operation of members' method for routinely dealing with such "problems."

The possibility of alternative versions or readings can provide a resource for the analyst. For example, should he attempt to provide for a specific piece of data as an attention-getter, then he is able to use and take account of the fact that he might be able to provide for the same piece of data as, for example, a joke. Insofar as members can routinely distinguish between jokes and attention-getters, then they must employ methods and practices which enable them to do so. Therefore, the analyst, wishing to describe how members perform attention-getters, must also be able to describe the methods which members use for distinguishing them from jokes, for example. This being so, the analyst is presented with a resource enabling him to see what might be involved in members "settling for" their version of the talk. He may be able to discover what methods members would require to use in order to preserve their version to the exclusion of other possible versions. this comparative method may therefore generate the rigorous provision of any one version of the talk. It is for this reason that we present multiple interpretations of our data.

[7] Schegloff (1968).

[8] See Sacks, Schegloff, and Jefferson (1974).

[9] See Sacks (n.d.) where the notion of "oriented-to" features is first propounded.

[10] See Atkinson, Cuff, and Lee (1973) where the nature of these three mutually implicative features and a methodological rationale for them are further discussed.

[11] Of course, we are not suggesting that there are conversational environments in which talk is unscheduled, in which topics are haphazardly introduced, in which participants may take vacations from the work of scheduling and controlling topical flow and monitoring topical relevances. Conversation is in these ways elaborately organized. What we are suggesting is obviously specific to activities in which the members may be said to have business; we also suggest that talk in meetings, though it may be organized in these ways, is also organized in a fashion that specifically enables members to accomplish the business of the meeting.

chapter 6

Some Sequential Negotiations in Conversation

UNEXPANDED AND EXPANDED VERSIONS OF PROJECTED ACTION SEQUENCES*

GAIL JEFFERSON AND JIM SCHENKEIN

The following is a transcribed excerpt of a multiparty conversation. Ted, John, Steven, and Richard are sitting around talking in a backyard patio; the excerpt begins just before the entrance of a newspaper salesboy who has walked down a driveway from the front of the house to deliver a sales appeal.[1]

TED:	I c'd play drums,	1
JOHN:	Y'ca:n, -- Hu:h. What *ki*:nd uh–a trap set? or uh	2
	*bon*go drums.	3

* This paper was originally published in *Sociology,* Vol. 11, No. 1, January, 1977 and is reprinted here with the permission of Oxford University Press. Work on it began at the School of Social Sciences, University of California at Irvine, in 1971; a preliminary report was presented to the Congress on Ethnomethodology at the University of Manchester in 1972; a revised version was distributed as a background paper for the International Conference on Sociolinguistics and Speech Act Theory, Zentrum für interdisciplinaire Forschung, Universität Bielefeld, Germany, in 1973. We would like to express our appreciation to E. C. Cuff, J. R. E. Lee, W. W. Sharrock, Fritz Schutze, and Roy Turner, and their colleagues and students for many comments at these earlier junctures.

TED:	*Trap* set.	4
JOHN:	*Hm.*	5
	((pause))	6
JOHN:	How long didjeh play the drums.	7
TED:	*Not* very long, just about uh::: three months	8
STEVEN:	( ).	9
	((pause))	10
SALESBOY:	G'n aftuhnoon sir, W'dju be innerested in subscribing	11
	to the Progress Bulletin t'help m'win a trip tuh Cape	12
	Kennedy to see the astronauts on the moon shot. You	13
	won'haftuh pay til nex'month en you get it ev'ry single	14
	day en I guarantee you ril good service. Jus' fer a few	15
	short weeks sir, tuh help me win my trip.	16
RICHARD:	Well I *live* in Los *An*geles. I don'live around here but	17
	these fellas live here, you might– ask the:m, I don'	18
	know	19
SALESBOY:	W'd eejer– any of you gen,tuhmen be innerested in	20
	subscribing to it,	21
TED:	Whaddi*you* think uh Beany,	22
	[	
STEVEN:	Na::w	23
STEVEN:	Naw. I don't *go* faw it.	24
	[	
SALESBOY:	Plea:se *just* fer a short weeks sir, Y'won'	25
	haftuh pay t'l next *month*	26
	[	
TED:	Well , you er talk t'the *la*dy of the house.	27
STEVEN:	Ye:h,	28
	[	
SALESBOY:	No. We knocked there no one w'z here.	29
STEVEN:	Well she's *here,*	30
TED:	She's here alright.	31
	[	
SALESBOY:	(Are you sure?)	32
STEVEN:	(Yeah.)	33
SALESBOY:	(okay.)	34
	((pause))	35

One way to begin an investigation of such materials is to elaborate
details of an intuitively observable interactional phenomenon. A beginning of this kind will focus our analytic attention immediately on
phenomena about which the members of a conversational community are

themselves analytic experts. We shall shortly have more to say about how this procedure can be only a beginning for the sort of research we are undertaking,[2] but for now, let us direct our attention to observations governed more directly by these data.

We will begin by developing some observations on the ways in which various recipients of the salesboy's subscription appeal avoid accepting or rejecting the appeal.[3]

The first recipient of the appeal, Richard, avoids the issue by "passing" it to some of the others:

RICHARD: Well I *live* in Los *An*geles. I don'live around here but   17
            these fellas live here, you might– ask the:m, I don'   18
            know,   19

In forwarding the salesboy to some others, Richard has formulated those others as qualified to accept or reject the appeal in just the way he has formulated himself as *in*eligible. Having selected his nonlocal residence to immediately disqualify himself from considering the appeal, Richard has found an exemption carefully fitted to prominent features of the appeal: The appeal is presented with a decidedly *local* service issue (" . . . you get it ev'ry single day en I guarantee you ril good service . . .") combined with an appreciation of *distant* newsworthy places (" . . . t'help me win a trip tuh Cape Kennedy to see the astronauts on the moon shot . . ."). That is, the sales pitch may be a coherent package, the "prize" selected in the first place for its locale-expansiveness. Obviously it is selected via its interest for potential subscribers as well as for its interest for the competing salesboys. The implication is that the newspaper, although local (with the virtues of a local paper) is cognizant of and covers "big news." Richard's "Well I *live* in Los *An*geles. I don'live around here . . ." undercuts the value of a local service. Simultaneously, by naming a place like Los Angeles as outside the scope of interest of the local paper, a place whose own *local* news could constitute *big* news for such a paper as the Progress Bulletin, he undercuts the locale-expansion proposed by ". . . Cape Kennedy . . . ."

With this display of his own disqualification[4] Richard is heard as neither assailing nor avoiding the subscription appeal, for he is simply not the candidate subscriber he was mistaken for. Richard has circumvented accepting or rejecting the appeal by forwarding the matter without prejudice to those bona fide local residents whose business it properly should be to respond to the subscription appeal with an acceptance or rejection. This kind of "passing" of the occasioned business at hand may be a local instance of a generally available interactional device to avoid performing some relevant next activity without harassing the propriety of its performance for someone else.

After the subscription appeal is redirected to the indicated local residents (20–21) and is rejected by Steven (23–24), Ted responds to continued pleadings from the salesboy (25–26) with an utterance similar in important ways to Richard's "pass":

TED: Well, you er uh, talk t'the *la*dy of the house.   27

Like Richard's utterance, Ted's remark forwards the salesboy to a potential subscriber as it forwards the acceptance or rejection of the appeal to the identified candidate. Both utterances appear to be instances of a particular sort of "pass," where the initiator of some sequence (in this case, the salesboy) is "processed" to alternative, legitimate, or in other ways preferred performers of the occasioned next action (here, accepting or rejecting the subscription appeal).

To emphasize both the processing of the initiator of a sequence and the passing of the occasioned next activity to someone else, we can refer to this kind of utterance as a *Processing Pass*.

As these data illustrate, Processing Passes can be used in different sequential environments and can have different sequential consequences. Richard's utterance is the first response to the subscription appeal; the utterance is not heard as proposing a termination of the salesboy's encounter, but only a disqualification of one among others present. By contrast, Ted's "Well, you er uh, talk t'the *la*dy of the house."(27) is offered after Richard's disqualification (17–19) and after the appeal has been rejected by Steven (23–24); the utterance specifically raises closure of the salesboy's encounter by directing him to continue his appeal somewhere else.[5]

Our data furnish us with an instance of an alternative kind of pass:

SALESBOY: W'd eejer–any of you gen,tuhmen be innerested in   20
          subscribing to it,   21
TED: Whaddi*you,* think uh Beany,   22
          [
STEVEN: Na::w,   23
STEVEN: Naw. I don't *go* faw it.   24
          [

Notice here that Ted's "Whaddi*you* think uh Beany,"(22) responds to the just redirected appeal with (again) something other than the relevant acceptance or rejection. In this respect, the utterance is a circumvention of the occasioned next activity, yet the circumvention is achieved under auspices substantially different from the Processing Passes we have considered.

To emphasize both that there is a passing of the occasioned next activity to someone else, and that it is via a conference with colleagues that a postponement of that activity is undertaken, we can refer to this kind of utterance as a *Conference Pass*.

While the Processing Passes provide direction to the salesboy who must redirect his appeal to realize an acceptance or rejection, the Conference Pass forwards the pending issue at once to its recipient without intermediary participation by the salesboy. In answering Ted's query, in "saying what he thinks," Steven unavoidably confronts the acceptance or rejection of the appeal.[6] Steven's subsequent "Na::w, —— Naw. I don't *go* faw it."(23–24), is heard as an explicit rejection of the subscription appeal which therefore inherits the pleadings to reconsider immediately following it.[7]

One resource Ted may be relying on for his Conference Pass, instead of accepting or rejecting the appeal, is that the redirected appeal to which he is responding was addressed to the ensemble "eejer– any of you gen,tuhmen" (20) who are presumably the "fellas" (18) Richard has indicated as the local residents. The salesboy, having been processed to, and subsequently addressing, an ensemble,[8] appears to provide for a conference among the members of that ensemble in advance of performing the acceptance or rejection of the pending appeal. The appropriate use of this kind of postponement of the occasioned business at hand may be a local instance of a collection of interactional devices which avoid performing some relevant next activity while being legitimately on the way to the performance of that activity.[9]

We have sketched out a characterization of the circumventing which ". . . *these* fellas live here, you might– ask the:m, I don'know" (18–19), "Whaddi*you* think uh Beany," (22), and ". . . talk t'the *la*dy of the house." (27) display in these materials. We have treated each instance of passing as a methodic interactional device and have suggested that there are different kinds of passes whose actual occurrences can be interrogated in detail with interesting reward. To propose that there are three instances of passing in the data we have been examining is not at all contrary to our intuitions about circumstances in which avoiding some relevant next action may be a likely component, and the details sketched out on these passes intimately corroborate our intuitions about the phenomenal world of conversational interaction.[10]

Our research interests, however, seek to move beyond these characterizations of intuitively available interactional phenomena. Our commitment is not to giving academic voice to the expertise of member conversationalists, or at least it is not only that.

Rather, we are entertaining the possibility of inquiries into a level of structural organization of conversational interaction for which the intuitions of member conversationalists are foreign. We are exploring certain organizational features of conversational interaction that may escape the scrutiny of ordinary intuitions. We are experimenting with analytic and methodological techniques for gaining access to those structural details of conversational interaction that may be arranged in domains remote from intuitive sensibilities typically defining for us the very phenomena of conversational interaction. We are, in the end, examining the prospects of a "nonintuitive" analytic mentality for investigating and describing organizational details of conversational interaction, not only thus far undescribed, but thus far unnoticed as resources for conversationalists.

One way to transact the kind of analytic shift being proposed is to review some prominent structural feature of the passes initially characterized. The features we have glossed with the labels Processing and Conference Passes will not be treated as final results, nor will they be treated as especially deserving of continued elaboration, comparative documentation, or any other career of devoted attention. Instead, we will treat these initially sketched features as problematically achieved phenomena that are responsive not only to conspicuous interactional contingencies, but responsive as well to intuitively *un*available structural details of conversational interaction.

The defining characteristic of the passes noted in the first collection of observations was a postponement of an occasioned next activity accomplished by the passer forwarding performance of it to someone else. If we review that feature, one thing that stands out is that postponement necessarily *expands* the interactional events between, on the one hand, whatever occasioned the activity which becomes postponed (in our data, the subscription appeal), and on the other hand, whatever would constitute recognizable performance of the relevant activity being postponed (in our data, accepting or rejecting the subscription appeal).

Having arrived at an analytic position that views the originally noted circumventions of accepting or rejecting the subscription appeal as "expansions" of an occasioned sequence, we can now take up the organization of conversational interaction around "unexpanded" and "expanded" versions of projected action sequences.

An appreciation of the organization of conversational interaction around "unexpanded" and "expanded" sequences can be initially drawn by comparing the conversational fragment we have thus far been considering (11–27) with another excerpt from the same encounter, somewhat later. Having returned to the backyard patio after an interchange with "the lady of the house," the salesboy eventually brings Steven to subscribe to the newspaper. After the order form has been completed, the following occurs:

SALESBOY:	Okay thanky'very much,	283
	[	
STEVEN:	Yah, *yer* welcome.	284
SALESBOY:	Would any of you other gen–tlemen be innerested,	285
	((pause))	286
SALESBOY:	Dju be innerested sir, ((addressed to Michael	287
	who joined the ensemble in his absence))	288
	((pause))	289
SALESBOY:	–Taking the Progress Bulletin,	290
STEVEN:	No, en *he* don'know nothin about it.	291
SALESBOY:	Okay.	292
SALESBOY:	Thank y'very much, ((brightly))	293
STEVEN:	Yeh *al*righty,	294
	((salesboy turns and walks away))	295

Here we have an instance of a sequence initiated by an appeal (285–290) representing the "unexpanded" version of the appeal sequence "expanded" by the passes we observed in the earlier excerpt from this encounter. In the data just cited, the salesboy's subscription appeal (285–290) occasions the relevance of an acceptance or rejection as the appropriate next action; when Steven follows the appeal with a rejection on behalf of Michael (291), the salesboy offers an acknowledgment (292) which paves the way for a subsequent closing to the encounter. We can schematize the progress of this unexpanded appeal sequence as follows:

(I)	A:	Appeal
(II)	B:	Acceptance/Rejection
(III)	A:	Acknowledgment

Technically, this unexpanded appeal sequence can be described as containing two actions beyond the occurrence of an appeal (I), with the next-to-last action (II) returning the floor to the initiator of the sequence for performance of the acknowledgment (III).

It is this unexpanded sequence that exerts a constraint upon, and provides resources for, the building of an appeal sequence successively "expanded" by the passes we observed initially. A stepwise schematization of that earlier excerpt can illustrate the technical dependence an expanded appeal sequence has on the materials of the unexpanded appeal sequence on which it is based.[11]

When the salesboy delivers his opening subscription appeal (11–16), the sequence his utterance sets up is the unexpanded appeal sequence projected upon the occurrence of an appeal:

(I)	A:	Appeal
(II)	B:	Acceptance/Rejection
(III)	A:	Acknowledgment

Richard's subsequent Processing Pass, instead of performing the occasioned next action, forwards performance of the (II) Acceptance/Rejection to "these fellas" (17–19) and thereby projects an expanded appeal sequence based on the initial projection:

(I)	A:	Appeal
	B:	Processing Pass
(I-r)	A:	Redirected Appeal
(II)	C:	Acceptance/Rejection
(III)	A:	Acknowledgment

The resulting expanded appeal sequence maintains not only the component parts of the unexpanded appeal sequence on which it is based, but also the order of the parts, and the distribution of the same parts to the initiator of the original projected sequence.

Now, as it happens, there then occurs a second expansion of this sequence; for instead of performing the forwarded (II) Acceptance/Rejection after the redirected appeal, Ted proffers a Conference Pass and the resulting sequence can be described as follows:

(I)	A:	Appeal
	B:	Processing Pass
(I-r)	A:	Redirected Appeal
	C:	Conference Pass
(II)	D:	Acceptance/Rejection
(III)	A:	Acknowledgment

Even with a second "expansion" on the originally projected unexpanded appeal sequence, the component parts are maintained in their same order, and the appropriate speakers of those parts are permitted by coparticipants to speak, and do speak, in the appropriate order.

Moreover, the passes that achieve the orderly "expansions" of the sequence are oriented to as on the way to the Acceptance/Rejection (II), and not as de facto rejections; although treating a sequence "expander" as a version of the activity it proposes to postpone is always an option open to the next speaker, all participants in this encounter "respect" the status of the passes as *sequence expanders*. Recall, for example, that the salesboy's pleading Acknowledgment (III) is finely timed to occur no sooner and no later than the performance of an explicit Rejection (II):

SALESBOY:	W'd eejer–any of you gen,tuhmen be innerested in	20
	subscribing to it,	21
TED:	Whaddi*you* think uh Beany,	22
	[	
STEVEN:	Na::w,	23
STEVEN:	Naw. I don't *go* faw it.	24
	[	
SALESBOY:	Plea:se, *just* fer a few short weeks, sir, y'won'	25
	haftuh pay t'l next *month*,	26
	[	

Only after Steven's "Na::w, –– Naw." (23–24) does the salesboy re-enter the conversation. We can see how Acknowledgments placed in this way are technically accomplished utterances sensitive to the performance of that event occasioning its own performance.[12]

While characterizing the passes in this excerpt as circumventions of the subscription appeal, we .noted how performance of Acceptance/ Rejection shifts from Richard to Ted, then from Ted to Steven. The passes with which Richard (or any "B") and Ted (or any "C") build an expanded sequence may reflect an alertness to the likelihood of inheriting the thrust of the Acknowledgment which will properly follow Acceptance/Rejection. That is, building an expanded sequence may be one of the ways speakers have of manipulating or negotiating performance of locally critical components of an initially projected unexpanded sequence. In our data, for example, since the performer of the next-to-last position (namely, Acceptance/Rejection) will be subsequently implicated in the kind of continuance (cf. 25–26) or the kind of closure (cf. 292) profferable by the last position (namely, Acknowledgment), the next-to-last position in the projected unexpanded sequence may be especially critical. We are suggesting that conversationalists design their utterances with such technical structures informing on their achieved fit between interactional enterprises and projected sequence structures.

We have sketched a technical, "nonintuitive" characterization of the observed passes. This has involved us in becoming alert not only to the availability of unexpanded and expanded sequences, but also to the possibility of selective deployment of those sequence-types in the service of distinctive interactional enterprises. As a next heuristic device to sustain our analyses, let us turn these resources to an investigation of some other materials. Using this heuristic device can generate an appreciation of the abstract status of these sequence-types, and as well, a sense for the detailed cooperation involved in the collaborative production of such sequences.

The following excerpt is taken from a telephone call between Patty and Gene, during which Patty's son, Ronald, is in the room with her as the telephone conversation proceeds; at some point Gene asks Patty about Ronald, and in responding, Patty is talking about Ronald in his presence when the following occurs:[13]

PATTY:	Oh I'd say he's about what five three enna half=	C1
PATTY:	=Aren'tchu Ronald	C2
RONALD:	Five *fou:r*.	C3
PATTY:	Five four,	C4
PATTY:	En 'e weighs about a hunnerd'n thirdy five	C5
	pounds.=	C6
RONALD:	**=Aauggh! Whadda–l–lie!**	C7
	⌈	
PATTY:	Well how–=	C8
PATTY:	=Owright? How much d'you weigh.	C9
RONALD:	One *twe*nty five.	C10
PATTY:	Oh one *twe*nny five.	C11
	⌈	
GENE:	What'r yuh tryina make a fatty	C12
	out'v'm?	C13
PATTY:	Hu:h?	C14
GENE:	Trina make a *fa*tty out'v'm?	C15
	⌈	
RONALD:	Y'make me sound like a *blimp*.	C16

Relying on Ronald's overhearing of her exchange with Gene (C1), Patty initiates an encounter with Ronald by soliciting a correction from him on her estimate of his weight (C2); Ronald offers the correction (C3), Patty acknowledges the correction (C4), and returns at once to her exchange with Gene (C5). The "unexpanded" character of the sequence devoted to the height correction (C2–C4) bears a striking similarity to the unexpanded appeal sequence we have already seen (285–292); in both, the occurrence of the first item projects two actions beyond it, with the next-to-last action returning the floor to the initiator of the sequence for an Acknowledgment of the next-to-last action:

Unexpanded Appeal Sequence

(I)   A: Appeal
(II)   B: Acceptance/Rejection
(III)   A: Acknowledgment

Unexpanded Correction Sequence

(I)   A: Correction Solicitor
(II)   B: Correction
(III)   A: Acknowledgment

In each instance, the initiator of the sequence (A) uses the return of the floor for Acknowledgment (III) to negotiate closure to an encounter. We have already seen how the salesboy's unprotesting "Okay." (292) acknowledges the just prior rejection and brings the encounter into a closing sequence. In the correction sequence now being considered, Patty uses an unelaborated repeat, "Five four," (C4) of Ronald's just prior correction to permit an immediate return to her encounter with Gene; packaging the unexpanded correction sequence within the syntactically tied utterance "Oh I'd say he's about what five three enna half. . . . En'e weighs about a hunnerd'n thirdy five pounds." (C1–C6) displays to both Ronald and Gene the intervals of height that, in describing Ronald, she is willing to treat as inconsequential.

In performing the Acknowledgment (III) to Ronald's just prior correction, Patty has the option to comment on the Correction (II) in some way that would generate resources for continuing the side encounter with Ronald; for example, the Acknowledgment (III) position can be used to apologize to Ronald for the error, to rebuke such a minor correction, to take notice of how much Ronald is growing or shrinking, and so forth. Patty's unelaborated repeat of the Correction (II) treats the difference between her own "five three enna half" (C1) and Ronald's "Five *fou:r*." (C3) as deserving no special notice by the estimator, and the side encounter with Ronald is brought to a close. Patty's immediate return to the encounter with Gene marks her part in the collaborative achievement of this unexpanded correction sequence.

As for Ronald's part, performance of the Correction (II) delivers the Acknowledgment (III) to Patty as we have seen; but this cooperation in achieving an unexpanded correction sequence stands as an alternative to an "expansion" he could undertake if, for example, he determined that the difference between Patty's estimate and his own knowledge of his height deserved another treatment. One characteristic "expansion" for such correction sequences involves following the first Correction Solicitor (I) with a return Correction Solicitor (r). The resulting sequence,

(I)	A:	Correction Solicitor
(r)	B:	Correction Solicitor
(II)	A:	Correction
(III)	B:	Acknowledgment

thus forwards performance of the Correction (II) to the initiator (A) of the sequence instead of its being performed by the second speaker (B) as originally projected in the unexpanded version of the sequence; as a consequence, the Acknowledgment (III) is delivered to (B) instead of to (A). By contrast, Ronald's performance of the Correction (II) in our data (C3) already reflects an anticipation that the difference his utterance will reveal can receive another's minimal Acknowledgment (III), and an "expansion" to forward the Correction (II) to Patty and deliver the Acknowledgment (III) to him is not warranted.[14]

On the matter of Ronald's weight, however, there is considerable flurry as these coparticipants negotiate an expanded correction sequence tossing the performance of the Correction (II) and its Acknowledgment (III) back and forth. The sequence is initiated this time by Ronald who asserts his outrage (C7) when Patty's resumption of her encounter with Gene commits a mistaken estimate of his weight:

PATTY: En 'e weighs about a hunnerd'n thirdy five   C5
             pounds.=   C6
RONALD: =*Aauggh! Whadda–l–lie!*   C7
                     [

Here, Ronald's utterance (C7) presents itself as a Correction Solicitor (I) initiating a correction sequence whose unexpanded projection,

	B:	Estimate
(I)	A:	Correction Solicitor
(II)	B:	Correction
(III)	A:	Acknowledgment

would have Patty (B) performing a Correction (II) to her own estimate of Ronald's weight, thus delivering to Ronald (A) the Acknowledgment (III) in which he can exercise the option to proffer continuance or closure to his apparent injury.[15]

Notwithstanding his outraged enthusiasm, Ronald has bypassed protesting at the point when the error was observable to him. Since his own knowledge of his weight is "One *twenty* five." (C10), an error of from 5 to 14 pounds is detectable by Ronald when Patty gets as far as "En 'e weighs about a hunnerd'n thirdy . . ." (C5). Instead of asserting a protest to the mistake at that point, Ronald allows Patty's utterance to go to completion. His outrage is delicately positioned at the point when he hears Patty's completed utterance has left uncorrected a mistake that is presumably self-correctable.[16] Following Patty's utterance with a Correction Solicitor (I) instead of asserting the correction himself provides Patty a chance to "look again" and offer her own Correction (II). Ronald's *"Aaugh! Whadda–l–lie!"* (C7) structurally reflects the disputed issue being a matter of appearance, not simply a matter of so many pounds, and it vigorously protests her estimate as an error his appearance will refute.[17]

But as it happens, Patty does not follow Ronald's protest (C7) with a revised estimate:

PATTY:	En 'e weighs about a hunnerd'n thirdy five	C5
	pounds.=	C6
RONALD:	=*Aauggh! Whadda– l–lie!*	C7
	[	
PATTY:	Well how–=	C8
PATTY:	=Owright? How much d'you weigh.	C9

In following Ronald's Correction Solicitor (I) with a return Correction Solicitor (r) instead of the Correction (II), the initially projected action sequence becomes an expanded correction sequence,

	B:	Estimate
(I)	A:	Correction Solicitor
(r)	B:	Correction Solicitor
(II)	A:	Correction
(III)	B:	Acknowledgment

thereby forwarding performance of the controversial Correction (II) to Ronald (A), and delivering the Acknowledgment (III) to Patty (B) instead of the other way around.

Upon the occurrence of each, both Ronald's and Patty's correction solicitors (I) and (r), respectively, project sequences returning the Acknowledgment (III) to their respective speakers. We are suggesting that in sequences such as these, incumbency of the Acknowledgment (III) position may be especially critical to coparticipants attempting to disarm another's victory. The negotiation of this expanded correction sequence reflects technical sensitivities to the uses of the Acknowledgment (III) position in such sequences. For an embattled issue,[18] Acknowledgment (III) can be used to control the disposition of the controversy with displays of its inconsequence—"Oh one *twe*nny five." (C11), or its injury—"Y'make me sound like a *blimp*." (C16). That conversationalists design their utterances, in part, by monitoring the positions being allocated in a projected action sequence is the recurring recommendation.

In elaborating the intuitively transparent circumventions observable in the salesboy data, we generated a detailed characterization of the passes used to avoid accepting or rejecting the subscription appeal. In turning those observations into reflections of underlying structural phenomena, we focused our attention on the sequential "expansions" achieved by those circumventions and explored the organization of the salesboy data around unexpanded and expanded versions of projected action sequences. That analysis was then turned to other materials.

In the salesboy data, it was the Acceptance/Rejection (II) that was successively forwarded by two passes, and we proposed that the negotiation of that expanded appeal sequence was technically sensitive to projected action sequence possibilities since the occurrence of the Rejection (II) would deliver the later Acknowledgment (III) to the salesboy and thereby inherit his efforts to continue the encounter until transformed into an Acceptance. In the subsequent materials, the Ronald-and-Patty exchange, it was the Correction (II) that was successively forwarded, and we proposed that the negotiation of that expanded correction sequence was similarly sensitive to projected action sequence possibilities since the occurrence of the Correction (II) would deliver the Acknowledgment (III) to the other participant and thereby place in the other's control the disposition of an energetically controversial matter.

The Acknowledgment (III) position and the next-to-last position (II) have an intimate technical relationship: Negotiations about their distribution involve their occurrence as a consecutive pair of events. The "expansion" of a sequence containing such a pair will consequently involve negotiation of the projected action sequence before the occurrence of the first component of such a pair; a review of our data will demonstrate that the components of these pairs (e.g., Acceptance/Rejection with its Acknowledgment or Correction with its Acknowledgment) are separated in none of the observed "expansions" (e.g., 23–24 or C8–C10). Since the occurrence of the first component in such a pair strongly controls the subsequent occurrence of the second, conversationalists may monitor them together, and they may be negotiating not merely incumbency of one position, but necessarily the distribution of incumbencies for both positions.[19]

NOTES

[1] This excerpt is from a larger corpus of conversations recorded in 1969 by Alan Ryave and Jim Schenkein at a halfway house for formerly institutionalized adult male "retardates" outside Los Angeles. Except for the salesboy, who is a "normal" boy of about 12, and Richard and John, who are "normal" adult male visitors to the house, all other participants are "retardate" residents. A more extensive consideration of the competencies exhibited by the "retardates" in the conduct of their conversational interaction can be found in Ryave (1973, 1977).

[2] This will be taken up on pp. 159–160.

[3] We might have developed instead observations on some other intuitively transparent activity as a way of breaking into these materials. For example, we could begin the investigation by building a characterization of the salesboy's opening utterance (11–16) as a recognizable sales pitch: We would observe the syntactic momentum employed for an uninterruptable delivery, the ordering of the component parts of the utterance, the construction of personal appeals and guarantees, the consequence of the utterance in now confronting its hearers with accepting or rejecting the sales appeal, and other features detailing the management of the sales pitch over the course of the utterance. It should be clear from this brief hint at one alternative beginning that these materials can support extensive analytic energies and can yield substantially different analyses. We should also point out that the procedure for beginning investigations of these materials suggested at the start of this paper—that is, "elaborate details of an intuitively observable interactional phenomenon"—was the result of retrospective examination of a research enterprise conducted unwise to a formulation of that policy. This research got started "somehow" and only a review of its history stimulated formulation of the policy reported. While at present we can offer no principled position for selecting one intuitively transparent observation over another as a point of investigative departure, some work has been done on a variety of other research predicaments requiring selection of one analytic direction over another; see Sacks (1971), Schenkein (1971, 1977a), Sudnow (1972).

[4] The explicit display of the grounds for his forwarding of the appeal to the others is a crucial part of an utterance designed to circumvent accepting or rejecting the appeal. Had Richard merely said something like "Ask these fellas here," he might well have avoided the issue for now, but without a display of adequate grounds for his own disqualification, he would not have secured resources for more permanent immunity to a redirection of the appeal to him by the salesboy somewhat later, or a "pass back" of the issue by those to whom he attempted passing the matter himself.

[5] In this regard, the Processing Pass of the housewife to her not-at-home husband is a notorious device to bring closure to encounters with door-to-door solicitors; to be sure, the countermoves available to such a Processing Pass occupy a critical place among the professional skills of salesmen.

[6] Of course, the query "Whaddi*you* think" is not guaranteed circumvention of the pending issue: Had Steven returned with "I think it's perfect for you" instead of "Naw. I don't *go* faw it," the issue would have been passed resoundingly *back* to Ted. Indeed,

successive passings back and forth sometimes become an occasion to specifically formulate the awkwardness, irony, or stalemate in such circumstances. But without regard to the *success* of the Conference Pass in committing its recipient to a position on the pending issue, a Conference Pass does confront its recipient with the issue being considered.

[7] These data reveal that a circumvention may be a preferred interactional strategy to an explicit rejection of the appeal. Richard's initial Processing Pass (17–19) avoided the practical and interactional consequences of considering the appeal further, for the salesboy turns at once to the others; Ted's subsequent Conference Pass (22) avoided for him performance of either an acceptance or rejection, and his continued participation in the encounter never jeopardizes his escape from the appeal; but Steven's rejection (23–24) is treated by the salesboy as a chance to extend Steven's consideration of the appeal (25–26). It is not unlikely that Passes used to circumvent the occasioned relevance of accepting or rejecting the subscription appeal are structurally wise to the extendibility of the encounter by the salesboy when a rejection of his appeal is proffered.

[8] The salesboy specifically corrects his utterance to contain not merely a term which covers two of the remaining three candidate subscribers (i.e., "eejer–" or 'either of you'), to a term which can include all three (i.e., "any of you"); in this way, John is not automatically excluded from "these fellas" being passed to by Richard, and he can decide for himself whether or not the paper is of interest to him no matter how selective Richard's "these fellas" may have been intended.

[9] The mere fact of a pass in some instances can invoke and rely upon elaborate ideologies that constrain the conduct of everyday social intercourse. Consider the tacitly rational distributions of authority and/or provinces of activity among certain categories of persons displayed in the pass of a man to the lady of the house for whole collections of issues, of the wife to the not-at-home husband, of the child to an adult, of the client to the attorney, of the psychiatrist to the patient, of the cashier to the floor manager, and so on. Both formulated displays of the grounds for a pass (as in Richard's disclaimer of local residence as a ground for passing to the others) and unformulated grounds (as in Ted's Conference Pass or his Processing Pass to the lady of the house) can bear inspection for those features of the taken-for-granted world underlying the design of conversational actions.

[10] The transparency of such heuristic initial observations (for example, "this is a sales pitch," "this is an evasion," and so on) can be appealed to for relief from our persistent suspicions that the phenomena we research are figments of our technical imaginations. Beginning with intuitively plain observations draws upon the resources lay conversationalists have for formulating their conversational enterprises. Conversationalists can recognize instances of such phenomena, they can elaborate subtleties of construction and debate with authority propositions about the phenomena, and they can locate situational contingencies having an impact on the appropriateness or artfulness of a given instance. The proposed beginning heuristic device offered here of course relies on our own membership within the conversational community we seek to study; more particularly, it asks that we formulate some aspects of our membership expertise concerning phenomena more or less known and observable to any competent member of the community.

[11] We intend the terms "unexpanded" and "expanded" as technical descriptions of action sequence possibilities, and not to suggest that the former is more impoverished than the latter; it is an unexpanded appeal sequence (285–292) that is used to negotiate the encounter into a closing sequence, and there are obviously large collections of interactional enterprises for which an unexpanded version of a sequence is the appropriate or preferred form. We might add that the particular appeal sequence being examined here in unexpanded and expanded forms (namely, an appeal sequence fitted to a newspaper subscription) has

observable generalizability to other sorts of appeals; we may well view this analysis as a prototype for appeal sequences of various kinds.

[12] While no such happening is exhibited in these data, it may be useful to point out that a series of sequence expansions heard to be circumventions of a relevant component in the projected action sequence (e.g., accepting/rejecting) can permit, and sometimes oblige, the initiator of the sequence to perform the avoided action himself (e.g., "Oh well, you probably wouldn't be interested"); notice that in this case, the initiator having performed the Accepting/Rejecting himself on the other's behalf has the consequence of yielding the Acknowledgment position to the others (e.g., "That's right"). We will have more to say shortly about the consequences of such negotiations for incumbency of one or another position in a projected action sequence (cf. pp. 167–168 and note 18). A more elaborate consideration of precise timing constraints such as the "no sooner and no later" placement of the salesboy's Acknowledgment in these data can be found in Jefferson (1973, 1974).

[13] This excerpt comes from a larger corpus of materials collected by Goldberg (1976), and we would like to record here our appreciation to her for making it available to us.

[14] When the difference between the estimate and the correction is somewhat more significant, or when the mistake in the estimate is heard as a different kind of error, the recipient of the first Correction Solicitor (I) may decide to "expand" the action sequence and respond with a returned Correction Solicitor (r) instead of the Correction (II) as in the following hypothetical instance:

> (I)　A:　You must be about five four.
> (r)　B:　Look again.
> (II)　A:　I mean *six* four.
> (III)　B:　That's better.

Notice that the "expansion" with a returned Correction Solicitor (r) results in B's incumbency of the Acknowledgment (III), whereas without this "expansion" A's incumbency of the Acknowledgment (III) would have to confront his prior error as in:

> (I)　A:　You must be about five four.
> (II)　B:　*Six* four.
> (III)　A:　Yeah, I *meant* six four.

These "expansions" can be used not only to make a fuss, but also to save an apology.

[15] Of more general interest is the observation that a Correction Solicitor can attach itself to some prior utterance, and thereby seek to gain control of a projected action sequence as it simultaneously proposes a review of its own precedent. In our data, Patty's estimate of Ronald's weight (C5–C6) does not generate the ensuing correction sequence, although it is the precedent for Ronald's Correction Solicitor (C7) which does. Correction Solicitors appear to have an across-the-board *second-position occurrence potential;* they can be asserted after estimates and assertions not necessarily wise to their own defect; they can occur after questions to inform the questioner that he already knows or ought to know the answer; and, what is emerging as organizationally critical, they can occur after a prior Correction Solicitor as a way to negotiate for control of the projected Acknowledgment (III) position.

[16] A detailed discussion of this fragment can be found in Jefferson (1972).

[17] In general, if one has made an estimate on something available to inspection for an estimate revision and is told in no uncertain terms that the estimate is in error, one can "look again" (actually, figuratively, or constructively) and see for himself the kind of error he has

committed. In this case, moreover, there exists a bias for generating low estimates of a person's weight since it is generally high estimates that are offensive. Ronald's Correction Solicitor (C7) not only proposes that his actual weight, as a matter of appearance, can be correctly observed by Patty, but it instructs her, just in case she cannot, that the direction her revision should take is downward.

[18] The same structural "expansion" can be used in another kind of correction sequence to negotiate the proper display of affinity, apology, or amazement. For example, in the following sequence:

	B:	I bet that sweater cost you thirty five dollars.
(I)	A:	Oh nowhere near that!
(r)	B:	Well how much *did* it cost.
(II)	A:	Five bucks.
(III)	B:	Incredible!

B's complimentary estimate is followed by A's Correction Solicitor (I); had B subsequently proffered a Correction (II) to the mistaken first estimate, A would be delivered the Acknowledgment (III) in which B's second guess would command attention—and since A's Correction Solicitor (I) illustrates not only the direction of the mistake but also the magnitude, B is in a position to substantially repair the mistake, and that would leave A an Acknowledgment (III) for either applauding B's second guess or affirming that a closer look at the sweater will convince you of its lesser value. By contrast, in treating A's Correction Solicitor (I) as a *claim* of correct information instead of a solicitation of correct information, B offers a return Correction Solicitor (r) which forwards to A performance of the Correction (II) and delivers to B the Acknowledgment (III) position in which to properly display the complimentary amazement. Negotiating performance of positions in projected action sequences is finely tuned to the interactional enterprises at hand.

[19] For those familiar with the emerging findings of conversation analysis, it is worth noting that the "consecutive pairs" being referred to in this discussion seem to behave differently from the "adjacency pairs" considered elsewhere (cf. Harvey Sacks, 1972a, Lectures 1–4). In an adjacency pair, the occurrence of the "first pair-part" occasions the occurrence of the second, such that the second occurs or it is noticeably absent. The "consecutive pairs" referred to here are not *pair* parts but *sequence* parts, such that the occurrence of the "first" has itself been occasioned by the large sequence in which the "pair" is structurally embedded. While we have not explored the implication of this distinction we suspect that it has some interesting analytic consequence.

chapter 7

On a Conversational Environment for Equivocality

W. W. SHARROCK AND ROY TURNER

The analysis we develop in this paper began with some relatively casual observations made on a corpus of citizen phone calls to a metropolitan police force. It was remarkably easy to see a subset of these calls as models of complaint giving: They were brief, "to the point," and intelligible both to us and (judging by results) to police. Other calls struck us as "rambling," packed with excessive detail, and unfocused. Further, we found that many of this second set of calls possessed another interesting property that we could notice with no more esoteric resource than our layman's ear for conversational strategies; namely, that without much difficulty we could derive from these calls a version of the events they narrated which was not teller's evidently preferred version, but which "made sense" as an alternative. When we say that the alternative versions we could "spontaneously" locate made sense, we mean that though we supposed they would be disavowed by callers themselves, equally with callers' own versions they provided an intelligible rationale for calling the police. Beginning with these crude glosses we sought to discover structural features of complaint deliveries which might underlie them. A methodological note is in order here. We did *not* take as our task, for example, to provide an analytic version of, say, "rambling discourse": That is to say, the analytical work did not consist in developing a technical version of the lay characterizations with which we began. Our initial glosses interested us in the data, but our analysis of the materials led us to considerations which we could not have entertained in the preanalysis stage. If our analysis has any merit, then the issues which it leads us to consider are of interest beyond our corpus and beyond the circumscribed domain of phone calls to the police. Our investigations no more dismiss our initial glosses than they technicalize them. As far as we are concerned, lay glosses and analyses of conversational structures live in peaceful coexistence—so long, at any rate, as their different spheres of relevance are not mistaken the one for the other.

I

When we speak in these pages of a "complaint" we shall be referring to a conversational event, that is, to some formulation of caller's trouble or problems which he delivers to the police. Although it is good idiomatic usage to use the same term for the troubles or problems themselves— persons possessed of "complaints" may decide to call the police—we shall use the less euphonious term *complainable* to refer to the state of affairs a complaint formulates. We do this so as to have a ready way of indicating when we are speaking of the conversational events we analyze and when we are referring to the states of affairs which occasion these conversational events.

Although we shall not elaborate the alternative sequences which a complaint's telling may engender, we need to note that upon a complaint's completion, a responsive recipient ought to produce an utterance–type which is hearable as a *complaint acknowledgment*. What this amounts to is perhaps not a simple matter, depending—as it presumably does—upon recipient's analysis of what the complaint delivery seeks; itself, perhaps, dependent upon recipient's analysis of the relationship that sanctions the delivery *to him,* as well as some assessment of how he might expectably be affected by the complainable itself. Minimally, it seems, complaints can seek remedy, sympathy, or shared indignation (in cases where what is a complainable for teller ought to be a complainable for recipient also), and thus minimally either the giving or denial of one of these reliefs stands to count as an adequate complaint acknowledgment. Nevertheless, the issue is more complex than this. Thus, if we take it that complaints are delivered to the police in search of remedial action, directed towards the complainable, then we can gloss the internal organization of "successful" calls to the police as first consisting of a complaint-delivery sequence (which may be single- or multiutterance, as we shall consider below), followed by a police-initiated fact-seeking sequence, the import of which, it seems, is that the facts are required for the implementation of remedial action; and hence the initiation of this sequence can signify acceptance of complaint and intention to deliver remedy, so that what otherwise might seem to be a disjunctive or topic-shifting utterance-type can perfectly well serve as an adequate complaint acknowledgment.

[VII-14]

P:	Newton Police.	1
C:	Hello; could I have a car down here at the Fir's Hotel, five seventy two Parkway?	2
P:	What's the trouble.	3
C:	Well the:hh (0.5) th' chambermaid sent in to clean a room an' there's a gun in ( ).	4
P:	Five seventy six Parkway.	5

When remedy, rather than, say, sympathy, is the sought response to a complaint, the issue of the timing of the complaint delivery with respect to the occurrence or discovery of the complainable is apparently crucial; and if no mention is made of the temporal relation between occurrence and delivery, then an inference is warranted, namely that the delivery has been made "as soon as possible" or in "reasonable time." Clearly with respect to many complainables, proper temporal placement of a remedy-seeking complaint delivery will be seen by callers to be a matter of efficacy; for example, informing the police of a stolen item ought to be undertaken "immediately" in order to expedite police recovery activities, whatever other considerations also operate. Thus there is a class of states of affairs which can be "seen at a glance" or verified after a short period of checking alternatives (that the jewels were not in another drawer; that the car was not parked on the next block) and which then legitimate, if not require, a soonest-possible complaint to the police (and perhaps others than the police).

Note in the following openings of calls to police that (*a*) a complainable of this class is extractable from the complaint, and (*b*) that the issue of the timing of the call is for the parties "no issue"—*and that this signifies not indeed that timing is no issue, but that the temporal placement of the complaint is deemed to be "normal" in the absence of evidence to the contrary.*

[III-5]

P: Newton Police,   1

C: eh my neighbor ah up the street ah thirty o::ne (1.0)
        (   ) forty five has locked herself out. (I ws jus')
        wonderin' if you could send a man up to help her to get
        en; she's an old lady over eighty.   2

[VI-17]

P: Newton Police.   1

C: Yes, I'd like to repar– report a car stolen.   2

[VIII-16]

P: Newton Police.   2
            (1.0)

C: Yi:p, I think ya need ta: shove ov'r there's a guy passed
        out, sleepin' on a garbage can at the back of the
        Parkway.   2

[XI-6]

P: Hello; Newton Police   1

C: Ah yes, I had my ca:r towed away from–eh Parkway
        and–eh Regent; it was in the alleyway. Could you
        tell me whereabouts it would be.   2

When the supposition concerning the temporal relation of call to
event is breached, caller may build notice of this in his first utterance.

[XVII-25]

P: Newton Police   1
            (0.5)

C: Yes, I was just wondering, my name is–eh Howard
        Kottingham, and–eh I parked my car (at) Cedar
        Boughs (0.5) ah not Cedar Boughs but in Locklin terri-
        tory, (0.5) and–eh, I went back there the other day,
        I: lost it, I don't know, (   ) I was just wondering if you
        picked it up or not.   2

This latter complaint formulation repays further study. While it is
true that caller can be heard to display attention to a breach in the "rule"
that complaints ought to be placed at earliest opportunity, the same
materials can be heard as informative as to the putative history of the
"lost" car, in that the passage of time suggests as a possible occurrence,

that police themselves had removed the car (an alternative to the car's being stolen). Again we notice that this appears in caller's first utterance. That a complaint is formulated in a single utterance, or in an extended utterance, or over the course of more than one utterance is an interactional achievement of both parties.[1] Clearly, for example, that a complaint is packaged over several of caller's utterances is the product of caller's being permitted or required to deliver more than a first utterance to formulate an "adequate complaint." Just what "adequate" amounts to here is not perhaps easy to specify; it may at least amount to telling "enough" so that police can determine whether or not the complainable is one which they will attend to, and to find what remedy is sought or is entailed by the complainable. That a single-utterance format may suffice in these terms is not interactionally indifferent; for in the first place *that* the first utterance has gone to completion is itself a collaborative achievement, and callers may well orient to packaging a complaint within a single utterance, since first utterance may be as much as they can expect to control. Thus regarded, the utterance we are currently looking at has some elegant features, if we consider (*a*) that caller's query is basically "I was wondering if you've picked up my car," and (*b*) that *that* format will not handle the problematics that caller needs to narrate if police are to have a sense of what the complainable is. Thus, caller begins with a query format, "I was just wondering," which he then suspends, so that recipient cannot find in what turns out to be the body of the utterance what the "wondering" is about, and then closes with a repeat which now goes to completion: "I was just wondering if you picked it up or not," where now the receiving officer has materials to process the query. First utterance thus manages to foreshadow a possibly complex narrative, and at the same time to offer enough to solicit a complaint acknowledgment.

Before turning to some of the structural features which may require complaints to be packaged as extended- or multiple-utterance formats, we would like to note a further taken-for-granted property of complaints, namely that caller "owns" the problem or trouble which occasions the call. When this is not the case, then it may be treated by caller as an accountable, and again such an account may be located in first utterance.

[III-5]

P:	Newton Police,	1
C:	eh my neighbor up the street ah thirty o::ne (1.0) ( ) forty five has locked herself out. (I ws jus') wonderin' if you could send a man up to help her to get en; she's an old lady over eighty.	2

"She's an old lady over eighty" simultaneously accounts for the

event occasioning a call to the police (rather than to a locksmith) *and*
accounts for caller delivering a complaint on behalf of its owner. Later in
the call, in response to a request for her own name, which she can perhaps
see as directed to the issue of the caller's failing to be the bona fide
complainant, caller directs her reply to just that matter.

> C: My name is Missis Henderson, she's just come to my
>   front door an' eh knocked an' asked me to phone
>   ya. . .

It is in this light that we can see, for example, "she's just come to my
front door an' eh knocked," not as reporting, as a matter of expectable
police interest, how the neighbor got to the house and secured caller's
attention, but as explaining how caller has found herself in the position of
making an "on-behalf" call to the police. "On-behalf" calls which are not
given an adequate accounting within first utterance may be subject to
query, placing possible police action in suspense until the query is an-
swered.

[V-10]

P:	Newton Police.	1
C:	eh eh I'm calling for my e::h for Mister D McDuff's–eh house.–eh They they have left for on a month's holiday at least. And–eh, they want–eh to have someone call there at night not in the daytime but at night. (1.5) To see (if it's–) you know, to look after the house at night.	2

>   [   ]

P:	Ya, well they should have phoned in themselves, you see. ( ).	3

>   [   ]

C:	Oh well, I'm her daugh ter.	4
P:	Oh, oh I see. ( )	

>   [   ]

C:	And–eh Mister D McDuff–eh worked on the department himself. She was going to call but she didn't have time this morning ( ) she would have missed her pla:ne if she had (1.0) taken the time she was just inna such a rush, you see.	5
P:	Yes, I'm sure.	
C:	So–ah this is the reason that–eh *I*'m phoning; I just got back from the airport.	

P: M–hm. (0.5) Fine, just a moment 'n' let me get the:h
          proper form an' I'll take the report.

In several ways we have been considering what various states of
affairs amount to as complainables when the issue is formulating a complaint for the police; we have seen that there is a possible preference for a
single-utterance format; and we have noted that accounting for other-
than-usual temporal ordering and on-behalf complaints may be oriented to
by callers. We can now look freshly at some of the ground covered:
Materials which upon a cursory reading of the transcript may give the
appearance of "ramblings," "embellishments," "redundant detail," or
whatever—such as one caller's telling that her neighbor came to the front
door, or another's that he had gone to look for his car "the other day"—
have been provided for as structurally occasioned in describable ways. So
far we have considered what we shall now term (for convenience) Class I
complainables (and, correspondingly, Class I complaints): states of affairs
for which it is true that no account need be given for finding them police
reportable. That the theft of a car should be reported as soon as possible
presupposes that, in the first place, the theft of a car ought to be reported.
Were the reporting of a stolen car to be perceived as an *optional* matter,
then some accounting of why *this* option—calling the police—might well
be in order.
          In contrast to Class I complainables, we want to take note of a class
(Class II), the formulation of which for complaint delivery involves complainants in narrating "details," as an essential part of telling the police
what constitutes the trouble and providing a basis for seeking remedial
action. In brief, such complainables can be characterized as follows: They
are states of affairs whose troublesome nature (as discerned by complainant) only becomes evident over time as a result of monitoring "developments" and deriving inferences; and hence, in order to establish the
bona fides of the complainable some documentation of noticings, realiza-
tions, suspicions, and so on, is required as an essential component of the
complaint—its absence occasioning questions as to its availability. For
the moment, then, we want to propose that where accumulating observations, monitoring events, making inferences over time, and so forth, are
seen as prelude to calling the police, then both *that* one calls, and that one
calls now may be standardly treatable as accountable.

[IV-9]

| P: | Newton Police. | 1 |
| C: | Yes; is this the stolen car eh (detail)?= | 2 |

P: = Well we take reports of
        stol en cars here (this is) emergency.   3
            [   ]
C: hh   well   eh:hm   4
        (This   ) I don't know whether it's stolen or not, it's
        been parked across the street from my house up
        against the schoo:l–eh yard;
P: It's against the schoolyard.   5
                    [   ]
C: for a week   today.   6
P: Against the schoolyard.   7
                    [   ]
C: the lic– ense number is three nine O,
        nine five seven. (1.0) It's a black, fifty-seven chev, I
        think; two-door. (1.5) There's no city test on it, I
        thought maybe it was from out of tow:n;   8
P: M–hm.   9
C: and there's a blue sign in one of the side windows (0.5)
        eh in the rear, (0.5) police.   10
            (1.5)
P: Blue sign, police,   11
C: Ya, it's a blue sign, police.   12
            (1.5)
P: I see,   13
C: It's–eh kind of an odd situation, I've been watching it= 14
            [   ]
P: Is it an obvious?   15
        Is it conspicu ous?
        [   ]
C: =oh=   =for a week now; I don't know when
        it was parked there because I don't very often go out
        the front or even look out the front windows of my
        house an' I live right across the street from it.   16

If our claim with respect to single-utterance complaint deliveries is
that though preferred, they must constitute candidate activators of remedial police activity, then Class II complainables are problematic for callers. If a single-utterance format is selected, it can at best initiate a
collaborative sequence developing the complaint. If callers are not assured that they can package a single-utterance complaint format which
will do that job, then they may initiate what will turn out on police
sufferance to be either an extended-utterance or a multiple-utterance
delivery. It may seem at first that there is little to choose between an

attempted single-utterance delivery and a design which already foreshadows extended- or multiple-utterance packaging. The interactionally consequential difference may amount to this: The former risks coming off as an inadequately delivered complaint, which puts the onus on police to solicit a more satisfactory version; the latter can give notice that a considerable amount of material will need to be heard before an assessment of adequacy can be made. It is on such slender considerations, after all, that persons can be found to be more or less cooperative or competent, more or less thoughtful as to what police will need to know. As an indicator of awareness that one's narrative may not be immediately transparent as an adequate complainable, caller can employ a prefatory component[2] (e.g., "I have a complaint") which instructs recipient that it may take some listening to find what it is thus proposed the completed narrative will turn out to be.

[I-2]

P:	Newton Police,	1
C:	Hello::?	2
P:	Yes,	3
C:	I ha:ve a complaint um my neighbor is (0.5) le– subl– well renting her garage out, end ah there are young boys, now they seem awfully nice an' everything but I don't know they're missing an awful lot of school, they're fifteen-year-old types, (0.5) an', they've got, apparently they've got seven old cars, I guess they buy these old cars, but about a month ago they went to town sma:shing one of them with a pick axe ju:st absolutely annoying you know pounding all day,=	4
P:	(Mm)	5
C:	= and I: have a dog that ba:rks a lot an' I guess he's not taking too kindly to these kids.	6

(See Appendix for continuation of complaint development over successive utterances.)

II

Let us now turn to a more focused consideration of some of the structural features of Class II complainables and their associated complaints. Though we might deal with these in more general fashion, our concerns will in fact be largely limited to the operation of a set of components of a subclass of Class II complaints. In order to provide for the intelligibility of this subclass we need to introduce briefly some aspects of complainables and complaints that we have hitherto neglected.

In many of the complaints in our corpus it occurs both that (*a*) the complainable is so conceived that some person(s) must be responsible for the state of affairs at issue, and (*b*) no mention of that fact is made within the delivery of the complaint (or anywhere else in the completed call). A stolen car, for example, presupposes a car thief,[3] but our complaints reporting stolen cars make no reference to such a key figure in the occurrence. Nevertheless, there are states of affairs which constitute complainables for citizens where it is the case that the complaint does, or can, involve persons known to the caller, that is, involve them as responsible for the complainable state of affairs. We shall refer to persons who figure in complaints in this capacity as *complained-againsts*. Despite the term's lack of elegance, it is descriptive of the part that such persons are assigned in the narratives which complainants offer. Our subclass of Class II complaints, then, is made up of those complaints, otherwise members of the class, which make reference to complained-againsts. It is important that we make clear our belief that this is not an arbitrary delimitation. We hope to show convincingly that the presence of complained-againsts is a feature of complaint formulation carefully oriented to by callers. Indeed, how that orientation is displayed, and some of the interactional concerns that display seems to cope with, will constitute the principle interest of the remainder of this paper.

We have already proposed that a caller's task in offering a complaint delivery to police is to provide for the reasonable character of the call, that is, to provide for the complainable as candidate police business, and in such a way that appropriate remedial action can be taken. Thus, where they are able to do so, callers make a clear distinction between a car's being "stolen" or "towed away," where in both cases the gloss "the car is gone" would in fact hold true, but where what caller expects from police turns upon the course of action which has led to the car's disappearance. When complained-againsts enter into a complaint, then, some formulation of such persons must of necessity be offered. It seems that there might be two views of preferred formulations: Names, if available, might be supposed maximally helpful to police in undertaking investigation; on the other hand, categorial formulations selected in accordance with some principled ways of constructing reasonable accounts might better serve caller's accomplishment of his task.[4] We do not suggest that these occasioned preferences need make for practical difficulties, for clearly each might be satisfied in some phase of the call; for example, categorial identifications in the complaint-delivery sequence, and names in the information-giving sequence that paradigmatically occupies the later part of a successful call. What we want to stress at the moment is that names are not in the first place necessarily preferred by either caller or police, and further that for callers the provision of names can turn out to be interactionally problematic in ways that illuminate components of complaints which are perhaps puzzling otherwise. We shall first look at selection procedures governing categorial formulations, and then turn to the issue of naming complained-againsts and the possible trouble this gives callers.

In assembling a complainable over time, *what* is occurring is not necessarily ascertained independently of *who* is seen to be responsible ("who" in this context standing for a category incumbency rather than a name as an identifier). Notice, for example, that in I-2 (see Appendix), complained-againsts are formulated as "young boys," "fifteen-year-old types," "these kids." While we can easily gloss what they are doing as, say, "dismantling cars," what *that* amounts to is perhaps not easily arrived at as a police-relevant matter. Indeed, what bothers complainant is perhaps that "these kids" are "sort of taking over the area," and that they are "pounding and pounding"; and if the complainable amounts to something like "causing a nuisance with noise and unsightly littering," then there is a sense in which cars are just the raw materials: "Kids" perhaps have plenty of ways of disfiguring and disrupting a neighborhood, and can find many resources to hand. "Just being kids," then, provides a possible way of seeing *what* is happening precisely by way of seeing *who* is doing it; it clearly, for example, has no effective contrast with such a nonidiomatic usage as "just being adults," and if the operations involving cars were indeed conducted by persons who could be viewed as "adults," we suggest that what they were/might be doing would perhaps find formulation as a possible criminal enterprise to which cars were central. And insofar as it might be that cars are central for the "kids," then their operations can be proposed as possibly the expression of "just [being] keen on cars." In short, there are two alternative ways in which the complainable can be tied to those responsible as a category-bound activity,[5] namely "kids" creating a neighborhood nuisance or "kids" going through a car phase. Either way, the fact of their status as children is used as grounds for formulating the complained-againsts as such persons who would do just what they are in fact doing.

In II-4 (see Appendix), complained-againsts are likewise both involved and characterized in ways intended to render intelligible the genesis of the complained-of state of affairs. Initially and elegantly, the status of the complained-againsts as potentially indifferent to the area and the comfort of its "permanent" residents is indicated by what on the face of it is "merely" a locational reference: "There is a house across the way rented," the force of which seems to hinge on the implicit contrast between "renters" and "property owners" (such as caller surely claims to be, and representatively so, by her invocation of the contrast). Further, the "renters" are more then just that, and other grounds (not at all incompatible) can be found by complainant for their indifference to the concerns of residents like herself; for the complained-againsts are "not exactly hippie element but – eh bordering on it." For such persons as caller, we take it, hippies, like children, if for different reasons, are prime candidates for the authorship of activities possessing side effects, the nuisance value of which they are ignorant of or indifferent to. What is offered here, it seems, is that the neighbors across the street not only *have* abandoned their car thoughtlessly, but are exactly such people who *would* do so. Again, then, the offense is clarified at least for complainant, and it is clarified in particular for police concerns, by the character of the offenders.

We return now to the issue of names as alternative forms of referral to complained-againsts, and our earlier suggestion that if there were differential preferences operating for names and for categorial formulations, then each could be satisfied in sequence. And whereas it may be caller's choice to employ categorial identifications in constructing the complaint, police can initiate second-phase references by direct inquiry.

[I-2]

| P: | Do you know the names of any of these boys? | 43 |
| C: | A:h gee I hate– I do? one of them; but I don't like to say anything you know. . . | 44 |

[II-4]

P:	You don't know the name of the party	
	( )	35
	[	
C:	No, I'm not sure.	36

Now, whereas there may be good reason for both parties to prefer categorial identifications for narrative construction, we have provided no resources so far to illuminate the kinds of interactional matters that may be at stake in callers "refusing" to give the names of those who, if police carry through remedial action, will likely find themselves in trouble. In order to argue on behalf of a determinate solution to what we have posed as an analytical problem, we need for a moment to turn to a somewhat grosser order of organization of talk and interaction.

Like other organizations and establishments dealing with self-selected clientele, seeking the products or services of the organization, police are oriented to the fact that some (unidentifiable) members of the population will invoke the standard routine contacts for subversive reasons, or will employ conventional resources for "doing business" in subversive ways. When customers and stores collaborate in the routines which amount to sale and purchase, for example, buyers can reasonably propose to make payment by check or credit card as "a matter of convenience." Suspicion as a fact of organizational life posits that "actually" some members of a check- and credit-card-using population will be motivated by the opportunity such arrangements provide for escaping payment altogether; and hence the routines which negotiate a sale may come to include activities which are visible as defensive action against that unknown component of the purchasing population which is ill motivated. Thus, it is a fact of organizational life that some of the "normal" contacts or transactions negotiated with clients are "fronts" for subversive courses of action, and more or less elaborate detection procedures can be devised to deter or frustrate would-be subversives.

For police (and not only police) one form of subversion is the "hoax," the mobilizing of police action for nonexistent complainables motivated by caller's search for amusement. Though we cannot vouch for members' intentions in employing the practice, we can notice that it is by no means uncommon for callers to offer in first-utterance position their names and addresses, in alternative to some formulation of a complaint. We further notice that on the occasions when this occurs, police typically take note of the "face sheet" information so offered, and we suggest that the interactional value of such an opening device is that it serves as an earnest of the bona fides of the call, that is, police assume that the prior delivery of such information warrants the seriousness of the call (not to be confused, of course, with the "degree of seriousness" of the complainable).

Our principle interest in something we might call subversion is not in hoaxes, but in quite a different matter. The activation of organizational routines can have what might be termed *side effects,* by which we mean consequences which are not merely additional to the standard outcomes of the routine, but are not avowedly sought as payoffs. With this in mind we return to our police data. Complainants in the course of seeking such remedies as the cessation of a nuisance, the removal of an abandoned car, and so on, may in the course of a complaint's delivery assign complained-againsts an identity derivable from the structure of the complainable, thus rendering incidental the fact that police remedial action will cause trouble for some (known) parties. Such trouble takes its proper place as side effect. Complainants who *name* those parties, then, perhaps risk the assessment that their complaint was motivated by just the intention to involve complained-againsts in police trouble, with the consequence that the complainable now can be retrospectively viewed as merely the occasion to set the machinery in action. Hence we are in a position to propose a rationality in callers' refusal to name complained-againsts: To do so—to name names—is to allow for the possibility that what they seek is other than what police action is designed for, namely, the settling of private scores.

III

It is this possibility which grounds *equivocality* as a phenomenon for members. Equivocal utterances are capable of "double interpretation." It is central to the notion of equivocality (which is thus distinguished from ambiguity) that the two interpretations of which such utterances are susceptible have a special relationship to one another. One interpretation, which we shall term "literal," trades on what the speaker "appears to say"; the other, the determinate alternative, in some way undercuts the literal version. Thus "damning with faint praise" crystallizes this structural relation between the alternative versions: An utterance which "seems" to praise can be heard as intending to do quite the opposite. An interesting question might be, Why praise at all, if the intention is to damn? Why not use strong pejoratives rather than faint praise? One possible answer relates the employment of equivocal utterances to the issue of *responsibility* for versions. For the record, and if challenged, speaker can claim the literal version as his, and can disavow a pejorative alternative, which is thus made out as recipient's "misunderstanding" (and hence recipient's responsibility). Speakers can have at least two motives for avoiding the voicing of pejoratives, even if they intend them to be understood. The first, which will not concern us much here, has to do with the preservation of relationships: Speakers may not wish to produce explicit (and possibly quotable) pejorative remarks in speaking of persons with whom they have (or are thought to have) relationships of friendship or trust. The second concern directs us to the consideration that sometimes to speak unequivocally is to deprive one's remarks of just those effects that equivocality accomplishes. One may hesitate to write clear pejoratives in a letter of recommendation for a colleague or friend, so as not to seem to betray trust; one may refrain from clearly stating one's hostilities to the police for fear that one's complaint will fail.

It is arguable that calls to the police which generate a narrative involving complained-againsts constitute an environment in which equivocality thrives, for what is available is a machinery for investigating and remedying neighborhood troubles, which simultaneously delivers embarrassment or worse to known parties. Thus, there are both *grounds* for equivocality and a *social organizational framework* which it can mobilize. A feature of such conversational environments is speaker sensitivity to the possible derivation of ill-motivated versions of their talk. That speakers can prefigure possible dispreferred hearings and uses of their talk is not restricted to environments in which equivocality has structural foundations. One of the fates of stories, narratives, and anecdotes is that their recipients may perform transforms on them, either in later retellings or "interpretively," that is, in figuring out for themselves the sense of what they have been told. We assume that this is a fact of conversational life known to tellers of narratives; we assume that tellers do not have control over such transforms and their uses; and we assume that nevertheless the possibility of transforms constrains tellers, and that they may employ devices intended to constrain the reworkings that their tellings may undergo. (A possible use of quoted remarks in narratives can thus be seen: The user can be heard as seeking to prevent his being held responsible for what he quotes—i.e., recipient when retelling the story ought to retain teller's quotes in some form: "George said that he heard X," rather than "George said X.") Under some conditions, tellers can and do find determinate transforms foreseeable, and engage in interactional work designed to protect their tellings against such metamorphoses. At least one significant transform is standardly foreseeable, and at least one set of conditions can be seen as grounds for activating it. Recipient can recast the part teller assigns himself in his telling, whith the result that the whole narrative undergoes a shift so as to "tell a different story"; and an assessment that the remarks are equivocal can motivate recipient to operate the transform. Thus "complaints" can undergo such a shift, so as to yield a story now focused on complainant, and complained-againsts can correspondingly appear in *this* version as victims.

One component of narrative material supplied by complainant is particularly pivotal for the kind of transformation we have in mind. We have already noted that it is part of complainant's task to provide formulations of complained-againsts which render the good sense of what is reported, there existing a preference for exhibiting a connection between "what happened" and "who was responsible." A comparable task for recipient, we suggest, is to find a formulation for caller which provides for the reasonableness of the complaint's delivery. In part, presumably, police can employ characteristics derived from attending to properties of voices, so as to find, for example, that caller is a "man," "woman," "foreigner," "elderly person," "drunk," and so on. In part, complainants will more or less explicitly provide information which makes some formulations possible: The fact that caller is home all day, and has a husband and child figured in her narrative, makes "housewife" available; that caller proposes that complained-againsts are renters, we suggested, displays caller as a "property owner." Now, although from caller's point of view, formulations of complained-againsts may be arrived at independently of any consideration of their own possible categorial incumbencies, police may indeed find otherwise. We do not need to attribute "cynicism" or "scepticism" to the police to warrant the claim that police formulations of callers may be structured by the very characterizations of complained-againsts they are offered. For insofar as there are categories of persons between whom typical troubles arise, hearing such a standard trouble, and finding that complained-againsts are just such persons as are typically "transgressors" for those matters, police may look to find, in the absence of counterinformation, that callers are incumbents of a corresponding class of "victims." Thus, "suburban housewives" may have ongoing and pervasive concerns with what "teenage boys" are doing in the locality, just as property owners may be subject to a variety of nuisances from such "transients" as "hippies." But just as such reasoning renders intelligible the instant complaint, it is also a possible license for the suspicion that the complaint itself is just one more event in a cold war between long-standing adversaries. The quest for remedy for a particular trouble—caller's version—is then susceptible of being transformed into a move in an ongoing feud in a version derived from treating the complaint's status as equivocal.

We can now look at one or two instances of narrative parts which appear to be designed by caller just in order to recognize and negate the possibly equivocal involvement of neighbors in the construction of a complaint.

In discussing the workings of Class I complainables and complaints, we emphasized the importance attributed by participants to soonest-possible reports. But if caller is motivated to avert the suspicion that his complaint masks vengefulness towards neighbors, then the temporal location of call with respect to occurrence may undergo a transform; for *now*, "call police at the earliest opportunity" may be discerned as a maxim governing spite calls. Thus, caller may specifically display that some earlier opportunities have been foregone.

[I-2]
    C: . . . about a month ago they went to town sma:shing
                one of them ewith a pick axe ju:st absolutely annoy-
                ing you know pounding all day=   4

[I-2]

C: . . . but I know some– somebody of one of these kids went into our garage one day; this is a couple of months ago, an' I don't like tha:t, they aren't allowed to go in *there*. 22

Similarly, if complainants can see that their accounts can undergo a transform which allocates them an active role in seeking materials out of which to accumulate enough for the police, they can convey that what they observe is incidental to their conduct of life as usual, or is information relayed to them and unsought, and is not the product of motivated search.

[I-2]

C: An' you know as I say I'm home most of the day an' I know that they're just pounding an' pounding half the time an', they'll *race* up the lane you know two or three ata time. . . 32

[I-2]

C: An' they're taking, you know these pa:rts, an' my daughter, (I got) a ten-year-old, was saying that she's seen all sorts of these parts down at the gully, I guess they go they follow the la:ne east, (it's inna) into the next blo:ck, and whether they're dumping or assembling something down there I really don't know. . . 16

We have already indicated that complainants who know the names of complained-againsts may refuse to give them. The same interactional work can be achieved by indicating that a ready means to discover names, for presentation to police, has been neglected.

[II-4]

P: =You see eh it takes us a week or ten days to establish
the–eh registered owner's identity ( ) 41
[ ]
C: Ya, I don't know whether
there's anything on the:eh (1.0) the steering–eh= 42
P: =M–hm= 43
C: =column, I haven't I haven't looked at it that closely . . . 44

In short, callers have available a repertoire of devices with which they can seek in effect to constrain recipients to find that their complaints *are* what they seem to be. Of course, a hearer who is determined to find the complaints equivocal can find further evidence in the use of these devices; for if callers in fact wish to make trouble for complained-againsts, there is no better strategy, presumably, than to assure police that the calls are bona fide, and thus to successfully set police routines in motion. We offer this as yet another demonstration of the structural complexity of equivocality, and not as an encouragement to find these narratives suspect.

Although our data has been restricted to a corpus of police calls, we do not intend that this limit the interest or application of the analysis. Materials in these calls have been analyzed to display sensitivities that speakers exhibit with respect to structurally founded transformations. We have tried to show that speakers can display an orientation to foreseeable transforms within the very utterances which are vulnerable; and while it is true that we have limited our interest to equivocality, since that phenomenon was located in the data, we do not believe that the concern of conversational participants with the transformability of their remarks is similarly limited. We would prefer to think that this brief treatment opens up analytical topics yet further removed from the glosses with which we began. And, finally, we would like to think that we have begun to squeeze the vagueness out of the common assertion that talk is open to "multiple interpretations," by demonstrating that for at least one class of utterances interpretability is both structurally provided for and foreseeable by participants. No doubt there are other participant-oriented—and describable—concerns with "more than one version."[6] If the "multiple-interpretations" assertion is not to remain vacuous, its proponents will need to concern themselves with the anchorage of versions in members' conversational practices.

APPENDIX

[I-2]

P:	Newton Police,	1
C:	Hello::?	2
P:	Yes,	3
C:	I ha:ve a complaint um my neighbor is (0.5) le– subl– well renting her garage out, and ah there are young boys, now they seem awfully nice an' everything but I don't know they're missing an awful lot of school, they're fifteen-year-old types, (0.5) an, they've got, apparently they've got seven old cars, I guess they buy these old cars, but about a month ago they went to town sma:shing one of	

	them ewith a pick axe ju:st absolutely annoying you know pounding all day,=	4
P:	(Mm)	5
C:	=and I: have a dog that ba:rks a lot an' I guess he's not taking too kindly to these kids.	6
P:	(Mm)	7
C:	But anyway there is two more cars in the–eh garage now: and–ah, the neighbor works in fact she's away all day 'n' she doesn't know what's going on but these kids are just spending their (h– e) one particular is spending most of the day there, and I know::? that he's taking parts like driveshaft I–I just saw the muffler going with him just now?, (0.5) They take them an' we live close by, it's in ((section of Newton)) Willow Heights an' it's by Gully-park; an' they take these (1.0) you know, big enough parts to ca:rry an' I: think they're dumping them into the gully; (1.0) and I'm *ju*st getting a little, annoyed about it because e–ah you know I I think they've got about seven cars, I talked to one of the boys and I didn't let on that I was you know (1.0) annoyed or anything but and I *was*n't at the time,	8
	[ ]	
P:	Do these cars all got license on them lady?	9
C:	A::h, e they're in a garage; I don't kn*ow*:, I really don't kn*ow* that.	10
P:	What is your name please.	11
C:	Ah my name is Missis Tho:mpson, and it's at her address is twenty-nine thirty-four west thirty-four.	12
P:	Thirty-nine,	13
C:	No twenty-nine twenty-fi– ah twen– ((rapidly)) I'm twenty-nine twenty-five. Twenty-nine, thirty-four (1.0) west thirty- four.	14
	[ ]	
P:	West thirty-four, (that's)=	15
C:	= An' they're taking, you know these pa:rts, an' my daughter, (I got) a ten-year-old, was saying that she's seen all sorts of these parts down at the gully, I guess they go they follow the la:ne east, (it's inna) into the next blo:ck, and whether they're dumping or assembling some-thing down there I really don't know but– (1.0) (i–e) they're sorta taking over the area with this business of eyou know, (smash ing up these things,=	16
	[ ]	
P:	(repairing)	17
C:	=an' I kn*ow* it's their their business if their dads allow them to do it but (0.5) they're not they're not doing it by *their* house they've they live further down this one particu-lar I know where he lives 'n' and ah	18
	[ ]	
P:	(a bout) what would you estimate their ages.	19

C: Pardonme?   20

P: What would you estimate their *a*ges.   21

C: A::h, Fourtee:n, fiftee–, Fifteen is one because he said he
        can't get his driver's license for ah till (0.5) this coming
        summer (1.0) when he's sixteen I guess 'n' and–ah, You
        know at ((high school)) West Hill for instance there's an
        automotive ah ah business, my husband is in an automo-
        tive business asa matter of fact of his own, but I know
        some– somebody of one of these kids went into our gar-
        age one day; this is a couple of months ago, an' I don't
        like tha:t, they aren't all*o*wed to go in th*e*re.   22

P: No.   Certainly not.   23
            [   ]

C: Because he has steam cleaner–ah parts (init), but
        anyway:–ah at West Hill I know they *do* have (0.5) that
        um (1.0) what is it a trade you know like the automotive
        trade?   24
                                   [   ]

P: (Yes   ) automo-
        tive trade (   )   25
                   [   ]

C: (   ) I ha– I mean I've got children of my
        own, I hate to be a complainer because–   26
                             [´   ]

P: Oh   I know   I understand,
        we appreciate your (   ). What is your phone
        number there Missis   Thompson.   27
                         [   ]

C: A::h   We're at a:h three   28
        five two,

P: Three five two,   29
            [   ]

C: O   O six one five.   30

P: O six one five,   31

C: An' you know as I say I'm home most of the day an' I
        know that they're just pounding an' pounding half the
        time an', they'll *race* up the lane you know two or three
        ata time an' as if they're doing something almost under-
        handed, probably not, probably just being kids, but but I
        do: you know I   I– *do*   object=   32
                      [   ]

P: I understand (this) completely.   33

C: =to them taking these parts an' dumping them in the
        gully.   34

P: Yes. (   ) some reason for it;   35

C: Ya: 36
        [   ]

P: (   ) stripping other cars you see or something.   37

C: Paronme?   38

P: They could be stripping other ca:rs.=   39

C: =Ya:s   40

P: (   )   41
        [   ]

C: I don't know really what in fact I: have an older car out
front that my dad ah   42

P: Do you know the names of any of these boys?   43
       (1.5)

C: A:h gee I hate– I do: one of them; but I don't like to say
anything you know.
I   mean I don't know he sounded like=   44

P: (   )   45
       [   ]

C: = he seemed like an awfully nice boy to ta:lk to an' yet,   46

P: Oh some of them a:re;
some of the worst crooks are very nice=   47
       [   ]

C: ya   ((whispered))   48
     Ya:: hh
     [   ]

P: =(   )
I married a woman that talks beautifully but o:h she's
rough on me:.   49

C: O::h ((laughs)) hhehhe you're te:rrible ((laughs)) ˙hh˙hh,
˙hh–hh˙hh; not even letting her=   50
       [   ]

P: (but I   51

C: =defend herself (hh hhh)   52
       [   ]

P: ((laughs))   53

C: Aw:: ( )   54
       [   ]

P: This   might be   worth   checking out Missis
Thompson, and ah–   55
       [ ]

C: Ya   56

P: (   )   57
     [   ]

C: We:ll elike you know I–I know–   58

P: They're there most of the day, are they?   59

C: Well off 'n' on, like today this one boy (en I said) he as I
say he looks idyllic an' he ta:lks rather nicely an' ( ) I
hate to get anybody into trouble I mean (if) they're just so
keen on cars, but I do think he must be skipping some–
they've got these kooky classes up at (this) school these
days where they have free periods you know,   60

P: Yes, that's right.   61

C: an' I just don't know, I mean he's no:t (of th–) horrible
hippie type he's just a–a real ambitious, you know,
looking um (0.5) as I say just interested in ( ) old ca:rs,
but I–I'd like to kind of know what's going on, since we
have (0.5) um you know vehicles out the front like
(I've) one of my dad's that he's given me over
the last couple o' years, it's an old car ande (1.0) bute
(0.5) and there's been nothing ever gone or or no reason
to suspect anybody even looking at it or anything, but it's

```
              just a matter ofe everything else, (1.0) they're just con-
              stantly back and forth in the lane, you know,                    62
P:            M–hm. (                    )=                                     63
                   [                     ]
C:                  e–and–ah if it's                                           64
P:            =(if) they're out of school not attending school at that age
              they should be–eh–                                               65
C:            That's it. Like this morning this boy came at I'd say
              tenish, (0.5) an' then went away: an' then e(    ) I
              watched the direction he we:nt in (I've got a child a' home
              an' I              ) but anyhow I watched ( ) he went
              towards the gully; well then (0.5) a little while ago before
              really school would have been out I saw him coming
              down this way again an' then this muffler thing went off,
              you know,                                                        66
P:            M–hm.                                                            67
C:            And–ah, I don't know,  ( I                )=                      68
                                     [                  ]
P:                                   (      I'll I'll    )                      69
C:            = she doesn't know anything– I mean I've told her once
              a–about it and she checked into it right away because this
              one day I don't know I think there was something to do
              with that United Appea?l I (          ) paper where they
              were smashing old cars whether they had a (kick) about it
              or something, you know (1.0); but  ah                            70
                                            [   ]
                                            ah this was a stunt for
P:            for publicity you see but this shouldn't be going on in your
              back lane.                                                       71
C:            NO:: a– an' (there are) some older=                              72
                 [                            ]
P:               (                            )                                73
C:            = neighbors you wonder if they maybe, you know, they
              don't know what to do about it (     they do'–) they don't
              know=                                                            74
                    [    ]
P:                  (mm)                                                       75
C:            = that maybe she's (0.5) go:t somebody there, you know,
              doing this for her, but–eh, they were just having a real
              noisy ti:me of it an' an' I had (a) friend in one day an' an' I
              know it was just– in fact they: suggested the:n to phone
              an' complain 'n' I think I (0.5) checked at the department
              but I didn'teh (0.5) say ( I said) they were making=            76
                         [                          ]
P:                       You (                      )                          77
C:            = a big                                                         78
                 [    ]
P:            No well I'll fill in a report Miss's Thompson and e–thank       79
              you so much for phoning.
C:            O?kay, thanks                                                    80
                 [     ]
P:                Bye, now.                                                    81
C:            Bye–bye.                                                        82
```

[II-4]

P:	Newton Police,	1
C:	(Ah) I (ethe) um, My name is Missie R B Toke, at thirty-five fifty-eight east forty-fifth. And I::e	2
	[ ]	
P:	e I didn't get that Missis Toke, I've gotta write this down, what was the address?	3
C:	eh Three five, five eight, east forty-fifth.	4
P:	East forty-five.	5
C:	And there has been a sma:ll blue Austin, license number four two six,	6
	[ ]	

P:	Just a minute (heh ˙hhh) I can only write so fa:st.
	                 [ ]
	                 sorry
		7

C:	Ah eh It's a small blue Austin, (2.0)	8
P:	License,	9
C:	Eh four two six (2.0) four, five, nine.	10
P:	M–hm.	11
C:	An' it's got the–eh righte ah front headlight bashed in, an' it's got an accident sticker on the windshield, an' it's been parked [ ]	
P:	Just a moment, plea:se, just slacken up a little bit,	13
C:	Oh (hh ˙hhh)=	14
P:	=(Ah um) We're trying to write this down lady an' I can't just continue on an' on,	15
C:	((short laugh)) hhhh–hehe No shorthand, eh? he–e,	16
P:	((laughing)) (No–e), not today,	17
C:	˙hh ah:=	18
P:	= Right headlight is smashed,	19
C:	Yes, and it has a:n accident sticker on the windshield. [ ]	20
P:	accident	21
C:	An' it's been parked between our place and the next door neighbor's in the front for six weeks to two months. (2.0)	22
P:	M–hm.	23
C:	And em, I'm *not* sure hh–who it belongs to,	24
P:	( ), (We'll) check it out, will you give me your phone number,=	25
	[ ]	
C:	ah	26
P:	= would you please?=	27
C:	= eh, Three five five, six two seven eight.	28
P:	Six two seven eight. [ ]	29
C:	A:nd I have my suspicions who it belongs to an' if it *is* thei:r's they've got an empty carport on their own property an' I think they could take it off the street.	30
P:	You think it belongs to somebody near you.	31

C: I think it does.   32

P: e–eh Who would you (   )   33
               [   ]

C: Well there there is a house across the way rented and it's (eh) (0.5) o:h a sort of eh more or less– (1.0) eh–hh well not exactly hippie element but–eh bordering on it; and–eh an awful lot of people in an' out of the place, an' I think it belongs to either them or someone, some friend of theirs.   34

P: You don't know the name of the party   35
          (   )
        [   ]

C: No, I'm not sure.   36

P: (oh) I see.   37
       ( )
       [   ]

C: A:nd (if) there is an empty carport at the back of the property that's not being used, and if they can't afford to have it fixed I think they could at least put it in the:re.=   38

P: = (in the) carport; you would naturally assume so.   39

C: Yes.=   40

P: = You see eh it takes us a week or ten days to establish the–eh registered owner's identity (   )   41
                                  [   ]

C: Ya. I don't know whether there's anything on the:eh (1.0) the steering–eh=   42

P: =M–hm=   43

C: = column, I haven't I haven't looked at it that closely; but it's a bit of an eyesore an' it's in the road for us you know company coming to our place=   44
       [   ]

P: Yes   yes
       = yes I can appreciate   45
       [   ]

C: =and the next door *neigh*bor's.   46

P: I can appreciate that Missis Toke.   47

C: An' it's been there, I think they've had a reasonable=   48
               [   ]

P: thank–   thank–   49

C: = length of time to remove it?   50

P: Yes,   51
          (2.5)

P: Thank you very much for phoning.   52
       [   ]

C: And–eh   Oh=   53
       =okay, thank you.

P: Bye now,   54

NOTES

[1] "Single utterance" and "extended utterance" may not appear to establish a satisfactory contrast. Nevertheless, as Sacks, Schegloff, and Jefferson have demonstrated in detail,

there are complex issues bound up with what they term the variability of turn size. For present purposes we simply want to indicate that *for participants* there is a difference between what can be projected as material for a single utterance, and what may come to be delivered over the course of talking beyond a series of possible completion points. See Sacks *et al.* (1974 and this volume).

[2] On story prefaces, see unpublished lectures by Harvey Sacks.

[3] We do not aim to use the notion of "presupposition" in conformity with its usage in recent linguistics, for example, the papers presented in Charles J. Fillmore and D. Terence Langendoen (1971).

[4] We owe something here to Sacks and Schegloff (1974) but we have not attempted to borrow or paraphrase their highly compressed and powerful analysis.

[5] We borrow the term category-bound activities from Harvey Sacks. See Sacks (1974).

[6] For a discussion of ambiguity as an interactional phenomenon, see Schegloff (1972).

chapter 8

Amplitude Shift

A MECHANISM FOR THE AFFILIATION OF UTTERANCES IN CONVERSATIONAL INTERACTION

JO ANN GOLDBERG

Over the course of natural conversational interaction speakers routinely produce gross shifts in the amplitude level of their successive utterances. There are a range of conversational environments in which the work of such amplitude shifts are intuitively apparent. Some instances:

1. Raised amplitude on the occasion of simultaneous speech appears to operate as one conversational resource for speakers to gain or hold the floor.
2. Adjusted amplitude by a speaker of his utterance, either upward or downward, in an environment where there is more than one possible recipient of that utterance can operate as a device to target the utterance to its proper recipient. So, by dramatically shifting upward the peak amplitude of his utterance, a speaker may indicate that the intended recipient of his summons is the party across the street and not the one standing in much closer proximity.
3. Modulation of amplitude by a speaker of his utterance, either

upward or downward, can operate as one agent for manipulation of the proxemic relationship between coconversationalists. Note the drawing power of the whisper.

This investigation will focus upon another domain in which amplitude shifts in speakers' utterances are conversationally organized. An argument will be presented that there exists in conversation an *Amplitude Shift Mechanism* by which a speaker may mark the relationship of his present utterance to his just prior utterance. By that we mean a speaker may mark some present utterance either as an *affiliate* or as a *disaffiliate* of his own prior utterance. We shall generally refer to that marking as *affiliation*. It is suggested that this Amplitude Shift Mechanism is (*a*) built for colloquy, that is, a speech-exchange system where present speaker spoke just previously and, (*b*) locally organized, that is, built to mark the affiliation of speakers' utterances on a turn-by-turn basis.

This chapter stands as a portion of a larger investigation of the operation of amplitude shifts as a major agent in the achievement of the affiliation of utterances in conversation.[1] The findings of the larger investigation are based on inspection of two conversational sequence types: the question/answer sequence and the closing sequence. In this discussion, focus will be exclusively upon the question/answer sequence. Two hundred question/answer exchanges were extracted for measurement from 22 two-party telephone interactions.

The auspices under which telephone interactions were selected for the data base needs to be indicated. Researchers of the organizational features of the conversational system have as a fundamental commitment the study of conversational data from natural settings. In light of this methodological stance, telephone interactions, despite some obvious measurements limitations pose two advantages: (*a*) Insofar as we can reasonably assume that coconversationalists were committed to producing mutually intelligible speech and that therefore each held the telephone transmitter in a relatively fixed position vis-à-vis their mouths, some constancy in measurement was maintained without violating the naturalness of the interaction; (*b*) by focus upon two-party telephone interaction we were able to exclude from occurrence other amplitude shift operations such as utterance targeting and manipulation of the proxemic positioning as mentioned above. The exclusion of these other amplitude shift operations enabled a heightened focus on amplitude shifts as an utterance affiliation mechanism in conversational interaction.

When we speak of the amplitude level of a speaker's turn-constructional component we mean to indicate peak amplitude in decibels.[2] Peak amplitude as opposed to average amplitude was selected as the unit of measure simply because it appeared to do the job at hand: to permit determination of the directionality of amplitude shifts in speakers' successive utterances. Clearly, the numerical values presented are relative and not absolute measures. Whether or not a more dramatic statement of findings is possible through use of other measurement mechanisms is a matter for later consideration.[3]

In our discussion we shall develop the following points:

1. Speakers' shifts in peak amplitude level of their own successive utterances over the course of a conversation are quite routine occurrences.
2. Shifts in peak amplitude of speakers' successive utterances over the course of a question/answer sequence are regularly patterned. The pattern is: Speakers' sequence-initial utterances are raised in peak amplitude relative to their own prior utterances and over the course of the sequence speakers lower the peak amplitude level of their own successive utterances.
3. Shifts in peak amplitude by speakers of their successive utterances operate as a mechanism for the affiliation and/or disaffiliation of such utterances relative to one another.
4. The Amplitude Shift Mechanism is a major conversational device for utterance affiliation. Some other such devices are mentioned and compared.

OVER THE COURSE OF A CONVERSATION, A SPEAKER'S SUCCESSIVE UTTERANCES WILL BE CHARACTERIZED BY VARYING PEAK AMPLITUDES[4]

In the data, peak amplitude values are indicated to the left of the utterance.

[JGP13] (1)

25.1	P:	Are you in charge a the swing shift?	←
	M:	Yes.	←
13.8	P:	Oh I see.	←
7.0	P:	Mhm.	←
27.0	P:	Well who's in charge out there t'morrow that I could talk with an get the few particulars on.	←

[JGP13]   (2)

27.0   P: Okay it uh pays two-fifteen? (1.0)
             t'start?   ←

        M: E'yea::h.

5.0   P: Jezus,   ←
                  (1.0)

23.6   P: Well hell that wouldn't hardly pay
             me t'come *out* there accordin'
             t'what I'm getting' on my unem-
             ployment.   ←

[JG3:11]   (3)

6.5   M: ·hh Oh it's not th*a*t far.   ←
17.0   R: Yeah I know.   ←
10.3   M: Well thanks f'r calling okay?=   ←
8.1   R: =Yeah.   ←
11.8   R: Okay.   ←

[JG6:3]   (4)

7.0   F: ·hh An so then I: will uh u::mh keep
             it here by the pho:ne, an I think ev-
             erything 'ill be– quite alright, you
             know.   ←

        S: Yeah.

        F: A:nduh hh

18.7   F: M'kay well the:n we'll look forward
             f– I hopė he has a good lesson on
             Friday.   ←

        S: Yeah.
                  [

[JGP7]   (5)

21.2   P:. ·hhh Well I got all the dope down
             here t'day at the temple so wez
             gonna discuss it t'marrah see.=

5.1   M: =Uh huh.

26.6   P: :hT·hh Well anyway I'll tell uh *A*ce
             then thet de uh you, if you ken make
             it you'll be down.

6.0   M: Yeah.

14.1   P: Ok yuh Mark.

SHIFTS IN PEAK AMPLITUDE OF A SPEAKER'S SUCCESSIVE UTTERANCES ARE ROUTINELY ASSOCIATED WITH INDEPENDENTLY DESCRIBABLE CONVERSATIONAL SEQUENCES

We shall use the term *sequence* to refer to commonly recurrent two-party-produced utterance exchange formats standing in a formally characterizable adjacency pair relationship.[5]

In the question/answer sequences inspected *a speaker's sequence initial utterance was found to be regularly raised in peak amplitude relative to his own just prior utterance.*

[NB-GH]   (6)

3.8	O:	Right.
		(1.2)
6.0	G:	Alright.=
16.5	G:	=Now from, Bay Side I jest– I don' haftuh dial one or anything aheada that do I? ←QU.
6.0	O:	Oh I'm sorry you'd haftuh ask yer Oh Operater. ←ANS.
	G:	Wh– oh a'right.

[NB-A/C]   (7)

4.2	C:	I w'z jist washin the dishes,
9.2	A:	Yeah, wir jis– cleanin up here *too*.
		(0.4)
9.8	C:	How'r you– How's yer *foot*. ←QU.
25.0	A:	Oh it's healing beautif'lly! ←ANS.
	C:	Goo ::d
		[

[NB-GH]   (8)

7.0	G:	Gotta nice smile on yer face, 'n ev'rything.
		[
--.--	E:	Yah(hh)
	G:	·hhhhhh
9.0	G:	Hey uh hh· My son 'n law's down, 'nd uh, thought w'might play a little golf either this afternoon er tomor-

    row, wouldju like tuh (0.9) hh·h get
    out?hh·   ←QU.

12.3   E: Well, this afternoon'd be alright, but
               I don't think I'd better tomorrow.   ←ANS.
               (0.7)

         G: Well?

[NB-A/C]   (9)

8.3   C: *Oh goo:d.*
               (0.4)

17.6   A: Yeah,

10.5   C: Whenjuh go, theh– yes–
                      [

         A: Uh.

25.1   A: Fridee.   ←ANS.

         C: O:h.

[JGP13]   (10)

28.0   P: Anu:h I wouldn't be able t'come out
               there is *e*vening anyway.

.7   M: Uh huh.

29.5   P: hT·hh But u:h could th– is there
               soneone out there t'morrah I come
               out 'n talk w*i*th?   ←QU.

4.2   M: eYea::h.   ←ANS.

Indeed, in the case that a speaker's sequence initial question was itself preceded by a question, the successively positioned question component was still raised in amplitude over its prior.[6,7]

[NB-G/A]   (11)

9.3   A: How yuh d*oi*n.   ←QU.

         G: Fine.
               (0.6)

20.0   A: Yih comin down early?   ←QU.
               (0.3)

         G: We::ll I gotta lot of, things tuh do
               don' know, I w– probly won' be t*o*o
               early,
               (0.2)

         A: Oka:y,

[NB-GH]   (12)

```
  ┌ 8.5        G:    E dudn' av a phone over there does
  │                  e?                                          ←QU.
  │            E:    No. (1.0) No.
  │            E:    ·hh I think yih c'get on San Juan
  ↑                  Hills, 'f you can'tche c'n get on San
  │                  Clemente.
  └ 13.6       G:    Well? uh, (2.0) Ev you gotta phone
                     number for San Juan?                        ←QU.
```

[NB-GH]   (13)

```
  ┌ 6.0        G:    What's the name San Juan Hills huh    ←QU.
  │            E:    I have the Hunnington Seacliff,
  ↑                  have– San Cleme nne
  │                              [
  └ 14.9       G:                    Hey how bout
                     Sh–How bout Shorecliffs, C'n yuh
                     get on there.                               ←QU.
```

If we can infer that speakers' shifts in peak amplitude are patterned, then for question/answer sequence-initial position, is the pattern ascending? Moreover, if question/answer sequence-initial utterances are raised in amplitude over their prior, where the prior is itself a question, is it exclusively ascending? Finally, if speakers are continuously raising the peak amplitude level of their successive utterances, how is it that conversation does not rapidly reach the level of a scream?

Over the course of a question/answer sequence, speakers lower the peak amplitude level of their successive utterances.

A question/answer sequence may reach completion in two turns, the question being the utterance of the first turn, the answer being the utterance of the second turn. But quite commonly the question/answer sequence will extend beyond those two positions. The auspices under which the extension will be produced will vary, but we notice that in each of the instances below the within-sequence successive utterances are lowered in amplitude relative to the sequence-initial component.

[JGP13]   (14)

```
  ┌ 25.1       P:    Are you in charge a the swing shift?    ←QU.
  │            M:    Yes.                                       ←ANS.
  └ 13.8       P:    Oh I see.                                  ←EXT.
```

[JGP4]   (15)

15.5	M:	Were you asleep.	←QU.
24.0	F:	Yeah.	←ANS.
9.2	M:	I'm sorry.	←EXT.
11.0	F:	M::hm.	←EXT.

[JGP4]   (16)

14.7	M:	(eu) Anyway t'work that?	←QU.
23.0	P:	No:::h	←ANS.
9.2	M:	Hm?	←EXT.
17.0	P:	No.	←EXT.

[JG-R/M]   (17)

12.0	M:	Uhm what– uh who wha– who is she.	←QU.
11.0	R:	Gross.	←ANS.
10.0	M:	Gro::ss?	←EXT.
9.1	R:	Yeah.=	←EXT.

For fragments (14)–(17), we note two commonly occurrent auspices under which speakers produce within-sequence successively positioned utterances:

1. For fragments (14) and (15) the successive units operate as first possible terminal position markers for the sequence under construction. Such lexical units as "mhm," "yeah," "okay," and so on, have elsewhere[8] been characterized as operating to signal, by the recipient of an utterance, that no issue is to be taken with the prior. They thereby operate as a potential final acceptance where otherwise issues of mishearing, misunderstanding, and the like, might be initiated. For our more immediate and narrower present interests, we wish to indicate—regarding such components—that they are back-referencing in their operation, attending some specifically within-sequence task, and are positioned in next turn by the same speaker of the utterance that is initial to the sequence.

2. For fragments (16) and (17), the successive utterances operate as repair initiators[9] positioned just following the utterances whose remedying they each attend. Here repair-type utterances such as "Hm/" and the partial repeat of prior "Gro::ss?" are suggested to be within-sequence operations on two grounds: (a) In their grammatical construction, repair utterances routinely employ as devices such back-referencing components as proterms and partial repetitions of prior speaker's utterance; (b)

recipients of repair initiator utterances routinely attend remedying of the utterance referenced and only upon the completion of the repair is the progress or termination of the sequence occasioned.[10]

It appears then that a partial answer to our problem ("If the amplitude pattern is exclusively ascendant, how is it that conversation does not rapidly reach the level of a scream?") is that the amplitude shift pattern is *not* exclusively ascendant. Lowerings were found to operate independently of the structurally diverse auspices by which a sequence achieves extension. Two commonly recurrent sequence extension formats inspected were terminal markers and repair initiators.

We might have correspondingly asked: If it is the case that speakers lower the peak amplitude level of their successive within-sequence utterances, how is it that conversation does not rapidly reach the level of a whisper? We need only return to our initial observation that there exists a sequentially specifiable locus in conversational interaction where speakers systematically raise the peak amplitude level of their successive utterances: Sequence-initial utterances of the question/answer sequence are raised in peak amplitude over their immediately prior utterances.

AMPLITUDE SHIFTS IN SUCCESSIVE UTTERANCES OPERATE AS A SPEAKER'S TECHNICAL MECHANISM FOR THE AFFILIATION AND/OR DISAFFILIATION OF SUCH UTTERANCES RELATIVE TO ONE ANOTHER

The discussion so far seems to have led us to an inconsistency. Speakers were found to raise the peak amplitude level of their sequence-initial questions even when the immediately prior utterance was itself a question. Yet later in the discussion of repair initiators, questions themselves (fragments [16] and [17]), it was observed that they were lowered in amplitude relative to their immediately prior utterance. This was so for cases where the prior was a question.

As a resolution of this inconsistency, we suggest that there exists a systematic distinction between the two question collections: In the case that a speaker produces in succession question components, where the successively positioned question component is a *within-sequence affiliate* of the prior, it will be *shifted downward* relative to its prior; correspondingly, where a successively positioned question component is a *new sequence disaffiliate* of the prior, it will be *shifted upward* in peak amplitude relative to its prior.

To suggest that a speaker might also disaffiliate an utterance from his own prior utterance is not meant to suggest disaffiliation from the conversation per se. Rather the notion of disaffiliation (as well as affiliation) attends a speaker's resource to signal the interturn relationship between utterances. Although more will be made of this point later, we wish only to say here that this mechanism may operate to signal to an utterance recipient to attend what was just said in light of what the speaker previously said; or, conversely, disattend, that is, disaffiliate what was just said from what was previously said. But, for now, the focus of discussion will be upon affiliation.

For now, we shall turn to evidence for the operation of the Amplitude Shift Mechanism in four different conversational environments. In each, a speaker's successively positioned utterance is lowered in peak amplitude relative to his own prior utterance. Hence, by our hypothesis, the successive utterance is thereby marked as an affiliate of its prior. Independent evidence will be provided for the treatment of those utterances as otherwise affiliated. Correspondingly, we will be providing evidence of the operation of the Amplitude Shift Mechanism's independence from any other single-type coherence agent. In addition, these materials will provide another basis for the suggestion that the Amplitude Shift Mechanism operates in a wider range of contexts than the question/answer sequence. (See note 7.)

Repair Questions

In our data corpus, speakers were found to routinely lower in peak amplitude their repair-type questions relative to their immediately prior question components. A single-type instance is presented here (see also fragments [16] and [17]).

```
[NB-A/G]                                                            (18)
    ┌ 10.1      G:    Whaddiyuh want f'm up here.       ←QU.
    │                 (.9)
    │           A:    t hhhhh Uh bring that u::h b– brown
    ↓                 e::n
    │                 [
    └ 7.3       G:    –brown 'n– brown check            REPAIR
                      dress?                            QU.
                A:    Yeah
                      [
```

In our earlier mention of repairs (pp. 206–207), we specified grounds whereby the repair question of an adjacent prior question displays constructional relatedness to it. We noted that components built in at the level of grammar operate to guide the utterance recipient to address in his next turn his own prior utterance. One mechanism that was mentioned as operating in the service of repair was the partial repeat. However, it must be emphasized that the sequential organization of the repair operation is a major point of reference in arguing the within-sequence status of the repair-type question and in appreciating the recipient's treatment of it. That is, the resources by which recipients of a repair initiator are able to achieve the appropriate repair are quite independent of the linguistic devices used to locate the repairable. The former hinges on speakers' knowledge of how repair sequences operate. That is, recipients routinely treat repair-type utterances as indicating back-referencing and once back-referenced to their just produced utterance, they routinely produce the appropriate repair operation. Only upon completion of the repair operation is the sequence in which it is embedded then terminated and the talk progressed.

Question Series

In the case of the repair initiator as a type of successive question affiliate, the sequential operation inspected was singularly back-referencing. In the case of the fragments below, speakers' successive questions appear to operate more on the order of a question series. Once again, there are multiple apparatuses that can be cited as operative in the service of cohesion of the series pair. For now, we cite only two such immediately apparent types: the proterm and the structure position marker.[11] In fragment (19), the "who" of the successively positioned question back-references to "someone" of the initial question. In fragment (20), the "he" of the successive question back-references to "Ward" of the initial. The placement of the proterm in each successive question component assures a grammatically based linkage of the utterance with the proterm to the utterance with its reference, the immediately prior question. In fragment (21), the structure position marker "and" placed just prior to the successive question establishes a formal relationship between it and its prior, transforming the two into a question series.

[JGP13]   (19)

	P:	Anu:h I wouldn't be able t'come out there this *e*vening anyway.
	M:	Uh huh.
29.5	P:	:hT· hh But u:h could th– is there someone out there t'morrah ←
		I come out n talk w*i*th?

```
 ⌐                M:     eYea::h.
 L  18.0          P:     Who– who                                        ←
                         [                    ]
                  M:       (A how 'bout)
                  M:     What I'd like you t'do . . .
```

[NB-A/G]   (20)

```
                  G:     We gotta dividin check here thet
                         needs yer signature. So I thought
                         "Well, I'll put the other one
                         through, ·hh en bring this one
                         down 'n (you c'd        )
                                         [
  ⌐ 28.2          A:                     Dinjeh call Wa:rd?             ←
  |                      (0.9)
  ⌡              G:     Yeah I talk'to im,
  L  15.0          A:     Whad 'e say.                                    ←
                  G:     "Put it through."
```

[JGP13]   (21)

```
                  P:     Well who's in charge out there
                         t'morrow that I could talk with an
                         get the few p'ticulars on it.
                  M:     Well whatdaya wanna know.
  ⌐ 24.9          P:     Well I mean uh where d'you– wha
  |                      d'ya do about parking your car
  |                      when y'come out there. Just pull in
  |                      the lot?                                         ←
  ⌡              M:     Uh huh.
  L  24.0          P:     An uh where do you go in 'nere t'go
                         t'work.                                          ←
                  M:     Well hh–hh I could explain that all
                         to you tomorrow night.
```

For the question series and repair questions considered above, the successive questions of otherwise affiliated pairs are lowered in peak amplitude relative to their priors; the downward shifts in amplitude by speakers of their successive utterances occurred independently of the varying auspices by which sequence extension was organized.

Reproductions

Not uncommonly in conversation a speaker will produce some utterance which in a general fashion reproduces his own just prior utterance.

For example, in fragment (22), the answer, "*I* don't know" by A, following a lapse, is followed by a reproduction of that answer, "I don't know." We note of the construction to which the reproduction is affixed that the completion of its turn's task does not depend upon the collective employment of itself plus its reproduction. Its duplicate is specifically reproducing. Affiliation here is evidenced by the phrasal duplication of the former by the latter. We notice for this collection, the lowered amplitude of the reproduction relative to its model.

Parenthetically, to claim of such an occurrence that is only reproducing is not to claim that it is doing nothing conversationally. At least one operation that a speaker may be performing in duplicating some utterance is "recompleting" the task of its model. Recompleting, both speaking yet saying nothing new, may stand as a speaker's resource to specifically decline to expand or progress the talk where he might otherwise have.

[NB-A/C] (22)

	C:	You gonna– be with er	
⌜ 16.9	A:	·hh *I* don' know	←
⎩		(0.7)	
⌞ 11.1	A:	I don't know	←

[NB-GH] (23)

	G:	He dudn' av a phone over there, does e.	
⌜ 8.5	E:	No.	←
⎩		(1.0)	
⌞ 5.0	E:	No.	←

[JGP9] (24)

	F:	Uh n*o*, ·hhh y'know the b*a*:nd thet hezin, y'know? hhh	
⌜ 16.6	O:	Oh yeah.	←
⌞ 15.4	O:	Oh yeah.	←

Interactively Grounded Affiliated Questions

Finally, we turn our attention to a fragment where the affiliative forces of grammatical and sequential mechanisms are relatively weak. Discussion will be directed to "interactive" grounds whereby two adjacently positioned questions might be considered affiliated. We contrast these data with the discussion on repair-type questions (pp. 208–209) which exhibit strong grammar-based links to the repair object and whose operations are most tightly sequentially organized. We present first the data:

[NB-GH]   (25a)

	G:	Ev *you* gotta phone number for San Juan?	1
		(0.4)	
	E:	Uh, I *think* so,	2
13.9	E:	You wanna hold on a minnit,	← 3
	G:	Yeah.	
10.3	E:	Are you calling long distance,	← 4
	G:	Well I'm uh I'::m in uh– No I'm not in l– in uh long distance, I'm in uh Bay Side.	
	E:	Alright.	
	E:	Well hold on, I'll see if I have a card.	5
	G:	A'right,	

In the conversation from which this fragment is excerpted G has called E to suggest an afternoon of golf. E accepts. Talk then turns to arrangements for the game. At the point where this fragment begins, G asks E whether or not he has the number for one of the courses under consideration (line 1). E returns with, "I think so," (line 2) and requests of G, "you wanna hold on a minnit," (line 3) possibly under the auspices of a search for the phone number. G consents. Then E produces a next question, "Are you calling long distance," (line 4). It is proposed that by lowering the peak amplitude of the successive question regarding where G is calling from relative to the initial request for a conversational lapse while he searches for the phone number, E indicates to G that the latter question is an affiliate of the former, that is, the former is marked as relevant to the interpretation of the latter. The nature of the affiliation and how it might be demonstrated will be considered. The argument for affiliation will depend on the position that if G (who has homes both in a distant community and the community in which the call takes place, the home of E and the site of the golf game now being arranged) is calling from the distant community and thereby long distance, then E's prior request for G to hold the phone so that he could search for the telephone number might be suspended and other means to get the number might be considered.

But, perhaps the more prominent underlying issue for E and G is the determination of the yet-to-be-allocated task of who's to make the extended series of calls that an arrangement for golf requires. These include a call to recruit another player, a call to the course to make a reservation, and return calls to all players to confirm game time: four calls, at minimum. It may be that distribution of this task is embodied in and decided by the question of who possesses the phone number for the course. (He who already has the number might be thereby treated as the one for whom the task would be "least" burdensome.) In light of this, G may not be so much "requesting" the number (line 1) as stating his nonpossession of it. As a counterstrategy, E may be ignoring the implied claim to nonpossession and exclusively attending the utterance's "request" potential. The transfer of the number would thereby at least leave as still open the question of who is to make the series of calls. But this strategy for E is viable only as long as G is not calling long distance. Here the issue might be that the one for whom the calls would be least costly as opposed to the one who possesses the number may be weightier in determining to whom the task is to be allocated. If G is calling long distance, the task would be clearly E's, the one for whom the calls would entail less expense. As it turns out, G is calling locally and shortly thereafter the conversational lapse is initiated.

So, it is argued here that E's questions are generally related insofar as each embodies alternative settlements of the question of which of them is to take on the task of arranging the game. Specifically, E's successive question is an affiliate of its prior insofar as it may represent a next move by E to settle the question.

But this possibly underlying issue and its negotiation as outlined above are based in part on other portions of the interaction and in part on this writer's knowledge as a member of the culture. However, materials within the fragment itself may provide a more local order documentation for the position that the "long distance" question is an affiliate of its prior, the request to "hold on." In line with this aim, a comparison is proposed between E's two utterances regarding whether or not he has the phone number.

[NB-GH]   (25b)
   G: Ev *you* gotta phone number for San Juan?
                   (0.4)
   E: Uh I *think* so,   ← 2
                   .

                   .

                   .

   E: Well hold on, I'll see if I have a card. I– I may   ← 5'
               have.

In answer to the question as to whether or not he has the number for the course, E responds, "I think so." Yet post the determination that G's call is local, E says, "I'll see if I have a card. I– I may have." We note of the latter relative to the former that it is a downgraded[12] (less forceful) formulation of possible possession. These two formulations, occurring on opposite boundaries of the questions to "hold on" and is the call "long distance" are informative for our interests.

It may be that the subsequent diminutive claim to possession of the number stands as E's implicit account to G as to the grounds by which the successive question regarding the origin of the call was generated, heretofore marked singularly by the successive's amplitude downshift relative to the prior. E now proposes that he is not at all sure whether or not he has the number such that a search for it, as well as the time consumed in the search, and the possible phone cost involved would be warranted. Parenthetically, in line with our earlier argument, now that possession of the number may once again be relevant for task distribution, E may likewise be presenting a weaker position with regard to ownership as well as formulating even the task of locating it as burdensome.

In sum, the argument was forwarded that E's two formulations as to whether or not he had the phone number in question gave us grounds to propose an interactively based affiliative relationship between E's adjacent questions, affiliation otherwise evidenced by the downward peak amplitude shift of the successive relative to the first.

Four environments were inspected in which a speaker's successively positioned utterance was lowered in peak amplitude relative to his own prior utterance. They were Repair Questions, Question Series, Reproductions, and Interactively Grounded Affiliated Questions. For each type, independent grounds for treating those utterances as affiliates were suggested. Our intent has been to provide evidence for the operation of an Amplitude Shift Mechanism for turn affiliation in a range of environments wider than the question/answer exchange and to suggest its independent operation from any other single type of affiliative agency.

THE AMPLITUDE SHIFT MECHANISM STANDS AS A MAJOR AGENT FOR THE AFFILIATION OF TURN-CONSTRUCTIONAL UNITS

We have argued here that the Amplitude Shift Mechanism is one order of speaker's resource for relating or detaching turn-constructional components, relating and detaching being omnipresent tasks for speakers. But, clearly, it is not the only conversational resource providing clues as to the relationship between turn-constructional components. Other mechanisms of this genre include structure position markers, proterms, and elliptical constructions.[13] Such mechanisms differ in terms of the directionality of linkage they indicate. Proterms and elliptical constructions are overwhelmingly back-referencing in their operation, while a range of structure position markers, including such lexical units as "now" and "then" and ordinals placed in turn-initial position, are forward-referencing. Such mechanisms display differing powers with regard to the number of turns they span in the establishment of affiliation. And, naturally, they vary in terms of the environments of applicability given the distinct affiliation-type task each performs.

A most prominent point of contrast between the Amplitude Shift Mechanism and these other affiliative devices hinges on this latter point. The Amplitude Shift Mechanism in the sequential environment studied and reported here displays the feature of being persistently operative. The ubiquitous affiliative work of this mechanism, operating on each and every turn, is no surprise given that amplitude is an integral aspect of speech and thereby an appropriate recruit. Such persistence of operation of the Amplitude Shift Mechanism within the conversational environments inspected as compared to other such affiliative mechanisms is one basis for proposing it as a more fundamental mechanism for the cohering of turns in conversational interaction.

In conclusion, we have reported on a segment of a larger investigation stimulated by two empirical observations: (*a*) Speakers' shifts in peak amplitude level of their own successive utterances over the course of a conversation are quite routine, and (*b*) such amplitude shifts are patterned. It was suggested that the patterning reflects the operation of a fundamental mechanism for the affiliation of utterances in conversation: an Amplitude Shift Mechanism. The features of this mechanism and its capacities were traced as they were evidenced over the course of a pervasively occurrent conversational sequence type: the question/answer exchange. Some of those features are briefly mentioned here.

A speaker may mark the affiliation or disaffiliation of his present utterance relative to his own prior utterance by use of an Amplitude Shift Mechanism. The Mechanism is two-valued, each with correspondingly different functions: A speaker may lower the peak amplitude level of his present utterance relative to his own just prior utterance to signal an affiliated relationship between the latter and the former. A speaker may raise the peak amplitude level of his present utterance relative to his own just prior utterance to signal a disaffiliated relationship between the latter and the former.

The Amplitude Shift Mechanism is self-managed. The achievement of affiliation of a speaker's present utterance to his just prior utterance is the task of the producer of those two utterances.

The Amplitude Shift Mechanism was found to be continuously operative over the course of the conversational environments inspected. Such constancy of presence was one basis for proposing it as a fundamental mechanism for the cohering of turns in conversational interaction.

ACKNOWLEDGMENTS

The author has benefited from the comments of Emanuel Schegloff and especially in many important matters the late Harvey Sacks.

NOTES

[1] Goldberg (1976).

[2] The reason amplitude level of speakers' turn-constructional components was selected for measurement needs to be indicated. Obviously, a more salient focus of measurement for the operations investigated here would be the intonational contour of which amplitude is only one modest element. Yet, spectrographic information is limited for the study of natural conversation. One major limitation is that it can only measure speech segments of 2.5 seconds, intervals usually far too brief to capture relevant natural speech segments. No such technological limitation existed in the case of machinery that could measure amplitude.

[3] Relevant portions of taped conversations were sent through a Bruel and Kjaer Sound Level Recorder Type 2305. The peak amplitudes of each turn-constructional component used in the construction of the question/answer pairs were established and compared. This included the question, the answer, and any relevant prior and subsequent components. Compared were a single speaker's own successive utterances to determine the direction in his amplitude shift. Peak amplitude values are indicated to the left of the utterances. Values to be compared are connected by lines: Arrows indicate the direction of the shift. An instance,

```
 ┌─ 3.8 O:   Right.                                                          ←
 │             (1.2)
 ├┬ 6.0 G:   Alright.=                                                       ←
 ├┼ 16.5 G:  Now from, Bay Side I jest– I don' haftuh dial one or            ←
 │           anything aheada that do I?
 │└─ 6.0 O:   Oh I'm sorry you'd haftuh ask yer Oh Operater.                 ←
 └── 6.0 G:   Wh– oh a'right.                                                ←
```

The Bruel and Kjaer Sound Level Recorder Type 2305 reports signal levels in the frequence range of 2 Hz to 200,000 Hz. The amplitude report is based on the magnitude of the voltage output of the sound source, in this case a Uher 4000 in which the tapes are played. A permanent record of the variations in voltage output is made by an inking unit on strip chart paper marked off in decibel (dB) units. Below is the collection of machine settings that have been used in the data run.

Input Attenuator	60 dB
Input Potentiometer	10 dB
Potentiometer Range	50 dB
Rectifier	RMS
Lower Limit Frequency	50 Hz
Drive Shaft Speed	1.2 rpm
Writing Speed	63 mm/sec
Paper Speed	30 mm/sec

[4] Commonly, speakers perform more than one conversational activity within a single turn. In the following discussion, we shall be referring by the term utterance to a single

turn-constructional component type such as a question or an answer. For example, in the fragment below we shall focus upon P's "Well who's in charge. . ." as the utterance-type question and exclude from consideration as a feature of that question the "Oh I see" and the "Mhm" that precedes it.

P: Are you in charge a the swing shift?
M: Yes.
P: Oh I see.   ←
P: Mhm.   ←
P: Well who's in charge out there t'morrow that I could talk   ←
   with an get the few particulars on.

Here, the terms utterance and turn-constructional component will be used interchangeably, but will refer to the same phenomenon. For a formal specification of the operations of the turn-constructional component, see Sacks et al. (1974).

[5] The most prominent features of adjacency pair sequences are outlined by Schegloff and Sacks (1973):

Adjacency pairs consist of sequences which properly have the following features: (1) two utterance length, (2) adjacent positioning of component utterances, (3) different speakers producing each utterance. . . . A given sequence will thus be composed of an utterance that if a first pair part produced by one speaker directly followed by the production by a different speaker of an utterance which is (a) a second pair part, and (b) if from the same pair type as the first utterance in the sequence is a member of. Adjacency pair sequence, then, exhibit the further feature (4) relative ordering of parts (i.e., first pair parts precede second pair parts) and (5) discriminative relations (i.e., the pair type of which a first pair part is a member is relevant to the selection among second pair parts).

The achievement of such orderliness in adjacency pair sequences require the recognizability of first pair part status for some utterances [pp. 295– 296]

See also Sacks et al. (1974).

[6] There arises the question of whether shifts in peak amplitude by a speaker of his successive turn-constructional components are not an artifact of articulatory properties of these adjacent utterances as would be the case were sequence-initial questions, produced in "normal" conversational volume, to be always preceded by a whisper. Were this the case, some order of regularity would have to be found in utterances positioned just prior to the sequence-initial construction. No formally characterizable prior to sequence-initial utterance type was found to exist either in terms of sequential task performed or in terms of articulatory properties internal to the utterance. Regarding the latter, clearly, the phonetic constitution of various constructions sets an inherent upper and lower productional limit on how weakly or forcefully an utterance may be produced. But the range between that upper and lower productional limit is fairly wide and well traversed in natural conversational interaction. In a sense, what we will propose here is a conversation-based account for observed orderliness by speakers in the selection of some particular point in the range for utterance production in natural verbal interaction.

[7] It is noted of the collection of fragments above that although the first component is grammatically a "question," such a characterization is by no means exhaustive. Commonly, the "questions" and the "answers" that attend them represent instances of a range of routinely occurrent, sequentially organized tasks not always nor necessarily cast in question/answer form. (See the request sequence of fragment [6], the invitation sequence of

fragment [8], and the topic initiation of fragment [7].) The recurrence of a range of commonly occurrent conversational sequence types captured in the question/answer exchanges investigated here is offered as one order of evidence for the wider applicability of finds on amplitude shift regularities beyond a single sequence type.

[8] Continuation markers is a term coined by Schegloff to refer to the general operation of such lexical components in conversation. Again, this class of lexical items appears to be commonly used by utterance recipients to signal to speakers in structurally identifiable loci, in the course of their ongoing talk, an acceptance where issues of understanding and/or possibly floor shift might otherwise have occurred.

[9] Inspection of any transcript will reveal a collection of conversational occurrences that are treated by interactants as being in some way faulted. Their occurrence commonly occasions one of a collection of devices that are put into operation for their repair. It is such order of operation that such utterances as "Hm?" and "Gro::ss?" are taken to attend.

Until now, the question/answer sequence has been defined in terms of adjacency pair organization (note 4). But, clearly, in some instances an adjacency pair question will operate as a subcomponent of a larger sequence of which it is a member, although it is sequence-initial for the adjacency pair it starts. A most prominent instance of this is evidenced in repair sequences. For a direct discussion on repair operations in conversation see Schegloff, Jefferson, and Sacks (1976).

[10] For the issues at hand, only a single-type repair initiator has been indicated: the partial repeat. By no means is this to say that the conversational repair machinery is solely limited to this order of difficulty. For a broader appreciation of the functioning of the repair machinery see Schegloff et al. (1976) and Jefferson et al. (1973).

[11] By the term structure position marker we refer to a collection of lexical items placed in turn initial position that operate to fix the position of the turn constructional unit within the sequence under construction. An obvious instance of such a type marker is that of the ordinal terms "first," "second," "third," and so on. "Now," "then," and "and," as inspected in recipe exchanges, seem also to position sequence-constructional components. Typically in instructional exchanges, "now" was found to be positioned directly after the enumeration of ingredients and just before the actions to be performed on them. Commonly, "and" either linked like instructional units within subsections of presignaled a last member of a series of like units within some section. See Goldberg (1975).

[12] The term "downgrade" is not casually selected to describe the materials at hand. A variety of data suggest that conversationalists mutually orient to ranking: downgrading, upgrading, and matching what they say to one another on a range of dimensions. For a treatment of such ranking in the production of assessment sequences see Pomerantz (1975).

[13] Ellipsis, contrary to the spirit of grammarians, is seen here as primarily an affiliation device. That is, a speaker may demonstrate at the level of grammar the affiliation of his present turn-constructional component with that of the just prior speaker by using as his constructional basis some portion of the prior speaker's utterance.

chapter 9

Sequential Aspects of Storytelling in Conversation[1]

GAIL JEFFERSON

In an investigation of stories told in conversation, Labov and Waletsky (1966) have shown that spontaneous stories can be subject to formal analysis, and under such analysis can be found to have a range of formal properties. While that study focuses on the story as the analytic unit, it suggests the relevance of "social context" to a story's telling (cf., e.g., Labov & Waletsky, 1966, pp. 12–13 and p. 34).

In a series of investigations, Harvey Sacks has focused on the contexted occurrence of stories told in conversation, and has made preliminary observations which indicate that stories are sequenced objects articulating with the particular context in which they are told.[2] For example, storytelling can involve a story preface with which a teller projects a forthcoming story, a next turn in which a coparticipant aligns himself as a story recipient, a next in which teller produces the story,[3] and a next in which story recipient talks by reference to the story. Further, the story preface can have consequences for the story's reception, and thus a rather extended series of turns at talk can be seen as a coherent conversational unit (cf., e.g., Sacks, 1972b, Lecture 2).

This chapter focuses on story beginnings and endings, sketching out two features via which a story can be seen to articulate with turn-by-turn talk: Stories emerge from turn-by-turn talk, that is, are *locally occasioned* by it, and, upon their completion, stories re-engage turn-by-turn talk, that is, are *sequentially implicative* for it.[4]

STORIES ARE LOCALLY OCCASIONED

In general, the occurrence of an utterance at a given moment is accountable, and a basic account is that a next utterance is produced by reference to the occurrence of a prior, that is, is occasioned by it (cf, e.g., Sacks, 1972b, Lecture 4 and Sacks, 1971, April 9). The local occasioning of a story by ongoing turn-by-turn talk can have two discrete aspects: (*a*) A story is "triggered" in the course of turn-by-turn talk. That is, something said at a particular moment in conversation can remind a participant (speaker or hearer) of a particular story, which may or may not be "topically coherent" with the talk in progress.[5] (*b*) A story is methodically introduced into turn-by-turn talk. That is, techniques are used to display a relationship between the story and prior talk and thus account for, and propose the appropriateness of, the story's telling.

In the following fragments, both aspects are readily observable. (*a*) An element of ongoing talk triggers a story which is (*b*) methodically introduced into that ongoing talk.

[GTS:II:2:64]   (1)
    ROGER: The *cops* don't do dat, don't gimme that shit I live in   1
           the Valley.   2
           (0.5)   3
 ● KEN: The cops, *o*ver the hill. There's a place up in   4
           *Mul*holland where they've– where they're building those 5
           hous ing projects?   6
            [
 ● ROGER: *Oh* have you ever taken them Mulhollan' time trials? 7
           'hh You go up there wid a girl. A buncha guys'r up there 8
           an' [STORY]   9

[Schenkein:I:7]   (2)
    ELLEN: Tuh relax er during this last illness, on top a' the   1
           antibiotics,   2
           (1.0)   3
 ● BEN: W–well on top a'thee, *cough* medicine.   4
 ● ELLEN: Yeah, and the cough medici– *inci*dentally. Did I tell you? 5

BILL:	No.	6
ELLEN:	That the d– he told us t'give uh Snookie a third of a	7
●	teaspoon of uh:: *cough* medicine. Cheracol, is there a–	8
	Is there a cou gh me dicine call'Cherac'l=	9
	⌈ ⌈	
BILL:	Yeah.	10
	⌈	
BEN:	Yeah,	11
ELLEN:	='hhh We happen'tuh have Vic's Forty Four [STORY]	12

[NB:IV:7:51]   (3)

LOTTI:	'hh (hh)en so 'hh when Duane lef'tuhday we took off ar	1
●	s– 'hh suits yihknow en, eh– *Oh* en she gave me the most	2
●	*beau*tiful *swim*suit you've ever seen in yer life.	3
EMMA:	*Gave* it to yuh?	4
LOTTIE:	Yeah,	5
EMMA:	Aww:: ::	6
	⌈	
LOTTIE:	A twunny two *do*llar one.	7
	⌈	
EMMA:	Aww:::.	8
	(0.6)	9
EMMA:	Well you've given *her* a lot in uh yer day Lottie,	10
LOTTIE:	I know ut. En when we *looked* w–one et Walter Clark's	11
	you know wir were gonna *buy* one cuz [STORY]	12

The technique used in these fragments consists of two discrete devices produced consecutively: (*a*) a 'disjunct marker' such as "*Oh*" (F.1.L.7 and F.3.L.2)[6] and "*inciden*tally" (F.2.L.5) signals that the talk to follow is not topically coherent with the adjacent prior talk, and (*b*) an 'embedded repetition' locates, but does not explicitly cite, the element of prior talk which triggered the story ("Mulholland," F.1.L.5. and 7., "cough medicine" F.2.L.4, 5, and 8, and "suits"/"swimsuit," F.3.L.2 and 3).

This appears to be a version of an explicit Speaking of X format in which a marked repeat (cf. Jefferson, 1972, pp. 295–296) cites a component of prior talk as the source of the story being introduced.[7]

[GTS:II:2:50:r:2]   (4)

ROGER:	*S*peakin about *for*ties. I *w*orked on a k–o::n	1
	Morga*ne*lli's Forty.	2

[SBL:2:5:12]   (5)

BEA:	Saying dahlias, I just cut some fresh dahlias	1
	at my neighbor's this evening. . .	2

Fragment (3) is of particular interest for the methodic construction of a disjunct plus repetition format. Assuming that speakers monitor their own talk (cf. Sacks, 1972b, Lecture 2) and assuming the "s–" in (L.1–2) ". . . we took off ar s–" is the beginning of the word "suits" (cf., e.g., Jefferson, 1974, pp. 185–188), then it is possible that having started to say "suits" speaker finds she has a story and cuts off, preparatory to introducing the story. Thereafter, to set up a disjunct plus repetition, she produces the word in full, ". . . we took off ar s– ˙hh suits. . ." and subsequently produces the display of sudden remembering, the disjunct marker "*Oh*" followed by the embedded repetition (L.1–3) ". . . we took off ar s– ˙hh suits yihknow en, eh– *Oh* en she gave me the most *beau*tiful *swims*uit. . . ."

The combined devices of disjunct and embedded repetition signal that the matter now being talked of, while not topically coherent with prior talk, had that talk as its source, that is, is a direct product of monitoring that talk. This stands in contrast to a story triggered at a particular moment but not by ongoing talk, for example:

[J:FN]   (6)
       ((three people walking together; someone passes them
                  wearing a photograph teeshirt))
       NETTIE:*Oh* that *tee*shirt reminded me [STORY]   1

The two devices need not occur in combination. A disjunct marker can be followed by something other than a repetition (cf. F.25.L.26), and an embedded repetition can follow something other than a disjunct marker. In the following fragment, a story is introduced as a topically coherent next utterance,[8] with a version of the once-upon-a-time format; that is, it starts with a temporal locator (F.7.L.7) "New Years we. . . ." Subsequently an embedded repetition of the trigger word occurs (L.13, cf.L.1 and 4).

[GTS:II:2:87:r]   (7)
● AL: ((To Roger)) *Probly poured glue* over it. ˈF I know you:,   1
                   (0.4)   2
      KEN: ˙hhhhh No:, yih gotta be careful evry so *o*ften ˈe takes   3
●   that *c*up'n ˈe takes a deep whiff he's gotta tube a'glue   4
                in it.   5
                   (0.7)   6
● ROGER: *N*ew Years we:: split up the *d*ues so we each hadda buck   7
                fifty tuh buy *b*ooze with fer the *N*ew Years party?   8
      AL: Mm hm,   9

```
ROGER:  So w'wen'around the room they were takin orders. 'hh So      10
        Lance k– So:, one guy bought a, dollar f'fty worth a'         11
        Ripple, 'hh next guy b(hh)ought a dollar fifty worth a'       12
•       glue:, uhh!                                                   13
(    ):  'hhh=                                                        14
KEN:    =heh huh– h u h                                               15
             [        ]
AL:             he–eh hehh he hh                                      16
                       [
ROGER:                 'hhh! 'ufff ff                                 17
                             [
AL:                          'hihhh!                                  18
(JIM):   hheh=                                                        19
ROGER:  ="Pl(h)anning on gittin ga:ssed. Huh La(h)nce."              20
                             [               ]=
AL:                          (V e r y )                               21
ROGER:  hh 'uhh hyihh 'hhh h                                          22
        =[[              ] [
AL:     (good   Roger)       'he:::h.                                 23
             (1.0)                                                    24
ROGER:  They were progressively gittin worse, ez we went
             aroun'                                                   25
        the circ(h)le,                                                26
KEN:    m–hhmhh(    )                                                 27
             [
AL:          he:h hehh' uh' hh nh                                     28
                   [
KEN:               (That's a true           ),                       29
                                  [
ROGER:                            I ordered rum'n                     30
        thought it wz ba:d y'(h)kno(h)ow                              31
```

The story is not produced as a sudden remembering, but as continuous with prior talk. It appears that the procedure used to introduce the story is consequential for the story's structure on this occasion of its occurrence. Specifically, the repetition does not occur as part of the introduction (cf. F.1–6), but as a component of the story's punch line (L.12–13). Some details of the fragment suggest that the repetition's punch line positioning is accompanied by a condensing of the story, with the repetition-bearing punch line occurring sooner than it might have, given the story's events.[9]

Subsequent to the punch line is a series of commentaries, one of which proposes an order in which the events occurred (L.25), one of which offers an event which might have occurred prior to that which constitutes the punch line (L.30–31). That is, the order of events might have been: They went around the room taking orders (L.10), progressively getting worse as they went around the circle (L.25); one guy ordered Ripple (L.11–12), Roger ordered rum and thought it was "*ba*:d" (L.30–31) until someone ordered glue (L.12–13 and 20).[10]

There are, then, a variety of devices and combinations of devices by which a triggered story can be appropriately introduced. The observable relationship between a story and prior turn-by-turn talk is a product of methodic displays, fitted to the talk so far and to the story to be told. Further, it appears that the particular circumstances under which a story is entered can have consequences for the structure of the actually told story, which itself is fitted to the manner of its introduction.

Entry into a story from turn-by-turn talk can be done economically or elaborately. So, for example, in the following fragments, entry is achieved via a conventional story-prefixed phrase.[11]

[Actors' Group:13]   (8)
JOE:	If they're supposed to hate you up there, they *do*.	1
B.J.:	eehaha ha	2
JOE:	You kn ow,	3
	[	
DARCY:	Tha ss–	4
	[	
B.J.:	They hold a grudge.	5
JOE:	Yeah!	6
AMY:	heh–heh–heh–heh	7
• DARCY:	Thass true now th–uh Hal's roommate Ron Bender [STORY]	8

[GTS:III:1:19]   (9)
KEN:	He was terrific the whole time we were there.	1
LOUISE:	I know what you mean. Wh'n they– my sister and her	2
	boyfriend [STORY]	3

[Adato:III:21]   (10)
VINNY:	The guy at the top's gonna make sure no one– knocks	1
	im *off*.	2
STAN:	The guy in the middle is playin both of 'em against	3
	the other, so *you* know, *wha*ddiyou got.	4
JAY:	hih! huh huh Ki(hh)nd of a me(hh)ess,	5
• STAN:	*Real*ly when you con*si*der it. It's– it's like uh I	6
	heard Senator Kennedy [STORY]	7

[Reilly:9]   (11)
FRAN:	I feel sorriest for Warren hh hh how he sits there an'	1
	listens to it I don'know? But, um.	2

HOLLY: Well he must'v known what she was like before 'e	3
married 'er.	4
FRAN: *I* guess. And–	5
• HOLLY: *He* can be a bastard too, he uh one– one day we [STORY]	6

[Carey:Bar:I:1] (12)

FRANK: What'r these freaks mostly?who'r goin t'this,=	1
GEORGE: =*No:* They're perfectly legitimate– `hh d– ezza	2
• mattera fact the g– `hh the *guy* [STORY]	3

[Frankel:US:I:4] (13)

PHIL: (*Yeh*) en the guy who broke it should c–certainly, clean	1
it *up.*	2
·VIC: But it don't *ha*ppen that way becuss nine chances outta	3
• ten matter a'fact I know duh, u–dih guy [STORY]	4

[D.A.:17] (14)

ANN: But nobody fought with huh like *I* fought with huh.	1
(1.4)	2
• ANN: Uhb–uh fer example, uh d–oh about two weeks before	3
she [STORY]	4

[Goldberg:II:I:23] (15)

MAGGIE: Very rarely do I get a Saturdee off, I mean I haf to like	1
• plan a *month* in advance for the Suh– for the *Sat*urdees	2
off, ez a matter a'fact I've [STORY]	3

The more elaborate procedures have a story emerging through longer stretches of turn-by-turn talk. The story emerges not only as topically coherent, as in fragments (8)–(15), but with coparticipant(s) specifically aligned as story recipients.

In the following fragment, a display of story triggering is produced (F.16.L.24–32) with a marked repeat (L.29) "And they *are* stars" which cites an element of prior talk (L.24) as the story trigger, and is followed by an embedded repetition (L.31–32; cf. also note 7). However, it appears that the story is actually triggered earlier, via a slightly more complex process than the one displayed here (cf. F.1–6).

[Labov:Battersea Park:B:3:r] (16)

LADY: It's *dy*ing *out* yihkno:w,=	1
• PARKY: =*Oh:* ye::s, Well they *got* s'm new,hh (·) new=	2
• PARKY: =They *got* th'*dol*phins in the:h=	3
MAN: =Mm.	4

```
TRACY:    They do :.                                                          5
             [
PARKY:          Fl ippah,hh                                                   6
                  [              ]
LADY:               B't even :=                                              7
PARKY:    =la hk you av i n Ameriker on the fi:lm,                            8
             [         ] [              [      ]
LADY:         s o : :.                                                        9
                     [                [       ]
TRACY:                  ˙h h h h h h h  O h :. Oh ye:s.=                       10
MAN:      =Ye:h, them.=                                                       11
PARKY:    =Well we got s ome in the:h.                                        12
                  [     ]
LADY:             P e e–                                                      13
TRACY:    I'll b e da:::rned.                                                 14
                             ]
LADY:            People uh co mplaining a'the pri:ce.=                        15
PARKY:    Ye:s th'pri:ce, Well et Oxf'd Street they've got'em the:uh.         16
             (0.2)                                                            17
MAN:      Ye :h.                                                             18
             [
TRACY:      Hhuh.                                                            19
PARKY:    And uh ther very good et Oxf'd Stree:t,                            20
TRACY:    Hhu:h.                                                             21
PARKY:    They've got fo'ovuh the:h,                                         22
             (0.4)                                                           23
● PARKY:   You s ee two: trainee:s, 'n then you see the two sta:hs.          24
               [
(    ):        I–                                                            25
             (0.2)                                                           26
(    ):    hhhh                                                              27
             (0.2)                                                           28
● PARKY:   En theh ah stah:s my Gawt.(·)I 'm sittin up e'the fro:nt=         29
                                           [
(    ):                                     Ah–                              30
PARKY:    =wiv, (mah two guhl), 'hhh Un:d uh h– all et once one a'           31
●          these stahs wen'up'n the ay didn'alf go up too.'n w'n 'e          32
           c(h)ome do:wn gow cracky I wz saturaite d.                        33
                                                       [
MAN:                                                    h–hheh
           hhehh hheh=                                                       34
MAN:      h e h,                                                             35
             =[[          ]
PARKY:       'E co me right this e:nd.                                       36
                [                ]
TRACY:           h a    h a!                                                37
```

```
PARKY:     F a : : c t,                                        38
         [[                  ]
MAN:       (Yeh that's) good.                                   39
         [[                      ]
(LADY): (M m m m m m M m m Yuh)                                 40
                   [   ]   ]
TRACY:                    ˙u::h h u h h a , h a, h a, ˙ha?      41
                   [   ]       ]   ]   ]    ]
PARKY:                    ' E dunnit pu:r posel y : .           42
                                         [    ]
MAN:                                     Mm.                    43
```

It appears that in the course of disputing a prior utterance which has proposed that amusement parks are dying out, a speaker is starting to invoke a general category—something like "new attractions" or "new acts" (L.2). Starting on that, he is reminded of an incumbent of that category, a particular new attraction (L.3) "the dolphins," about which he has a story to tell. And he proceeds in much the same fashion as does speaker in fragment(3) (L.1–2) ". . . we took off ar s–˙hh suits. . ."; that is, he stops prior to completion of the unit "new–" and then starts to recycle it (L.2.) ". . . they got some new,hh (·) new. . . ." Thereafter he takes a different tack, abandoning the entire sentence-so-far and replacing it with (L.3) "They got the dolphins in there." His subsequent talk may specifically "mask" the fact that a story has been triggered; that is, reference to the dolphins is preserved through turn-by-turn talk without a repetition of that word (L.6–8, 12, 16, 20, 22, 24). Rather, the particular new attraction is used as a base for topical talk, with teller proposing a special interest that one of his coparticipants might have in talk about dolphins (L.6–8) "Flipper. . . like you have in America. . .," coparticipant producing tokens of special interest (L.10) " ˙hhhhh O h:. Oh ye:s." With these tokens, while coparticipant does not herself offer topical talk about dolphins, she displays herself as receptive to talk on that topic; that is, she aligns herself as a recipient.

Thereafter, two of teller's three coparticipants produce tokens of appreciation/understanding as the talk moves toward the ˙storytelling (L.11, 14, 18, 19, 20). These two may be relevantly identified as "potential story recipients." The third, however, competes with the talk out of which the story is emerging, overlapping both teller (L.6–8 and 12–13) and one recipient (L.14–15) with a single coherent sentence continuing the ongoing dispute (L.7–9, 13–15) "But even so:. . . . Pee– . . . People are complaining of the pri:ce." (cf. Sacks, 1967b, Lecture 13, and 1972, Lecture 4).

The disparate alignment of coparticipants prior to the story's telling seems to have consequences for its reception. The two recipients produce laughter (L.34–35, 37, 41.) while the disputer does not—that is, the positions taken by coparticipants prior to the story's telling are preserved in its reception. Thus, the elaborated turn-by-turn emergence of a story from topical talk may be methodically constructed, not only by reference to its appropriate, locally occasioned occurrence, but by reference to its projected reception.

STORIES ARE SEQUENTIALLY IMPLICATIVE

In general, an utterance "projects for the sequentially following turn(s), the relevance of a determinate range of occurrences. . . . It thus has sequentially organized implications." Further, there are ways of "methodically providing for such implicativeness [Schegloff & Sacks, 1973, p. 296]." The re-engagement of turn-by-turn talk at a story's completion is a matter of sequential implicativeness in both senses; that is, at a story's ending two discrete aspects similar to those observed for local occasioning can be found. (a) A story can serve as a source for triggered or topically coherent subsequent talk, and (b) a range of techniques are used to display a relationship between the story and subsequent talk— techniques which provide that the story is implicative for subsequent talk and thus propose the appropriateness of its having been told.

As an initial approach to sequential implicativeness, an instance is shown in which it is absent. Here, a story (F.17.L.17–29) may have been triggered by an element of prior talk, the word "Brentwood" (L.13) which is being used to refer to a mental hospital (L.15–16), it happening that the hospital is located in a high-income suburb (cf. L.17–18). The story is introduced as continuous with prior talk (L.17; cf. F.7.L.7) and is elaborately told, but when its telling stops (L.29), ongoing talk is picked up where it left off (L.30). For clarity, the transcript has the story indented.

[GTS:IV:1:12]   (17)
DAN:	Alright, except that again, you're–you're–you're using an	1
	example of maybe one or two individuals,	2
ROGER:	Yes,	3
DAN:	Uh::m and saying well look what these people did. And the	4
	other idea is that most schizophrenics, most psychotics	5
	are not really able to produce very much of any thing.	6
	[	
ROGER:	I'm not	7
	saying don't cure schi– I'm taking it as an individual	8

```
              case. I'm taking this individual and referring to only=      9
                          [
DAN:                      Mm hm, it's true–                                10
ROGER:    =this individual.                                                11
DAN:      'S true, and I'm sure that his artwork uhm all you have to       12
          do is go over t'Brentwood and see some very interesting          13
●         artwork I find it interesting.                                   14
                        [
ROGER:                  Where at the hospital?                             15
DAN:      That's right,                                                    16
● KEN:    Yeah and you c'n also go into some of these                      17
          millionaires' hou–homes. And they've bot– boughten               18
          some of these uh artworks from different places in               19
          the world? You c'n look at 'em and– I mean I don't               20
          know anything about art, I can't–I can't draw that               21
          well, I can draw cars, and junk like this when I                 22
          want to, but uh::go into some of these houses and                23
          they–it looks like somebody took a squirtgun with                24
          paint in it an'just squirted it. Justa buncha lines              25
          goin every which way an' "Oh isn't that terrific?"               26
          "Yeah. What is it." Y'kno(h)w? "Didjer child have                27
          a good time when he was drawing that?" "Whad-diyuh               28
          mean that cost me–" Y'know hhh                                    29
DAN:      See but the other al– the alternative that you're giving         30
          me is to say well look, m–m–maybe uh maybe a person has          31
          to be sick in order to be able to see these things,              32
ROGER:    No, this man–                                                    33
     [[
DAN:      And I don't think–                                               34
DAN:      And I don't think that's true.                                   35
ROGER:    I don't think so either. But this man. . .                       36
```

This is a dramatic instance; the story is treated as utterly irrelevant to the ongoing talk and is sequentially deleted.[12] More routinely, the relationship of a story to subsequent talk is negotiated between teller and recipients. For example, recipients will not actively move to delete a story, but will withhold talk which demonstrates the story's sequential implicativeness, and teller will search for ways to elicit recipient talk, deploying story components as story exit devices.

In the following fragment a story reaches a point of possible completion (F.18.L.3) and is followed by a pause (L.4). Thereafter is a series of postscripts and commentaries, each followed by a pause (L.5–8 and 9, L.10–12 and 13, L.14–16 and 17). Finally, a commentary is followed by turn-by-turn talk (L.22–25 and 27 ff.). Across the series of story components there is an observable progression away from the story, toward tangential and more general, but yet recognizably related, issues. And it is at the point where teller offers a general topic that recipients engage in turn-by-turn talk (L.22 ff.).

[GTS:II;2:64:r]   (18)
```
    ROGER:  [STORY] 'n were back t'the pizza joint we started from.      1
            Y'know, En we spend a whole night doin that, 'n waste a      2
            lotta money on gas'n, 'hh Buh we hadda ba:ll.                3
                (0.8)
  • ROGER:  En there's only two guys t'each car. That's th' thing        5
                                            [       ]=
    DAN:                                           mkhhh                  6
    DAN:    mkhhhm, ((throat clearing))                                  7
            =[[           ]
    ROGER:  y'know?                                                      8
                (0.5)                                                    9
  • ROGER:  Ih wz during the su:mmer en we do it lo:tsa times yuh       10
            know, W'call it a crui:se y'know, En the club enjoys        11
            doing that.                                                 12
                (1.0)                     .                             13
  • ROGER:  'hhh B'd now most'the guys in th'club through'hh one        14
            method'r another are either not driving'r don't have a      15
            ca:r. 'k–'ghh?                                              16
                (1.2)                                                   17
  • ROGER:  So,                                                         18
    (KEN):  hhhh                                                        19
    DAN:    hmh, hm,                                                    20
                (0.9)                                                   21
  • ROGER:  'hhhhh Kids don't drive long.They start off w't their si–  22
            by the time– when they're sixteen b'the time they're       23
            eighteen they're back wa–alking:hh:::'ehh–'eh th(h)rough    24
            c(h)irc(h)umsta(h)a(h)nces.=                                25
    ROGER:  'uffffffffff                                                26
            =[[                  ]
    AL:     beyond their con tro::::::::::::l.                          27
                           [             ]
    DAN:                       beyond their c'n tro ::l.                28
                                       [
    ROGER:                              Uh!hhY(h)e(h)s.=               29
    ROGER:  ='ihhh'uh=                                                  30
```

```
AL:      =˙uhhh hh                                          31
          [
ROGER:              ˙hhh Hot rodders (don't)                32
              [                    ]
AL:                         Bec'z it's a:ll th'cops'f ault,  33
                              [
ROGER:                              Now the Soshes          34
          keep drivin'. Daddy's car'n evrythin:g y'know, ˙hh=  35
(   ):  (   )–                                               36
          =[[
DAN:     'T's all the cops' fault.                          37
AL:      Yeah it's not ours.We're pri–=                     38
ROGER:   =I t's the insurance companies'n the cops.        39
          [
              We're be tter (     )                         40
AL:      Damn right.                                        41
```

A prototypical display of story completion, a return 'home' (L.1.) "'n were back t'the pizza joint we started from," is followed by commentary (L.2–3) and a secondary ending, now not of the story, but of the storytelling; an assessment (L.3) "'hh Buh we hadda ba:ll." There is no talk whatsoever at completion (L.3 and 4), nor over three recycles of a "transition-relevance place [Sacks *et al.*, 1974, p. 703]," a place at which turn-by-turn talk might be re-engaged (L.5–8 and 9, 10–12, and 13, 14–16, and 17), and a request for recipient comment (L.18) "So,"[13] receives minimal tokens of appreciation (L.19 and 20) which, although they acknowledge and are occasioned by prior talk, are not themselves implicative for subsequent talk. These are followed by still another pause (L.21). The absence of recipient talk is dramatic.

Equally dramatic is the manner in which turn-by-turn talk is re-engaged. Teller himself provides a topical utterance which demonstrates the sequential implicativeness of the story (L.22–25). If recipients talk by reference to it, then the story will have re-engaged turn-by-turn talk. In the course of that utterance, he produces an object which can provide for the utterance's implicativeness and thus for the story's implicativeness; that is, teller offers a first half of an idiom (L.24–25) "through circumstances. . . ." It appears that he has specifically offered a first half; that is, immediately thereafter he produces, not its second half, but a form of laughter (L.26. cf. F.7.L.17). The second half of the idiom is produced by two recipients (L.27 and 28), and it is a second half fitted to the entire utterance; that is, ". . .beyond *their* control" (emphasis added) understands and talks by reference to the prior "Kids . . . they . . . they're . . ." and so on (L.22–24). This is a powerful demonstration of an object's sequential implicativeness, with multiple parties producing a second part, given the occurrence of a first—the utterance has not merely implicated ''a determinate range of occurrences,'' but a single one, and a single one for more than one coparticipant. The fuguelike tumble thereafter might well be seen as a celebration of the re-engagement of turn-by-turn talk, of a return to a state of talking together.

A range of materials, in which it initially seems that a teller is indulging in story expansion, can be seen via sequential analysis as a teller searching for recipient talk by reference to the story, using story components as exit devices. In the following fragment it may be as a by-product of such a pursuit that teller provides a series of statements which progress from excoriation of an individual (F.19.L.4 and 10) to a denouncing of his entire family (L.15).[14]

[Goldberg:II:2:23:r]		(19)
MAGGIE:	[STORY] A::n uh: I guess once wz *enough*.	1
GENE:	Yeah. (·) Yeah.	2
	(1.0)	3
MAGGIE:	˙tlk But ez far ez *I'm* concerned he [ex-husband] hez,	4
	shown his *col*or::s to the point where:: ˙hhh n:*no*body	5
	in iz right *mi*:nd who's even got a: *de*cent breath left	6
	in them.˙hhh wou:ld think thet he wz ec*cep*table.	7
GENE:	Yeah.	8
	(0.7)	9
● MAGGIE:	˙t En it's a sure damn thing thet whenever:: this *kid*	10
	[her son] grows *up* he'll have n:*no*buddy tuh thank fer	11
	*an*ythaing. ˙hh uh: of *that* family [ex-husband's].	12
GENE:	Yeah. (·) Yeah.	13
	(1.0)	14
● MAGGIE:	I wouldn't spit on the best side of'm en I've yet t'	15
	see the best *si*:de.	16
GENE:	hhhehh heh-heh-heh ˙hhhh Well how a*bout* the rest	17
	a'the fam'ly. . .	18

Following an assessment (L.1) ''And I guess once was *enough*'' (cf. F.18.L.3), and over two recycles of a transition place (L.4–7 and 10–12) there is token acknowledgment by recipient (cf. F.18.L.19 and 20) followed by a pause (L.2 and 3, 8 and 9, 13 and 14). A third recycle (L.15–16) is followed by appreciation (L.17.; cf.F.16.L.34.ff. and F.18.L.18–20) and thereafter by an object which formally re-engages turn-by-turn talk; that is, a question which is observably occasioned by the prior utterance and itself implicates at least a next utterance.[15]

While re-engagement of turn-by-turn talk may be the primary issue upon a story's completion, there are other matters to which a storyteller may be oriented. Specifically, there may be orientation to what a recipient makes of the story and thus what the story has amounted to. Following is a dramatic instance in which recipient displays appreciation and understanding of a story at a possible completion point (F.20.L.2–4). It turns out that only a story segment has been completed and were the storytelling to stop at that point, recipient would be left with a misapprehension of the events being reported. That is, following recipient's response (L.4.) is a story component which contradicts the sense to be made of the story so far (L.1–2 and 6–7).

[MC:I:15]   (20)

HARMON: I said "And–and–and–" "What ih–" "Is her boyfriend a nice 1
         ma:n Joey?" He sz "Oh he's very nice, he's a colored man." 2
         hhh*hhhh HAH* hah!   3
                 [
● LIL: Oh no::: the poor kid yer kidding.   4
                            [
HARMON: I said–   5
HARMON: No waita second I said "Joseph, that's, not your mother's 6
         boyfriend. That colored man is the man (   ) she–   7
         eh he takes her tuh work every day.   8
LIL: *Uh* huh.   9
HARMON: This colored man. (   )–   10
                           [
LIL: Sure– What *diffe*rence does it make, sure. 11

A generalizable feature of this fragment is that tellers can propose and recipients accept that a response was premature, that there is more story to come, and that upon a next completion point, recipients have a next opportunity to respond via their corrected understanding of the story.

Such a feature can serve as a resource for negotiations as to what a story shall have amounted to. Roughly, talk which demonstrates a story's implicativeness may be tangential to it, as is teller's commentary and subsequent turn-by-turn talk in fragments (18) and (19). In those fragments the tangential talk is clearly alternative to and remedial of recipient *silence*. When recipient *talk* follows directly on story completion, then silence may not be a relevant alternative; rather, the relevant alternatives are two types of talk—tangential talk as observably contrastive to talk which is directly continuous with and fitted to the story.

Storytellers do not explicitly challenge or complain of tangential recipient talk (as they do not complain of recipient silence). Instead, they propose that the story was not yet completed by offering a next story component. Upon completion of that component, a next point occurs at which the story can be responded to (cf. F.20), and thus, at least an opportunity for, and perhaps an invitation to, a different order of response—in the case of tangential talk, a more fitted response—is provided by an added story component.

In the following fragment a story reaches a point of possible completion (F.21.L.5–7) and a recipient initiates tangential talk (L.9 and 12–13). In overlap with that talk, teller provides two recognizable next story components (L.10–11 and 14).

```
[Labov:T.A.:4:r]                                                    (21)
    RITA:   She didn'have time tuh cook yesterday she got home la;te,   1
            (0.4)                                                        2
    RITA:   So ah met'er et (Promtiers).                                 3
            (0.2)                                                        4
    RITA:   She had a:, (0.3) a broi:led hambuhrger, (0.6) with no:      5
            gravy awnnit, (0.5) She hadda serving of cabbage, 'n she     6
            hadda salad.                                                 7
            (0.3)                                                        8
    MARGE:  Very– It's terrific I bec ause I'm tellin yih–               9
                             [                        ]
  • RITA:                          E n she couldn' ev en=               10
    RITA:   =fini–ish :: i(h) t,=                                       11
                    [      ]
                    There's                                            12
    MARGE:  =E:vrybody's e ncouraging her there. ¹⁶                     13
                      [              [            ]
  • RITA:                      Enna cuppa ca:wf e e.                    14
```

And in the following, story-tangential talk (F.22.L.2.) which overlaps a story commentary (L.1.) is met with an added story component (L.5.).

```
[Rose:I:1]                                                          (22)
    COLEY:  Really Har ry pulled a gun on me.                           1
                      [
    MICKEY:             We wanna bring a suit against im fer            2
            discrimination.                                            3
            (0.3)                                                       4
  • COLEY:  An' plus he, he– he hit me inna mou:th.                     5
```

It appears that added story components can be deployed for a range of contingencies. So, for example, in the following fragment a recipient wisecrack in the course of a story (F.23.L.3) is met with an added story component (L.6).

```
[Gaye:A:4:r]                                                          (23)
  LEN:    [STORY] go getta– (0.2) cuppa co:ffee'n, (0.7) have a        1
          c igare::tte 'n, hnh                                         2
          [              ]
  RAY:    Smoke twelve ci garettes uh!                                 3
                         [
  LEN:                   n–hn                                          4
  RAY:    ˙hh hh                                                       5
          [
• LEN:      'n have another cuppa co:ffee 'n::                         6
```

And in the following, an interchange between two parties (F.24.L.2–3, 5 and 6) who have so far been recipients of an ongoing story (data not shown) is overlapped by an added story component (L.7.).

```
[Freas:A:4:r]                                                         (24)
  LORI:   [STORY] And– heels or loafers: or, s a d d l e–              1
                                  [                   ]
  BILL:                           ((whispered)) Shouldn' you check=    2
  BILL:   the                                                          3
          =[[
  LORI:   oxfe rds,                                                    4
             [
  JAN:       Hm?                                                       5
  BILL:   ((w)) Shouldn't you check the (      )?                      6
                                        [
• LORI:                                 And ponytails,                 7
```

In a fragment shown earlier (see below, F.16a), following a completion point (L.33), teller produces two recycles (L.36) "He come right this e:nd" and (L.38–42) "Fa:ct, . . .He done it purposely" although recipients are offering appreciation (L.34–35, 37, 39, 40, and 41). Since appreciation of a prior does not itself implicate subsequent talk, when the appreciation stops the storytelling will have its sequential implicativeness yet to be demonstrated (cf. F.18 and 19). The second recycle may constitute one solution to that problem, providing materials for (and perhaps specifically designed to elicit) a query by recipient (L.48) "Purposely?" However, the query does not occur immediately after, and it appears that a secondary solution is offered; that is, teller proposes a return to the dispute with (L.45) "No: Oxford Street,". When recipient offers the query (L.48), thus formally re-engaging turn-by-turn talk (cf. fragment F.19), the initial solution is, after all, successful and teller abandons the dispute, providing a response to recipient's query (L.50) "*YE::S.* . . ." In this case, the response leads to a next story segment (L.50–58).

[Labov:Battersea Park:B:3:r]   (16a)
```
    PARKY: . . .gow cracky I wz saturaite d.                          33
                                 [
    MAN:                           h–hheh hhehh hheh=               34
    MAN:   h e h,                                                     35
           =[[        ]
    PARKY: 'E co me right this e:nd.                                  36
             [       ]
    TRACY:        h a  h a!                                           37
  • PARKY: F a : : c t,                                               38
           [[        ]
    MAN:   (Yeh that's) good.                                         39
           [[        ]     ]
  (LADY): (M m m m m m M m m Yuh)                                     40
               [    [  ]
    TRACY:          'u::h h u h h a , h a, h a, 'ha?                  41
                    [   [   ]   ]   ]   ]
  • PARKY:            ' E dunnit pu:r posel y : . =                   42
                                   [     ]
    MAN:                             M m.                             43
    (   ):  =(     )=                                                 44
    PARKY: =Nao: Ox 'n S treet,                                       45
              [     ]      ]
    MAN:        In O xf'd S tre et.=                                  46
                [        ]   ]
    TRACY:           huh–ha hu–                                       47
  • TRACY: ='hhhh Pu: rpose ly?                                       48
               [       ]
    PARKY:      Pa:r–                                                 49
  • PARKY:          YE:::: S::.T h e– t h e                           50
                          [      ]    ]
    MAN:                    Yes they're uh they're very good=        51
    MAN:   (dolphin acts)                                            52
           =[[              ]
  • PARKY: The bloke 'oo gives'em thee– instru:ction on th'wissowl=  53
    PARKY: = n ::                                                     54
             [
    TRACY:    Ah hah?                                                 55
              (0.2)                                                   56
    MAN:   (          )                                              57
           [       ]
  • PARKY: This thing come up'n eez ovuh theh [NEXT SEGMENT]  58
```

Thus, a series of utterances which can be extracted from a conversation and identified as parts of "a story" can be sequentially analyzed as parts of "a storytelling," with recognizable story components deployed as story-entry and -exit devices, providing transition from a state of turn-by-turn talk among conversational coparticipants into a story told by a storyteller to story recipient(s), and a return from the latter to the former state of talk. Conversely, utterances which might not otherwise constitute parts of "a story" can be sequentially analyzed as parts of "a storytelling," with recognizable topical talk used to engage conversational coparticipants as story recipients, and to negotiate whether, and how, the story will be told, whether it is completed or in progress, and what, if anything, it will have amounted to as a conversational event.

A STORYTELLING

In this section, resources considered so far are turned to a partial analysis of a single extended fragment in which a storytelling is approached through turn-by-turn talk, where features of the story's emergence are consequential for its reception and its sequential implicativeness.

[GTS:II:2:50:r2]   (25)

AL:	I'm gonna'z thinkin about building that Healey up to	1
	compe*ti*tion *u*:se.	2
	((door slides open))	3
ROGER:	Good *lu*:ck.	4
	((door slides shut))	5
(KEN):	Hi–i:,	6
	(0.3)	7
ROGER:	I'll *te*'yuh. hh	8
	[ ]	
( ):	( )	9
	(·)	10
● ROGER:	*I* wanna bui:ld, (·) the *ho*ttest street machine in *W*est	11
	L.A.	12
	(0.2)	13
AL:	*I'd* like to do that too.	14
	[ ]	
● ROGER:	' N *cha*llenge *V*oodoo to a race I	15
	*m*ean the *hell* with *d*rag strips *y*ou gotta have ten	16
●	thous'n bucks ready t'spe– 'hh *I* wanna build a *h*ot	17
	*s*treet machine.	18
	(0.7)	19

ROGER: I mean–   20
       [   ]
AL: (   ) dz– a hundred'n fo:rty in the stree :ts,   21
                                          [   ]
ROGER: Pull into   22
     A 'n W, hhhehh'hh en challenge, *an*ybody to a go, heh   23
•   'hh th'*R*oad Runner Voodoo hehh'khh "C'm on"
       y'know,=   24
AL: Ey wuh–   25
    =[[   ]
ROGER: 'hhhhhh *Oh* there's a twenny sev'n–   26
               [   ]
• AL: *What's* the Voodoo,   27
       (·)   28
AL: I've *h*eard about it.   29
       (·)   30
ROGER: Oh *that* is a ru– it's uhm:: (0.3) a *myth*. Ih–it– Well   31
    the *Voo*doo is the *f*astest *c*ar, I've ever seen, inna   32
    streets.   33
       (0.3)   34
AL: What *is* it.   35
       (0.4)   36
• ROGER: It's a *f*ifty five Chevvy. It's *b*right orange, (0.5) and 37
    it has, (·) it *ha*:d 'hh *u*–lemme tell y'bout this car.   38
    'hh A *th*ree twunny seven:.(·)*V*et in it. (uhyih) an' if   39
    wuz uh, 'hh *du*al quads, 'hh hadda *f*ull roller cam (0.3)   40
    four speed neon hydrostick, four f'fty six positraction,   41
    (·) big slicks, 'hh An' it wuz *thee* fastest car. I've   42
    ever seen in th'streets.   43
       (·)   44
• ROGER: 'hh I'll *t*ell y'something there wz a big *d*rag (in out'n)   45
    th'Valley?   46
       (·)   47
ROGER: Y'know *wa*:::*y* out there ih wz.'hhh bout *ni:net*y miles,   48
(   ): hhhh=   49
ROGER: =So, (·) We *a*ll the whole b–evrybody met et Scott's'n we   50
    went *o*ut there it wz a (·) *b*ig caravan.   51
       (·)   52
• ROGER: So the *Voo*doo doesn', it has the–p–*grill* blanked *o*:ff.Y' 53
    know,'hh so it couldn'git'ny *a*ir in the rad'er.So on the   54
    *f*reeway, (·) he over*h*eats.   55
       (0.2)   56
ROGER: Y'know. 'hh *Big* water shoot'n out, 'hh He's been *d*riving 57

fer *two hours* mindja on the *freeway.*˙hh He over*heats.*Well   58
we *figured scratch* one *Voodoo.*   59
    (0.2)   60
• ROGER: Y'know cz izzih–(˙)ih wz over*hea*ted. So we left widout im,   61
    (0.4)   62
ROGER: So th'*dr*ag starts,   63
    (0.7)   64
ROGER: u–Everybody hear a *big* loud, n–*n*oi:se like a *c*annon. ˙hh   65
Here comes Voodoo *w*indin end a *p*uffin *up* there, ˙hh *We*   66
thought he ez *d*ead fer sure–He doesn't shut off the   67
*e*ngine.˙hh He jus' *k*eeps on going, (˙) *O*ne after a*n*other   68
'e *s*huts down e:*vry car (offa) Valley.*Sup*erstock *a*nything   69
they had.˙hh He didn' *shut* off iz *e*ngine'n–˙hh *p*o*lished   70
'em *o*:ff.one after another,   71
    (0.3)   72
ROGER: Turns aroun'n goes home.   73
    (0.4)   74
(   ): hhmh   75
    (0.3)   76
ROGER: *I* gained a lotta res*p*ect fer *th*at car.   77
    (˙)   78
(   ): hhhh   79
    (˙)   80
ROGER: ˙hh Y'know what *h*appened once?˙hh He wz *t*unin the car.   81
*li*ttle tiny screw dropped down the ju:g, ˙hh lodged in   82
the valve en (*t*hen) went the *e*ngine.˙hh=   83
AL: =(N: n o   s h i t.)   84
    [   ]
ROGER: So'e dropped in a four sixty *sev*'n.*Do*:dge.   85
    (0.6)   86
(ROGER): Whhhew.   87
    (0.5)   88
AL: There wzay uh:m (0.3) u̦–u̦–Bill *Rei*lly rode in a car uh,   89
en he toh–wz *t*elling me about it.I:'ve *s*een it.*arou*:nd.   90
•   it's a:, *s*ixty one *Fo*:rd with a three ninety bored out   91
tuh four ten *two* four barrels (˙) straight (differn) cam   92
'n all this, four speed close'spline,˙hh four fifty *s*i:x,   93
big slicks,   94
    (˙)   95
ROGER: *S*peakin about *f*orties.   96
    (0.2)   97

ROGER: I worked on a k–o::n Morganelli's Forty.   98
       (·)   99
(   ): (   )=   100
ROGER: =The guy's a (trip) but yihkno:w,   101
       (·)   102
ROGER: He's sorta wierd.   103
         [   ]
AL: (Hey.)   104
       (·)   105
AL: D'you know (   )–   106
      [   ]
ROGER: He's gotta forty Fo:rd,   107
        [   ]
AL: (Hey.)   108
      (0.4)   109
ROGER: He took outta– (·) t–uh: two ninety six Chrysler'n put   110
    inna three: (uh) fifty Chrysler with dual qua:ds?   111
       (·)   112
ROGER: Eh he:– He hates drag strips. Y'll never find im etta   113
    drag strip,   114
       (·)   115
ROGER: 'S one a'these street me:n y'know,=   116
KEN: =(   )   117
      [   ]   ]
AL: 'hh hk   118
       [   ]]
ROGER: Run 'n fm th'fu:zz'hh That car's pretty fast,   119
      (·)   120
ROGER: Then I also worked o:n, w't is pobly.(·) ↑ thee fastest[17]   121
●   car.faster'n Voodoo.   122
      (·)   123
ROGER: He acshlly doesn'live around here. 'e lives in Manha–u–   124
    uh:in uhm. (0.3) Y'know where Lance I fergot th'name a'   125
    th'place.   126
      (·)   127
ROGER: Well it's uhm twenny sev'n Tee with a full blown   128
    Chrysler in it. (·) (Dual) quads. An' he dyives it in   129
    the stree:t.   130
      (0.3)   131
ROGER: Guy's'n asshole. I mean he c'd i:dle et thirty miles   132
    'n hour.   133

The story appears to be triggered via a mechanism similar to that described for fragment (16); that is, the naming of a category evokes an

SEQUENTIAL ASPECTS OF STORYTELLING

incumbent of it. In the course of turn-by-turn talk a participant produces a description of a car he would like to build (L.11–12) "the *ho*ttest street machine in West L.A." In his next utterance he names a car against which his would compete for such a status (L.15) "'N *cha*llenge *Voo*doo to a race." And the story is about the car called Voodoo (L.45–77). It is possible that the descriptive phrase is specifically a title—a category which at any given time has a single current incumbent, determined by means of contest, and Voodoo is that category's current incumbent, such that the category, used as a descriptor, has evoked a story about its incumbent.

With the premise that the Voodoo story is triggered at lines 11–12, a series of approaches to and veerings away from a storytelling can be sketched in which it appears that the story will not be told unless coparticipant aligns himself as recipient of talk about Voodoo.

While the naming of Voodoo (L.15) might serve as a basis for topical talk (cf. F.7 and F.16.L.3ff.), or set up a same-speaker story introduction via a disjunct plus embedded repetition (cf. F.2 and F.3) or a version of the Speaking of X format (cf. F.16.L.24ff.), features of the next several utterances suggest that in this case teller provides a trigger for his *coparticipant* and thereafter, consecutively, produces talk by reference to (*a*) the potential initiation of further talk about Voodoo by coparticipant, and (*b*) its nonoccurrence.

(*a*) Latched to the sentence in which Voodoo is named is a next sentence which embeds the naming into ongoing topical talk.(L.15–17) "I *m*ean the *hell* with *d*rag strips. . ." is topically coherent with prior talk, proposing a contrast between dragstrip racing (cf. L.2. "competition use") and street racing (L.11.; cf. also L.113–116).

The positioning of this sentence is systematically vulnerable to overlap by coparticipant, since triggered talk by a noncurrent speaker routinely is initiated in overlap with the utterance-part adjacent to the trigger word. So, for example, fragment (1) contains an overlapping disjunct plus repetition story introduction (L.6–7) and the following fragment has an overlapping disjunct plus repetition query (F.26.L.7) which is followed not only by further talk about the triggered topic (L.8) but by a story (L.9).

[MC:I:14]   (26)

LIL:	I still say that the sewing machine's quicker,	1
HARMON:	Oh it c'n be quicker but it doesn' do the jo:b,	2

```
LIL:          Oh really, We:ll,                                        3
              [
HARMON:                   Not– Not like I c'n do it,                  4
LIL:          Well I, I (  )                                          5
              [
● HARMON:                 with my little ha:: nds,                    6
                          [
● LIL:                                    Say how's yer little boy,   7
HARMON:  Oh he's fi:ne. He's just fine (              he's–) hheh     8
         something. 'hh I, I bought im a pair'v underpants
         [STORY]                                                     9
```

(b) Coparticipant offers neither story nor query in the course of the continuing utterance. If this utterance reaches completion, a transition-relevance place will occur, a place where coparticipant can produce a next utterance, one which is topically coherent with the prior (in this case, e.g., further talk about competition versus street racing).

Just prior to completion, teller cuts off (L.16–17) ". . . you gotta have ten thous'n bucks ready t'spe–." A cutoff in a nonoverlapped utterance is a recognizable initiator of self-repair (cf. Jefferson, 1974, pp. 185–188 and Schegloff et al., 1976, pp. 9–10), which means that a repair of an error in the utterance-so-far will follow. As a consequence of the repair, transition will be delayed beyond its initially projected point, and thus coparticipant should delay initiation of his next utterance.

Latched to the cutoff is, not a repair, but a new sentence (cf. F.17.L.7–9), a reissue of a prior utterance (L.17–18; cf. also L.11–12) " 'hh I wanna build a hot street machine." [18] Thus, in the absence of coparticipant-initiated further talk about Voodoo, teller returns to the point at which the story was triggered, and thereafter, Voodoo is named again (L.23–24) ". . .en challenge, anybody to a go, heh'hh th'Road Runner Voodoo hehh. . . ." [19]

Again, it appears that teller offers coparticipant a chance to initiate further talk about Voodoo and thereafter consecutively talks by reference to (a) the potential nonoccurrence and (b) the actual occurrence of such an initiation.

(a) Latched to the sentence in which Voodoo is renamed is a disjunct plus story introduction in which a car is identified. The car is not Voodoo. If it were, then the slot in which identification is occurring—i.e., (L.26) ". . . a twenny sev'n. . ." would contain a repetition of "Voodoo" (cf. F.1.L.8, F.2.L.8, F.3.L.3, F.4.L.2, F.5.L.1, and F.16.L.29). That is, teller is recognizably initiating another story, perhaps specifically as a substitute for, and literally in the place of, the Voodoo story. Again, this utterance is vulnerable to overlap by coparticipant, should he, now, choose to initiate further talk about Voodoo.

(b) Simultaneously with the substitute story, coparticipant initiates a disjunct plus query (L.25.; cf. also F.26.L.7) "Ey wuh–," cuts off as teller produces a prespeech inbreath (cf. note 10), and recycles and completes the query (L.27) "*What's* the Voodoo," at a 'recognition point' in the identification component (cf. Jefferson, 1973, pp. 56–69 and F.2.L.9–11) thus, aligning himself as a recipient of information about Voodoo. Thereupon, teller abandons the substitute story (L.26) and initiates a response to recipient's request (L.31, cf. F.16a.L.45–50).

While the response to recipient's query might constitute a piece of information, it is also a 'superlative assessment' (L.32–33) ". . .the *Voo*doo[20] is the *f*astest car, I've ever seen, inna streets." Superlative assessments belong to a class of objects which can elicit a "newsmark" or "solicit" from a coparticipant (cf. Terasaki, 1975). Recipient may produce general tokens like "Really?" "No kidding,' etc., or tokens fitted to a prior utterance, for example, (F.16a.L.42 and 48) "He done it *pur*posely." "*Pur*posely?" Such tokens align coparticipant as a recipient of whatever is to follow. So, for example, in fragment (3), a similarly structured superlative assessment[21] receives a fitted newsmark/solicit.

LOTTIE: . . .she gave me the most *beau*tiful *swim*suit you've
          ever seen in yer life.
EMMA: *Gave* it to yuh?

However, recipient does not offer such a token. Instead, he recycles his request for information (L.35; cf.L.27) "What *is* it." thus aligning himself, not as a recipient of whatever is to follow, perhaps a story (cf. F.26), but as a recipient of information. And teller produces information about Voodoo, an elaborate technical description of the car's features (L.37ff.). Teller caps the description with an escalated recycle of the superlative assessment (L.42–43; cf.L.32–33) "An' it wuz *thee* fastest car. I've ever seen in th'streets."

This can constitute a next chance for recipient to offer a solicit (cf. L.24 vis-à-vis L.15), and again, teller's subsequent talk may be produced by reference to the potential occurrence or nonoccurrence of a delayed solicit (cf.L.25–27). Following the escalated recycle of a story prefatory superlative assessment is a secondary preface (L.45) " 'hh I'll *t*ell you something." Should recipient overlap with a solicit, the secondary preface can be abandoned. Should he not, the secondary preface is one of a range of utterances which serve as story prefixes (cf.F.8–15)[22] and the story can appropriately occur with no observable absence of a solicit, directly thereafter.[23] Recipient offers no solicit and, upon completion of the secondary preface, teller initiates the story proper (L.45) ". . .there wz a big *d*rag (in out'n) the Valley?"

Thus, over a series of utterances, coparticipant is aligned as teller's recipient, but not as a story recipient. When the story is told, it is told on a volunteer basis, and this may have consequences for the story's sequential implicativeness.

At the story's completion, teller engages in a search for recipient response. He produces a prototypical story-ending device (L.73; cf.F.18.L.1) "Turns around and goes home." This is followed by a pause (L.74), a token of appreciation (L.75) and another pause (L.76). Thereafter, he offers a prototypical telling-ending device, an assessment (L.77; cf.F.18.L.3) "*I* gained a lotta res*p*ect fer *th*at car" which is followed by a token of appreciation (L.79). Over a series of recycled completion points, then, turn-by-turn talk has yet to be re-engaged; the story's sequential implicativeness is yet to be demonstrated.

Teller produces a story tag (L.81–85) which is topically coherent with, and upon its occurrence can be seen to have been projected by, the sort of technical talk which preceded the story (L.37ff., particularly L.37–38 "and it has, it *ha*:d. . ."). Recipient's subsequent talk is consistent with the story tag's technical aspects (L.89–94). Although it is *consistent with* and thus demonstrates a sequential implicativeness of the story tag, and via the tag, of the story itself, recipient's talk is *intensely fitted to* the utterance elicited by his recycled request for information (cf. L.37–42).

Both utterances follow the same format. Both start with a car's year and make (L.37) "It's a *f*ifty five *C*hevvy" and (L.91) "It's a *s*ixty one Ford" and both run through a list of components in identical order: *engine* (L.39) "a three twenty seven *Vet*" and (L.91–92) "a three ninety bored out to four ten," *carburetor* (L.40) "dual quads" and (L.92) "two four barrels," *cam* (L.40) "full roller cam" and (L.92) "straight (differn) cam", *transmission* (L.41) "four speed neon hydrostick" and (L.93) "four speed closed spline," *traction* (L.41) "four fifty six positraction" and (L.93) "four fifty six," and *tires* (L.42) "big slicks" and (L.94) "big slicks."[24] Thus, it is the utterance specifically requested by recipient to which his subsequent talk is fitted; that is, his alignment prior to the story's telling is powerfully preserved in his response to it. Further, the response tacitly disputes Voodoo's status; that is, the story, which depicts an unsurpassable combination of car and driver in action, is encapsulated by technical talk in which a car is adequately characterized as a set of components, and via such a characterization, recipient's "sixty one Ford" is comparable, perhaps equivalent, to teller's "fifty five Chevvy."

It appears that teller's subsequent talk, at least in part, disputes recipient's treatment of the story and its protagonist. Voodoo is mentioned once more; this time as a basis for comparion with yet another car, a "twenty seven Tee" (L.128; cf. L.26), which is announced as "faster than Voodoo" (L.122). While the comparison proposes Voodoo as the lesser car by reference to one feature—speed—it establishes a context in which implicit comparison is provided for two other features relevant to Voodoo's status; that is, relevant to incumbency in the category The Hottest Street Machine in West L.A. By reference to those two features, the twenty seven Tee is not a candidate incumbent. It is neither from the relevant area (L.124–126) "He *ac*tually doesn't *li*ve around here," nor, crucially, is it a proper street machine, but a competition car illegitimately driven in the streets (L.129–133) "And *he* drives it in the *stree*:ts. Guy's an *ass*hole." By implicit comparison, Voodoo re-emerges as best in its class, where, further, its class is to be seen as the better class (cf., e.g., L.113).

These sorts of considerations yield an extended fragment of conversation as heavily occupied by activities relevant to the telling of a story, where the story itself occupies but a portion of that fragment.

NOTES

[1] This is a revised version of a paper presented at Seminars in Ethnomethodology, Graduate Center, City University of New York, April 1973. Great appreciation is extended to Doug Maynard, Candy West, Tom Wilson, Don Zimmerman, and Roger Mandlebaum.

[2] Several of Harvey Sacks' unpublished lectures deal with storytelling in conversation, for example, Lectures 1–8, Spring 1970 and Lectures 1–16, Fall 1971. (A version of Lectures 9–12, Fall 1971, appears in this volume under the title "A Technical Consideration of a Dirty Joke.") There are numerous references to Sacks' work in this paper. These are best treated, not so much as support for an argument, but as pointers to very interesting talk.

[3] There is preliminary evidence that a story not only articulates with turn-by-turn talk at its edges, but throughout. Roughly, a story is not, in principle, a block of talk, but is constructed of "segments" via which teller's talk can alternate with recipient's. The segmental construction of the story itself will be considered in a later report.

[4] The pair of features, local occasioning and sequential implicativeness, are regularly present in a single utterance; that is, a methodic display of local "occasionedness" is also a demonstration of the sequential implicativeness of a prior. Since this paper tends to treat the story as protagonist, focusing on its emergence from and re-engagement of turn-by-turn talk, the *inter*relationship of prior talk to story to subsequent talk is obscured.

[5] Topical coherence is roughly defined as a current utterance standing in an appropriate, continuous relationship to ongoing talk; cf. Sacks (1968, April 17).

[6] Abbreviations refer to fragments (F) contained in this chapter and their respective line numbers (L).

[7] Routinely, the marked repeat is followed by an embedded repetition. It appears that the disjunct marker and the Speaking of X device perform a similar task, and *placement* is criterial to selection between the two. The disjunct is used prior to completion of the utterance containing the trigger word (cf. F.1–3) and a Speaking of X is used after completion of that utterance (for F.4. cf. F.25.L.96, data not shown for F.5., see also F.16.L.24).

[8] Next positioning is a basic device for relating two utterances (cf., e.g., Sacks 1972b, Lecture 4). Disjunct-marked overlap and postcompletion Speaking of X may be used for triggered talk because without such devices the "next" positioning of an utterance can lead coparticipants to monitor it as topically coherent with prior talk; cf. Sacks (1968, April 17).

[9] The repetition may have been *removed* from an earlier to a later position. At lines 10–12 there is a shift in person reference, "So Lance k– So:, *one* guy bought a dollar fifty worth of Ripple." While the shift could be a repair of reference-type, from known-to-coparticipant to unknown-to-coparticipant (cf. Sacks, 1971, Lecture 5), at line 20 it appears that Lance is not the one who ordered Ripple, but the one who ordered glue, "Planning on gettin *ga*:ssed. *Huh* Lance." Thus, the shift in person reference may be a matter of reorganizing the story's events and the actors associated with those events.

[10] "Thought" is a sequencing object, a 'first verb', which implicates a next, "realized" (cf. Sacks, 1968, May 2 and 1970, Lecture 2). Its occurrence in lines 30–31 positions speaker in a series of activities, in this case, as prior to the order of glue.

[11] These fragments were collected as instances of single-turn story-entry devices for next speaker (F.8–11) and current speaker (F.12–15). When the collection was examined, it was noticed that in seven of the eight cases (F.8–14) some form of *perturbation* occurred adjacent to the entry device. Schegloff is noticing regularities in the occurrence of perturbation, for example, upon resolution of overlap and at various unit-initial positions (personal communication). It appears that perturbation occurs at junctures between discrete activity types, and its presence can serve as an index to junctures between discrete activities in otherwise apparently continuous activities like 'story preface' and 'story entry'. Another phenomenon which may indicate activity junctures is the *audible inbreath* (cf., e.g., F.1.L.8; F.2.L.12; F.3.L.1; F.7.L.10,12; F.12.L.3, etc.).

[12] This fragment and others designated "GTS" are taken from a series of group therapy sessions recorded in 1964 with teenage patients and an adult therapist. A feature of the therapy setting which may be relevant here is that it is one in which business is done, that business superseding personal talk, but in which some forms of personal talk constitute business talk and thus the relevance and admissibility of personal talk may be problematic. In this case it appears that personal talk is superseded by nonpersonal but recognizably "therapeutic" talk.

[13] The 'request' operation of postcompletion "So" is among the phenomena being considered in the forthcoming report on story segmenting (cf. note 3).

[14] In a consideration of gossip, Sacks notes that person attributes are expandable from an individual to related others (cf., e.g., Sacks, 1967b, Lecture 2), those others being co-members of some "membership categorization device" category (cf., e.g., Sacks, 1972). Fragment (19) may not only constitute an instance of such an expansion, but may locate a context in which it would routinely occur; i.e., in a series of story-exit devices. If the story is about an individual, recognizably related talk can be found by application of the device "family." Or, for example, if, as in fragment (18), a story is about a teenage car club, recognizably related talk can be found by application of the device "age group" which yields "kids" (L.22).

[15] A question is a prototypical Adjacency Pair first pair-part, an object which has powerful sequential implicativeness (cf., e.g., Sacks, 1972. Lectures 1 and 4).

[16] "There" refers to a weight-loss organization to which teller, tangential speaker, and story protagonist belong.

[17] The notation " ↑*thee*" (F.25.L.121) is used to indicate higher pitch and amplitude than "*thee*" (L.42). It appears that the shift in intonation contour is analogous to the immediately subsequent lexical unit "Faster than Voodoo" (L.122), that is, is produced by reference to a distanced prior. Cf., for example, Sacks (1967, Lecture 13) and (1972, Lecture 4).

[18] A repair initiator produced just prior to possible completion, followed by a new sentence, may be one solution to the "two-sentence problem" (Sacks, 1969, Lecture 9); that is, a second sentence is produced without a first ever having reached completion.

[19] There is a difference between lines 17–18 and 23–24 which permits the following consideration. The second occurrence bears no traces of, and perhaps specifically masks, the trigger mechanism (cf. F.16); that is, the descriptor "a hot street machine" is not a category with an exclusive incumbent, but one which can contain multiples, and the contest is no longer with one car, which might be the prior category's exclusive incumbent, but with "*any*body," with more than one instance of "anybody" provided ("the Road Runner" and "Voodoo").

[20] Teller, in his initial references to the car, calls it "Voodoo" (L.15 and 24). Coparticipant, in his query, calls it "the Voodoo" (L.27), and teller, in his response, calls it "the Voodoo" (L.32). Technically, this series constitutes an 'unmarked correction sequence' which has as criterial features that, for a same referent, (*a*) a current speaker uses a term; (*b*) a next speaker uses an alternate term; and (*c*) prior speaker uses the alternate term. The abstract format is [X]–[Y]–[Y]. It appears in actual sequences like the following: For an identification of law enforcement officers [police]–[cops]–[cops], for an identification of the ridges on a metal pipe [wales]–[threads]–[threads].

[GTS:2:2:60]   (27)

KEN:	. . .the police have said this to us.	1
ROGER:	*That* makes it even *bet*ter. The *cha*llenge of runnin	2
	from the *cops!*	3
KEN:	The cops *say* if you wanna race, uh go out at four or	4
	five in the morning on the freeway . . .	5

[J:FN:Hardware Store]   (28)

CUSTOMER:	((examining a length of pipe)) Mm, the wales are wider	1
	apart than that.	2
SALESMAN:	Okay, let me see if I can find one with wider threads.	3
	((selects another piece of pipe)) How's this.	4
CUSTOMER:	Nope, the threads are even wider than that.	5

The offer and acceptance of a [Y] is embedded into ongoing talk; that is, the replacement is done in unmarked form. In fragment (25), teller's acceptance of coparticipant's [Y] may be a matter of accommodating a not quite correct usage, the accommodation done by reference to the pair of relevant categories—candidate storyteller vis-à-vis candidate story recipient. Teller's accommodation of recipient's misuse is preserved in the story itself; that is, when the car is first mentioned (L.53) it is "the Voodoo," but is abandoned at the story's climax (L.66) "*Here* comes Voodoo," and the final reference (L.122) is to "Voodoo."

[21] For a consideration of assessments as sequenced objects, see Pomerantz (1975) and (1977).

[22] Preliminary inspection of conversational data indicates that a range of constructs like "I'll tell you something" and their request-correlate "Tell me something" occur as prefixes with no place provided for a solicit.

[23] While superlative assessments *can* initiate a sequence in which a storytelling is requested by recipient, that potential is not always utilized by teller, who can move directly from preface to story, for example, in fragment (16), someone attempting to talk after a superlative assessment (L.29) "And they *are* stars *my* God," finds that teller has already started the story (cf. also F.25.L.81). But there are conditions under which a preface can be seen as a failed attempt to get a solicit. For example, in fragment (14), a superlative assessment (L.1) "But nobody fought with her like *I* fought with her" is followed by a substantial pause (L.2) and a secondary preface, one which does not admit the relevance of a solicit (L.3) "for example." The secondary preface may constitute a repair of the initial preface's failure to get a solicit. Fragment (25) shares features with both fragment (16) and fragment (14); that is, while teller does not provide a place for a solicit, he does produce a secondary preface which can be abandoned if a solicit occurs or can be directly followed by the story if a solicit does not occur, with no recognizable failure present.

[24] These two segments, with their series of proper nouns, are a transcriber's nightmare (cf. Sacks, 1967b, Lecture 12). A noun may be heard as an unintelligible sound, for example, F.25.L.92 "straight (differn) cam," and F.21.L.3. "So I met her at (*Prom*tiers)." Worse, it may be heard as perfectly intelligible and turn out to be misheard. For example, over multiple rehearings, F.25.L.41 was heard as "four fifty six poundsa traction." Rich Frankel mentioned that it ought to be "positraction." On rehearing it was, unequivocally, "positraction." Further, a name may be correctly heard, but not understood. So, for example, although the two segments were seen to be closely fitted, they did not appear to be so utterly equivalent until Frankel pointed out that (L.40) "dual quads" and (L.92) "two four barrels" have the same referrent.

chapter 10

Some Technical Considerations of a Dirty Joke*

HARVEY SACKS

I'm going to give a presentation that will involve an analysis of a dirty joke,[1] eventually leading up to a theory of some of the business of dirty jokes. Roughly, I want to make a case for the dirty joke as a technical object worth attention. One way I think of this investigation is under a title like "A Detoxification Program for Dirty Jokes." Which is to say, while one might imagine that dirty jokes are kind of frivolous objects, or that what's interesting about dirty jokes is necessarily the ways that they're dirty, I will suggest that there may be ways in which that's not so;

---

* The materials that appear here were originally delivered as four consecutive lectures to an undergraduate social science class at the University of California at Irvine during November of 1971. They have been edited by Gail Jefferson into a condensed and continuous presentation and are published here posthumously. Harvey Sacks routinely taped his lectures and had them transcribed. Initially this was a way to organize his materials, but it subsequently developed into an informal publication system distributing his lectures and other unpublished manuscripts free of charge to anyone who asked for them. A large collection of his transcribed lectures and other manuscripts are available and will be published shortly (Sacks: forthcoming) [J. S.].

that they are serious technical sources of information (and not merely, at all, sexual information). We'll get to that kind of a position rather later on.

To start off, I want to argue the artfulness of this joke. By its artfulness I mean that not only is it, as you'll see, elaborately organized, but that some aspects of its elaborate organization can be found to be occupied with the following kind of job: concealing some of the ways the joke works on its recipients from those recipients, while directing them to attend it in rather sharp ways. I'll begin with an overview of some sorts of organization the joke has, and then proceed to take it apart rather more closely. The joke goes like this:

[GTS:II:2:16]

KEN:	You wanna hear– My sister told me a story last night.
ROGER:	I don't wanna hear it. But if you must.
	(0.7)
AL:	What's purple and an island. Grape, Britain. That's what his sister told him.
KEN:	*No.* To *stun* me she says uh,
	(0.8)
KEN:	There was these three girls and they just got married?
ROGER:	hhhh–hhh
AL:	heh heh heh
	[[
KEN:	And uh,
KEN:	(They were)
	[[
ROGER:	Hey waita second. Drag that by again heh
KEN:	There was these three girls. And they were all sisters. And they'd just got married to three *bro*thers.
ROGER:	You better have a long talk with your sister.
AL:	Waita second heh!
ROGER:	*Oh.* Three *bro*thers.
KEN:	And uh, so,
AL:	The brothers of these sisters.
KEN:	No they're *dif*ferent you know *dif*ferent families.
ROGER:	That's closer than be*fore* (I think).
KEN:	So–
	[[

AL: hhhh*hah*
                     (0.7)
KEN: *Qui*et.
AL: °(   )
KEN: So, *first* of all, that night they're on their honeymoon the mother in law says well why don't you all spend the night here and then you can go on your honeymoon in the morning. The *f*irst night, the mother walks up to the first door and she hears this "*uu*ooo–ooo–ooo," second door is *"HHHOHHhhh,"* third door there's *NO*thin. She stands there for about twenty five minutes waitin for somethin to happen. *N*othin.
                     (1.0)
KEN: Next morning she talks to the first daughter and she says "How come you– how come you went *YAAAaaa* last night" and the daughter says "Well it *ti*ckled, Mommy." Second girl, "How come you *scre*amed." "*Oh, Mo*mmy it *hu*rts." Third girl, walks up to her. "Why didn't you *say* anything last night." "Well *you* told me it was always impolite to talk with my mouth full."
                     (1.3)
KEN: hhhhyok hyok. Hyok.
                     (2.5)
AL: *HA–A–A–A!*
KEN: heh–heh–huh–huh
ROGER: Delayed reaction.
AL: I had to think about it awhile you know?
ROGER: Sure.
                     (1.0)
ROGER: hih heh You mean the *deep* hidden *m*eaning there doesn't *h*it you right away heh
AL: hhih
             [[
(DAN):   (It's pretty interesting.)
AL: What he *m*eant to say is that– that um,
ROGER: Kinda got psychological overtones.
KEN: Little sister's gettin older.
AL: eh–hih–hih

KEN: yihh hih–hih That's what I *m*ean to say.
DAN: *Sounds* like it.
KEN: For twelve years old tellin me– *I* didn't even
              know–
ROGER: How do you know she's just not repeating
              what she heard and doesn't know what it
              means.
AL: Did she have to explain it to you Ken?
KEN: Yeah she had to explain it in detail to me,
AL: Okay Ken, glad you got a sister that knows
              somethin.
KEN: She told me she was eatin a hot dog,
                   (3.0)
ROGER: What does *th*at mean.
AL: Yeah come on. Explain it to us. Explain–
KEN: *I DON'T KNOW* I just said that.
              [[
AL: Explain everything you know, Ken.
AL: Explain everything.[2]

A first, very gross pair of related facts is that the joke is both
temporally and sequentially organized. With regard to its *temporal* organization, it has the "canonical form for narratives"; i.e., the story
proceeds in a simple temporal order, an order which might be seen to be
directly preserving the temporal format of the events it reports. But we
have to keep very well in mind, and I won't let you forget it, that it's made
up. There weren't such events. And in that regard it *adopts* a format
which such events might have. With regard to its *sequential* organization,
it is constructed such that an appreciation of some point in it turns on an
appreciation of its position as subsequent to some other point. For example, in these materials "next morning" and the events thereof, requires
for its understanding that there was a "first night" with its events.

The two types of organization are distinct, that is, one could have a
sequential organization which did not employ the format of events-in-
order which temporal organization provides, e.g., "The mother stood at
the third door and heard nothing, after having heard sounds at the first two
doors." And one could have a temporal organization which did not
employ the connectedness which sequential organization provides, e.g.,
"At 11:39 p.m. Mrs. Smith stood at Nancy's door and heard a sound. At
11:40 p.m. Mrs. Smith stood at Sally's door and heard a sound. At 11:41
p.m. Mrs. Smith stood at Carol's door and heard nothing." In combination, these two types of organization can do a range of jobs. And one of

those jobs, which we'll get to in due course, is to array events in such a fashion as to have an otherwise extraordinarily implausible series of events appear plausible.

Now the body of the joke is composed of two sequences, the "first night" sequence and the "next morning" sequence, and the two are specifically sequentially connected, not only by their titles, but by such features as, e.g., it appears that the mother interrogates the daughters in the second sequence in the same order she investigated the doors in the first. The "first night" sequence yields a puzzle and the "next morning" sequence yields a solution to the puzzle (where that itself is an ordered business; first puzzle, then solution). And the solution is nicely positioned; i.e., its occurrence matches the arrival at the joke's punch line. We want to see that the arrival at the story's puzzle solution and the joke's punch line with that kind of fit might take some kind of constructional work; i.e., there could be a puzzle posed at some point in a story and a solution to the puzzle positioned at some point in that story. If the thing is also a joke, the punch line of the joke will occur somewhere relative to the solution of the puzzle. A more or less perfect meshing would involve that the punch line of the joke is the same event as the solution to the story's puzzle. We have, then, a story structure-type perfectly co-operating with a joke structure-type in these two sequences.

We'll start with the first sequence.

KEN: The *first* night, the mother walks up to the first door and she hears this "*uu*ooo–ooo–ooo," second door is "*HHHOHHhhh,*" third door there's *NO*thin. She stands there for about twenty five minutes waitin for somethin to happen. *No*thin.

First of all this looks like simply an ordering of the mother's behavior relative to a series of doors behind which we know are the newly married couples, where this just happens to be the order in which she approaches the doors. But on close inspection we find that the sequence's components are "sequentially organized in fine detail." And by that I mean, e.g., the mother "walks up to" the first door, "and she hears this" sound. She doesn't "walk up to" the second door, and she doesn't "hear this" sound; it's just reported as "second door is *HHHOHHhhh.*" We employ the description of events at the first door to understand that object, and find that there was a second event which was identical to the first, except for a difference in the sound itself. We don't get, or need, the whole description repeated for the second event, nor for the third, "Third door there's *NO*thin.'' (We'll see this detailed sequential organization operating in a more elaborate way in the second sequence.)

This array of events provides the mother with a puzzle: Why no sound at the third door? Now there is a constructional element to the puzzle sequence (which appears as well in the solution sequence) and that is the use of three components in a particular order: two sounds followed by one silence. This is an ideal construction; a perfect economical use of a number of components to get a puzzle; i.e., it turns out that you need *at least* three to get the silence as a puzzle, and you also need *no more than* three to get the silence as a puzzle. Suppose there were two daughters; at the first door sound, at the second door silence. So? One was sound and one was silence. There's no particular issue as to why there was silence; we could equally well wonder why there was sound. But the two sounds suffice to make the silence noticeable. And you don't need four, five, or eleven doors—the mother goes to each door, ten of them she hears sounds, by the eleventh, if she got silence we'd say "Huh! Wonder why that was." Three suffice. Three is the minimal but sufficient number for making the minority event peculiar and therefore focusable-on as a puzzle. And the arrangement which has the silence occurring last works to build up an appreciation of the expectable, normal, majority character of the sounds.

The mother gets a puzzle from this sequence. Now think of the figure of "the mother" as something like a shill in the story to direct its recipient's attention; to lead its recipient to hear the story in certain ways, so that if the mother is puzzled, then the recipient can come to adopt that puzzle as his own. Though a recipient thinks of "the mother" as a person, we want to see "the mother" as something operating as a guide for this story. How does "the mother" operate as a guide? There's apparently a merely temporal ordering to her going to the doors, and there is no statement in the story of what she's interested in. But her interest is very powerfully conveyed by her behavior. She goes to the first door and, as soon as she gets there, she hears a sound and then directly proceeds to the second door where, again as soon as she gets there, she hears a sound and then directly proceeds to the third door where she hears nothing when she gets there, waits, and still hears nothing. This collection of events and behaviors leads us to see that what she's interested in are the sounds, and what then puzzles her is the absence of sounds.

Plainly one could have a story where she goes to the first door and hears a sound, and then stands there listening for some extended period of time, and a whole range of happenings could be reported. By the fact that at each door where she hears a sound she moves promptly on, we know that she's interested in hearing some sound. And her nonchalantly received luck of encountering the sounds at the moment she arrives at the first two doors sets up a consistency under which, at the third door, she (and a recipient) can become puzzled immediately. And that immediacy, for one, provides that the extended wait at the third door becomes an observable additional event and thus underscores the oddness of the silence. So, from the way the story reports on the mother's movements, and on what seems adequate to have her move on or stop, we get the puzzle she has. Further, we get *only* the puzzle she has, and not other possible puzzles; for example, it could be quite puzzling, could seem quite implausible, that at the first two doors we get a sound then and there. But since there is no issue for "the mother," e.g., she doesn't wonder if each couple is waiting for her arrival at the door, whereupon they issue a sound, then there is no issue for us as recipients of the story. And by the end of the first sequence we know that the puzzle is, and is exclusively, why no sound at the third door.

Now to the second sequence.

KEN: Next morning she talks to the first daughter and she says "How come you– how come you went *YAAAaaa* last night" and the daughter says "Well it *ti*ckled, Mommy." Second girl, "How come you *scre*amed." "*Oh, Mo*mmy it *hu*rts." Third girl, walks up to her, "Why didn't you *say* anything last night." "Well *you* told me it was always impolite to talk with my mouth full."

As I said, the second sequence specifically connects to the first via its use of "next morning," and now we get, again, an apparently natural sequence: first daughter, then second, then third. And here we find another instance of the potentially implausible consistency I mentioned with regard to sound-upon-arrival at the first two doors. Here, while we don't know from the first sequence, we learn from the second, that each of the sounds was produced by a daughter, although we know that there were two people in each room, and presumably at least one of the sounds could have been made by a son-in-law. The sounds are unremarkably exclusively the daughters' sounds. Now the apparently natural sequence is given as a temporal thing (i.e., the exchanges are reported in an order in which they are to be supposed to have occurred) and it works as a sequential thing (i.e., we employ features of a prior event to understand a subsequent). So, e.g., while "she talks to" the first daughter "and she says" the question, for the second we simply get "Second girl, 'How come you screamed.' '' The absence of the temporal locator "last night" in the second question is of interest. It tells us that the question is addressed to someone who has been a listener to the first exchange. Imagine this question asked in isolation: "How come you screamed?" Such a statement properly occurs when somebody has just screamed, and she hasn't just screamed. That it's last night's scream which is being asked about is found by reference to the question to the first daughter and that one's answer, which the second daughter, we now understand, has heard.

The copresence of the parties is kind of crucial, not just to getting the second daughter to know what's being asked, but to getting the third daughter to know what's being asked, because in a way, the question being asked her is rather more bizarre yet. "How come you didn't say anything last night?" In the first place, the reappearance of the temporal locator might be designed to solve a special problem raised by this particular question; a problem which the temporal/sequential array might not solve; i.e., the one to whom this question is directed has, just now, been silent; hasn't said anything, and thus this question is positioned after an instance of the activity it's asking about. "Last night" locates the silence being asked about, and excludes the current one. But even with "last night" as a resource, well, that's a large span of time, and third daughter presumably could refer to any number of things she did say at any point in it. But she knows what's being asked about, and knows it, in part, by virtue of the questions that have been asked the others, and the answers they've given.

The first daughter says "it tickled" and the second daughter says "it hurts." Both use a same format for answering, in which there is a something-or-other "it" which has no prior-named referent, which nevertheless permits of a common interpretation; that interpretability in part provided by earlier information (that they just got married, that it was the "first night," etc.). That is, the answers so far have been consistent with regard to their allusion to sexual activity. And this common interpretability permits of an interpretation of the third answer, as well. In the first place, "Well you told me it was always impolite to talk with my mouth full" itself poses a puzzle as to what could this be talking about. The so-far-consistently-applicable sexual interpretation of the prior two answers sets up an interpretability of the third which makes its puzzle "what, sexually, could this be talking about?" And the solution to that puzzle is extractable from the answer.

This is another instance of the unremarked consistency we've been picking up throughout this story. Again, were this a series of actual events, then it's perfectly possible that, instead of, e.g., "it hurts," the answer would be "I stubbed my toe." But the intrusion of such an event into the story would be problematic for the common interpretability of the first two answers; where the common interpretability of the first two is needed to set up the interpretability and thus the solvability of the third.

It turns out that such a consistency is characteristic for stories and yields the kind of starkness which stories tend to have. In a book on Gogol, Nabokov has a beautiful discussion of this phenomenon. He considers it in terms of conventions in fiction, particularly in the theater. In the discussion, Nabokov is talking about one of the things that Gogol did to Western literature, and he says something like this. Before Gogol, if, when the curtain rises, there's a gun on the mantlepiece, you can be sure the gun will go off before the end of the play. Or, if, at the beginning of the play, one of the characters says "I wonder what happened to Uncle Harry. He's been in Africa all these years," you can be sure that Uncle Harry will turn up. Now, what Gogol did was to introduce characters into his fiction who were mentioned in a paragraph and never appeared again. And if you think of the development of the literature of the Absurd, one characteristic feature of it is this sort of de-economizing, where events occur and have nothing to do with anything except that they occur. The consequence is taking, e.g., a detective story as a model, you can't then latch onto anything to know "If I take good account of this, then it will turn out to matter." In the joke we are examining, each event turns out to matter.[3]

So. The joke employs a series of cooccurrent coincidences which turn out to be organizationally crucial; i.e., without them we wouldn't have the joke. That they all happen together, just as they're needed, is rather implausible. For the joke to come off, it is central that they not be attended to as implausible coincident events. Now, this kind of harkens to a really ancient theme in the construction of things with storylike form; i.e., something like Aristotle's notion that we engage in a "willing suspension of disbelief." Now the notion that what we do is willingly suspend disbelief is, if actual stories are examined, nonsense. The thing to see is that while, for the story to come off, we may need to accept its events, the story is in the first place built in such a way as to have it not occur to us that "this is implausible but we shall suspend disbelief." And the thing then is to look to see in what ways a recipient is *led* to not have that occur.

The canonical temporal ordering; i.e., the sheer narration of the thing as having happened in just this order, does some of that work. The burden of work, however, seems to be accomplished in the following way. I've made a good deal of the fact that the story is intensely sequentially constructed. Now this means that a recipient is engaged in doing a job of analysis on, say, roughly, each sentence of the story. He is continually engaged in figuring out what each sentence means, using the prior-so-far and what it looks like it's developing into, to do that work. And, having done that work, a recipient finds himself in a position of indeed understanding the story so far; i.e., the story's sequential organization poses jobs whose success is demonstrable when the next thing happens and is understood.

Furthermore, there are characters in the thing who seem to be doing a parallel task, and in that they seem to understand what's going on, and the recipient can find that he can understand it in the way that the parties seem to, then the parties' understandings can serve as further confirmation that the recipient is doing the right sort of work on it. It's imaginable that a recipient, having no guide as to the work he must do, might, e.g., engage in a consideration of the implausibility of some collection of components, or, e.g., become interested in alternative possible interpretations of "ambiguous" references. Notice, for example, that this joke's recipients, at what is perhaps a prototypically as-yet-unguided moment in the story, the introductory sentence, "There was these three girls and they just got married," are free to find an alternate sense of it, and treat it as ". . . they just got married to each other." But, in part, the behavior of the characters acts as a guide. So, for example, there are plenty of places the characters could be puzzled. The girls could be altogether puzzled as to what's being inquired of them, or how the mother came to be in a position to ask, or, e.g., given an answer like "it tickled" the mother could perfectly well wonder what tickled. But there is a sufficiency to these things by virtue of the fact that nobody in the scene questions them. If one of the characters at some point said "What are you asking me about?" or "How did you know what was happening last night?" or "What tickled?" then it would be available for a recipient to notice the problematic aspect of those events.

Crucially, both the temporal/sequential organization of the joke and the behavior of its characters, guide a recipient to see a particular puzzle as the joke's puzzle, and to take on as a task the solving of that puzzle. In the course of the joke, one is not ever in a position to assess the complex of its components, but is fully occupied in understanding it, piece by piece, so that, arriving at its end, one can solve the punch line as fast as possible. This is a critical task posed for a joke's recipient. And it is characteristic for jokes, and present in this one, that while the puzzle is solvable from the punch line, the solution isn't asserted in the punch line but will have to be interpreted out of it. That is, the third daughter's answer is not itself a solution to the puzzle. It's what does the answer *mean* that's a solution to the puzzle. And recipient's task is to "get" what the answer means. It is not only a task provided by the array of events, but, since failing to "get" the joke can be treated as, e.g., a sign of one's lack of sophistication, then the social circumstances, as well, urge a recipient to be working to find what the punch line means. And from the joke's beginning, that will be the test of him. Recipients will be working to come up with an interpretation of the punch line which they can exhibit by, e.g., laughing, and laughing as soon as possible. And the whole thing is over as soon as they've laughed.

Thus, while the joke needs a total concatenation of events which can thereby have an extraordinary implausibility, it need not be left to whether people will or will not grant their plausibility. Recipients can have their minds directed in ways that will involve them in not at all seeing an implausibility. There can be no room in the story to engage in assessing its plausibility when it emerges sequentially, piece by piece; one is hearing it as it's being told, going through it and understanding it, and seeing that it's characters are understanding it as one is understanding it. In these ways a recipient will not see that the joke which is testing him is crucially implausible; i.e., that without this implausible concatenation of events, the joke collapses.

So far the interest has been to see that there are extremely well developed constructional forms that can handle a collection of components in ways that allow for a story to be built out of them. The story, then, acts as a coherent package for a bunch of components. We'll now begin to look at those components as pieces of information; to pull them out and look at them as information packaged in the story/joke form. First, I want to consider some similarities and differences between stories, jokes, and dirty jokes.

Stories are plainly ways of packaging experiences. And most characteristically, stories report an experience in which the teller figures and figures as the story's hero—which doesn't mean that teller has done something heroic, but that the story is organized around the teller's circumstances. I'll give you what can pass as bizarre instances, though they're not bizarre but altogether characteristic. Here are two stories told shortly after the assassination of Robert Kennedy. In the first, two ladies are talking on the phone. One of them mentions the place where the body was flown by helicopter out of Los Angeles.

EMMA:	Hey that was the same spot we took off for Honolulu. Where they put him on.
	(1.0)
EMMA:	At that chartered place.
NANCY:	Oh really?
EMMA:	Yeah.

NANCY: Oh for heaven sakes.

EMMA: Exactly. It said "on West Imperial
            Boulevard" and I could see the building, and
            then the World Airways was on the side there
            where it comes in and that's just where *we*
            took off.

NANCY: Well I'll be darned.

EMMA: Yeah.

NANCY: Oh, well I'm glad it didn't happen while *you*
            were trying to get off,

EMMA: Oh my God.

NANCY: God *that* would of been a mess, you'd of
            never gotten to Hawaii.

That is, an event which, in the "objective reality," has the teller figuring
altogether incidentally, gets turned into an event in his life specifically (or,
as in this case, an almost-event). In the second, the same teller is talking
to her sister and is telling about her daughter Marian's response to the
assassination. Marian is first proposed to be highly political, having done
a variety of things in the primaries, and having been really depressed by
the assassination.

EMMA: So the *next* night they had a big baseball game
            and the Lions are losing by one, that's
            Michael's [Marian's son] *team*. So they put
            some of these other kids in that can't play as
            good as he, you know, give them a chance. So
            finally they put *him* in at the last five innings
            there, and he made a home run with a little kid
            on first, and the kid came in and Michael made
            a home run, there's *two* runs, so they won and
            they *picked* him up, and Marian says it was
            really the cutest thing, they picked him up and
            held him up in the air, and everybody was
            lovin him and huggin him, even Sy [Marian's
            husband] had tears in his eyes.

LOTTIE: uh uh uh

EMMA: huh heh! *He* won the game! uh uh uh!

LOTTIE: huh! Oh God love'im.

EMMA: She says that's the only good thing this week.

In this story, Marian's life is what it is that the assassination has happened to. It happened to her as something depressing her, such that something that also happened to her could lift her depression somewhat.

Now, not only does teller figure in the story, and figure with the story organized around his circumstances, but it's pretty much teller's business to tell the story with respect to its import for him, and it is his involvement in it that provides for the story's telling. That is, teller can tell it to somebody who knows and cares about him, and maybe recipient can tell it to someone who also knows and cares about initial teller, but it goes very little further than that. So, e.g., the second story involves this little boy; his mother tells it as organized around her circumstances, as a respite from the depression engendered by the assassination; i.e., it is sequentially connected to the prior night's assassination via "So the *next* night" and is summarized as "She says that's the only good thing this week." His mother tells it to her mother and her mother is now telling it to her sister (the boy's great-aunt, his mother's aunt). The story is not going to go much further on this track; it has no base for going much further. So there's an initial power, but it's shortlived.

Further, recipient of a story has as one business to display his understanding of it, e.g., Nancy's "God *that* would of been a mess, you'd of never gotten to Hawaii.", and/or to affiliate to it by showing its particular relevance to him. Lottie's "Oh God love'im." is one form such affiliation takes. Another form involves recipient telling a second story, in which recipient figures as teller had figured [cf., e.g., Sacks, 1970, Lecture 5, April 30].

Finally, one constraint on telling a story is that it needs to be fitted into the conversation. It doesn't make its own place, and at any free time that there might be, e.g., a silence occurring, or whatever, that's not an occasion for telling some or any story. So that stories, for their occurrence, have to be put into a place appropriate for that story in the conversation, and stories are very carefully placed.

Now, while jokes characteristically have a story format—i.e., they report some sort of single experience in which someone is some sort of hero—a first difference is that the teller is specifically *not* a character in the joke. One may tell funny stories in which one figures, but that's something different than a joke. In a joke, the teller is not a character; there is a specific disaffiliation between teller and the characters. Obviously, insofar as one is a character in the story one tells, then one is permitting or encouraging or desiring to have others get a view of one (as courageous, thoughtful, frank, God only knows, whatever it is that stories will convey of someone). Jokes, then, can contain different sorts of events than stories will characteristically contain, since the characters in jokes can do things that tellers might not like themselves to be thought to be doing if what were heard were that the teller is a character in it. And any recipient of a joke is a possible future teller. Having heard a joke, having "gotten" it, that's enough to be able to tell it.

Further, recipient does not affiliate to a joke and does not indicate he's had experiences similar to the joke's hero. Rather, he shows his understanding of the joke by appropriately laughing.

Finally, jokes are not placed in the ways that stories are. Jokes can make their place in a conversation. If nobody is talking one can say "I gotta joke," tell the joke, and it has no bearing on the conversation so far or thereafter. So that, as compared to stories, jokes "go around" rather more extendedly than any particular story does.

While what holds for jokes holds for dirty jokes, there's one serious addition. Because of their obscene components, dirty jokes circulate with a restriction on them that says "Pass it, but pass it with discretion"; i.e., dirty jokes are not to be told to just anyone.

With that kind of differentiation, let's suppose that the elaborate constructional aspects we considered earlier warrant our treating these objects as "rational institutions" directed to packaging and transmitting information. Now, what sort of rational institution might dirty jokes be? One might be led to figure that the information in a dirty joke is its obscene information. That would be irrational, since their obscene character serves as a restriction on their passage. A vehicle which, by virtue of its obscenity, has a restriction on its passage, would be rationally exploited if it were used to pass information other than that which restricts that passage. Thus, if there are any sorts of information which it's relevant to pass, which it's also relevant to pass restrictedly, then such things could be put into dirty jokes, where the obscenity serves as a "cover" for other information. The dirtiness aspect of the dirty joke might, then, be simply a formal aspect of the joke having to do with its *transmission* and not particularly with its *information*, so that in some ideal form one might have dirty jokes whose information had nothing to do with sex.

Consider the transmission issues involved in something put into a story format. A story format has a short motive power. Turn it into a joke and you increase its motive power. Use the joke format for building a dirty joke and you preserve its increased motive power while adding a restriction on its transmission. Furthermore, that information which you might put into a dirty joke format has a sort of safety to it, in that teller is not a character. So, insofar as the joke contains possibly embarrassing or denegrating information, it isn't information to be affiliated to teller, and recipient need not affiliate to it.

With those kinds of features to jokes, and the possibility that the dirty joke can be a vehicle for passing information which is intendedly restricted, I want to argue that the joke we're examining is a joke with information relevant for, and passage intendedly restricted to, 12-year-old girls. In our data it's told by a 17-year-old boy to other 17-year-old boys, and it's specifically told by the boy as having been told him by his 12-year-old sister. Now, the boys know they understand it and figure it's not very funny, and they also doubt that the girl would have understood it. I'll argue that the *boys* don't understand it, that the girl would, and that it involves some information distinctly interesting to 12-year-old girls.

We can start off by asking who would be attracted to this joke's components so as to find it capturing of their interests. For example, some groups would and other groups wouldn't find it interesting that the girls in the joke get married together. While it occasionally happens that, say, two sisters get married on the same occasion, and maybe conceivably three, we might ask why that component is put into the joke, and whether putting it into the joke reflects some interest that could be attractive to some particular group, e.g., 12-year-old girls. I'd like to suggest that 12-year-old girls are perhaps in some way interested in sex and marriage and things like that, but I think it can be found that what they are rather more interested in is each other. That is to say, one of the really distinct features of that age group of girls is that they travel in packs; i.e., they have a group life among themselves. And they know that in the future there will be an end to their traveling in packs which will be replaced by, e.g., getting married and ending up in two-person relationships, the other person being a male. When they fantasy about the future, one thing they do is attempt to project their pack traveling into that future. And one characteristic such fantasy is that they get married together. That the marriage takes place in a pack is a way in which the future of a marriage for each of them that splits the group apart, can be accommodated to their pleasure in their pack status. Notice, for example, that males play virtually no part in the joke. They appear only as a way to clarify the introductory sentence after it has been subjected to heckling by other males. So the event of the three sisters all getting married together can project a common fantasy that 12-year-old girls have.

If this is a dirty joke for 12-year-old girls, then it may contain information of distinct interest to them and not of interest to others; information extractable by them and perhaps not by others. Such information seems to be present, and we'll spend some time looking at it.

A first sort of information is found in the punch line. Now, one aspect of the punch line is characteristic for dirty jokes: An altogether well known expression—an idiom, a proverb, a rule—has a properly obscene interpretation which it is recipient's job to find. And that's one aspect of this punch line's work. In this joke, however, something new has been added. In the second sequence, all three answers constitute explanations of why something was or wasn't done. But the third also operates as a *squelch* of the mother by the daughter. It is an explanation which says, "What I did that might violate a rule, I did by reference to some other rule which *you* told me to follow." And that is one standard form for squelches.

Given the squelch operation, some components of the story become rather more crucial than they might initially have seemed. For example, that it is a "mother" interacting with a "daughter." Had someone else interrogated the girls, then each of the answers is a satisfactory and understandable explanation. But for the third answer to be a squelch, it needs a "mother" doing the asking of "her daughter." That explanation, to someone else, i.e., "My mother told me it was impolite to talk with my mouth full," wouldn't be a squelch of asker. So, while there is a series of identities of the girls in the joke (they're introduced as "girls," they're collected as "sisters," that they got married makes them "wives"), they largely function as "daughters," and that identity is crucial for this event, which is the surprise of the joke's structure. While we're prepared for some sort of interpretably obscene punch line, we have not been led to expect a squelch, as well.

I want to propose that with this squelch, specifically with the invocation of a rule to explain a violation, we have captured here aspects of an altogether characteristic problem for children. Children learn rules in various ways: by inducing them from events and by being told them. And a routine occasion for being told a rule is upon the relevance of that rule's application; the rule being used to correct some action the child did or didn't do. Now a thing that children can and do suppose is that they can be freed of correction (and whatever accompanies correction, e.g., punishment, sanction, being treated as a child), by learning to use rules. Living under rules can provide a source of freedom for them—freedom from corrections, sanctions, etc. All they have to do (it's not a small "all," but "all they have to do") is to have their activities conform with rules. And they can learn to do this by determining under what circumstances a particular rule should be used. It turns out that they discover, or are taught, something else besides this. And that something else is that the domain of a rule's *possible* application is not the same as the scope of its *actual proper* application. Instead, rules are to be used more narrowly; i.e., not each occasion on which any given rule might apply is an occasion on which it should be applied. This is an altogether pervasive problem, e.g., it's a problem in language use, where following the apparent rules of a language, one comes across places where, using a rule, one ends up talking incorrectly, it happening that the language has "irregular forms" which need to be learned separately. And one very characteristic source of children's erroneous talk is that their talk is in ways more lawful than the language. It isn't that they're simply making an error. Their error is due to having applied some rule of grammar beyond its actual scope of application. The same goes for many, if not all, other rules.

That poses a variety of distinct problems for children, since some of the time, in following a rule, they turn out to be behaving incorrectly and are then corrected or sanctioned by adults, and come to learn that they aren't freed from adult supervision by virtue of the fact that they follow the rules they're told. And they can't get a handle on the size of the problem; i.e., they can't come up with a systematic, general solution. They can only "learn by experience" when a rule will turn out to be incorrectly applied. And, that rules will turn out to be incorrectly applied by them operates to preserve adult authority over them, which allows the adults to engage in correction, sanction, etc., for what might seem like private, capricious interests. So the dream, that acquiring rule use can lead to freedom from authority, never materializes, and one is nonetheless subject to the authority of those who seem to simply introduce assertions that this rule doesn't hold here, some other does. And that is one characteristic way a violation of this type is proposed; i.e., by juxtaposing a pair of rules: "You applied Rule X here, but Rule X doesn't apply here, Rule Y applies here." Thus, what children are learning about problems of rule use is that some places where a rule might apply, it's not that nothing applies, but that some different rule applies.

In evolving ways of dealing with that problem, a special skill is to be learned. As adults characteristically use a rule to correct a child's intendedly rule-governed activity, so the child learns to use a rule to counterpose a proposed violation. Children learn (and get a special kick out of being able) to answer complaints about possible rule violations by introducing another applicable rule, which they offer as the thing which yielded the activity being treated as a violation; i.e., they acquire skill in using rules to do things like make excuses. Having been accused of doing something wrong, they can come up with a rule and offer it as the explanation for their action. And ideally, it's a rule that they were told to follow by the one who is now threatening to sanction them.

So, while there are various sorts of squelches, the one present in this joke catches a specific way that children dream of turning the tables on adults. Indeed, it appears that a specific occupation of this joke, one which has nothing particularly to do with sex, is setting up child-as-victor. Now there is a particular type of joke for which squelches are distinctly characteristic, and those are political jokes—political in the sense of, say, group conflicts. And certain things are present in such jokes. One is that they involve a member of some known-to-be-lower category squelching a member of some known-to-be-higher category, e.g., a citizen squelching a government official, an employee squelching a boss, etc. And a characteristic of such jokes vis-à-vis the groups in which they circulate is that the victor in the joke will have an identity which the teller has, and also the recipient has; i.e., we find a common identity between the victor, the teller, and the recipient. In this joke we have a child-desired squelch; an aspect of the joke which kids who have come to deal with the problem of the scope and domain of rules' applicability can understand and appreciate; an aspect which others would hardly see as interesting; and thus, the joke is distinctly for circulating among children.

There's another sort of issue. For any given child who experiences the situation of having learned a rule and, following it, it turning out that sometimes, at times they wouldn't have known about beforehand, they nonetheless did wrong, then the question is: Is it this given child's problem, or a problem that is not particularly theirs? After all, it's their parents who taught them or from whom they induced what seem to be general rules, rules having nothing to do with their parents, but it's their parents who inform them of the violation that their rule use has produced. Question is, "Is it that *my* parents are introducing all these exceptions, or is that the nature of the game?" It's easy enough to suppose that insofar as it's my parents who introduce the corrections and it's my parents who obviously have an interest in preserving their authority over me that way, then it's my parents who use rules against me that way. How would anybody ever learn that it's not a "my problem," but an "anybody's problem"?

In that regard, the dirty joke contains information which, again, has nothing particularly to do with sex, but does have particular interest for a group within which it might be passed, where this group does not have obvious other sorts of vehicles for transmitting information relevant just for them; i.e., there's no child's newsletter. But, given the transmissability of jokes and the transmissability of dirty jokes with a "discretion" marker on them, then these sorts of things can move within the groups interested in them, informing its members of problems, solutions, fantasies, possible outcomes, etc., of distinct interest to just those groups, in the way that, e.g., private newsletters can do that job for stockholders, or a motorcycle magazine can do that job for motorcyclists.

Now, it so happens that the joke involves sex. In part, the sex is there as a restriction on the joke's passage. But given that sex is there, we might consider its relevance, and ask, e.g., if there is a drama in the joke with certain parties involved in it, then, by reference to real persons, for whom is such a drama characteristic? I suggest that it isn't for just anyone that the drama of sex involves mother and daughter. But for 12-year-old girls, to some considerable extent, the drama of sex involves, not their relationship with males, but their relationship with their parents, perhaps, in particular with their mothers. Conflicts about sex, dating, etc., concern what mother will and will not allow, what mother wants to find out, etc. So that the mother–daughter drama of the joke can indeed capture a specific drama in the lives of some persons, whereas for other groups, that would hardly be a relevant circumstance in their lives. Further, recalling the feature I mentioned earlier, of the common identity between victor, teller, and recipient, this joke, with its drama and its outcome, can be of distinct interest to, not children in general, but girl-children; i.e., it's not merely parent–child with child as victor, but mother–daughter with daughter as victor.

Another kind of information involved here seems to be specifically sexual. And, again, specifically something for girls—girls old enough to be interested in what is sex, and young enough to have only particular sorts of experiences; experiences like encountering sex from behind a closed door. That is, something is going on behind a door, your parents are participants, it may be sex. Encountering sex that way, a question is, what is it like? Where it's specifically ambiguous by virtue of the fact that the sounds of sex are ambiguous—i.e., hearing them, one sometimes hears sounds that seem like pleasure, sometimes sounds that seem like pain, and sometimes no sounds. So, encountering sex that way, overhearing it (whether intendedly or not), one doesn't get a solution to what is sex like? but finds instead that a problem is posed: What is sex like? Furthermore, encountering it that way, one faces a similar situation to the one attendant to rule use: Whatever the sounds may mean, the question is, is that the way it is for my parents, or is that the way it is: Do only they make such noises, or does everyone?

The problem, with its information so encountered, plainly has difficulties getting an answer. It's presumably illicitly acquired. And that raises still another question: Is it just me, or has anybody else acquired the information that way? So the illicitness of the knowledge will serve as a partial constraint on presenting the information so as to get it checked out. And that it's about my parents can provide a source for not saying to a friend, e.g., "Listening at my folks' door I heard these noises. What does it mean, and is that the way it is?" So the means and source of acquisition of the information can themselves serve to constrain getting a solution to the problem that the acquisition of that information yielded. In that regard, then, if there were a package of information floating around that could be transmitted without revealing whether its teller or its recipient had the experiences it preserves—its teller because teller is not a character, its recipient because recipient, laughing, doesn't reveal that he had such experiences—such a package would have distinct transmission virtues for both the rule-use problem and the ambiguous-sounds-of-sex problem. In both cases we're dealing with information which is learned in the first place as possibly unique, carrying with it possibly unique problems: possibly just my parents' problems, possibly just my problems, and, in the case of rule use, possibly just my fantasy solution to it, and, in the case of the sounds of sex, possibly just my lack of knowledge of what it means. The joke can then serve to package information which persons interested in such information can pull out of it and see to be not merely mine, but ours.

Finally, let me note that while this joke's guise as an oral sex joke can initially restrict its passage, it in no way discriminates in terms of its transmission among those who do circulate oral sex jokes; i.e., not all oral sex jokes are equivalently tellable and not all groups who tell oral sex jokes would tell this one. In that regard, a chance feature of these data, that the joke is told by and to 17-year-old boys, turns out to be relevant. Its current teller specifically marks it as something his little sister did, which he is now describing to them. Nonetheless, he gets ridiculed for telling it, and it's pretty clear its recipients don't like it. But the fact that its recipients don't like this one doesn't mean that they wouldn't enjoy and retell other oral sex jokes. That is to say, its obscenity can provide an initial restriction, but it is other aspects of it which discriminate among that initially located population and find a still narrower population, among which the joke circulates.

This discrimination may be a "rational" feature of the joke, in the following sense. While the abstract information it carries is, in its abstract form, applicable to a larger population than is its concrete instance, in its abstract form (e.g., rule use, source and acquisition of data) the information is not readily accessible to someone dealing with events as he encounters them in his concrete circumstances. Packaging the information in a way which locates and addresses a set of concrete circumstances can provide for its accessibility. But it can have as a consequence that only those who are encountering the circumstances located by a particular package will readily see what that package has to offer them. A joke could pass among others than those for whom it is distinctly relevant, and those others wouldn't know what they had, wouldn't inquire into what it might possibly have for them, and wouldn't see what's in it for anyone else. In the case of this joke told among 17-year-old boys, they figure they understand it and see what's in it, and there's not much in it. And they specifically doubt that a 12-year-old girl (one for whom it happens to be relevant) would understand it. They understand it by reference to its oral sex; i.e., *what* they understand is not the same sort of thing a 12-year-old girl would see in it. So the joke gets into their hands and goes nowhere. But it continues to circulate among those for whom it is relevant and who understand it for the information it contains specifically for them. And that information is in the first place tagged as information for them by still other aspects of the joke which appeal distinctly to such a group (e.g., that "daughters" are involved, that they get married in a pack, etc.), i.e., aspects which can alert them to its possible special interest for them. And it's the girls who can directly understand the power of the squelch in the joke's punch line; it is they who are the victors in it.

NOTES

[1] An article entitled "An Analysis of the Course of a Joke's Telling in Conversation" has also been published by Sacks (1975). This earlier article deals with the same conversational fragment, addressing itself to aspects of the joke's telling; that is, how it is introduced, told, and responded to. In a footnote to that earlier paper, Sacks says "The examination of the joke itself will be reserved for a later report." The materials presented here might be seen as a version of that "later report." The four lectures have been edited into a continuous presentation with two discrete parts: (*a*) a discussion of the joke's sequential organization, and (*b*) a consideration of a dirty joke as a device for packaging and transmitting information [G. J.].

[2] This is a simplified version of the transcript which accompanied the four lectures. The original transcript is not provided, but may be found in "An Analysis of the Course of a Joke's Telling" (Sacks, 1975 , pp. 338–340. A more recent and more detailed transcript is available [G. J.].

[3] This paragraph does not occur in the four lectures, but in Lecture 3, April 16, 1970, p. 24. It seemed appropriate to include it here [G. J.].

References

Albert, E.
1964 "Rhetoric," "logic," and "poetics" in Burundi: Culture patterning of speech behavior, *American Anthropologist*, *66*, 6, part 2.
Atkinson, M. A., Cuff, E. C., & Lee, J. R. E.
1973 "Right ——— e:r": Prolegomena to the analysis of "meeting talk" with special reference to the problem of "beginnings." (Didsbury Conversational Analysis Workshop, August 1973, Working Paper No. 1). Unpublished manuscript.
Bales, R. F.
1950 *Interaction process analysis*. Cambridge: Addison Wesley.
1970 *Personality and interpersonal behavior*. New York: Holt, Rinehart & Winston.
Bales, R. F., Strodtbeck, F. L., Mills, T. M., & Roseborough, M. E.
1951 Channels of communication in small groups. *American Sociological Review*, *16*, 461–468.
Barker, R. G., & Wright, H. F.
1951 *One boy's day*. New York: Harper.
Beardsley, R. K., Hall, J. W., & Ward, R. E.
1959 *Village Japan*. Chicago: University of Chicago Press.
Beckett, S.
1972 *The lost ones*. New York: Grove Press.

Coleman, J.
1960 The mathematical study of small groups. In H. Solomon (Ed.), *Mathematical thinking in the measurement of behavior: Small groups, utility factor analysis.* Glencoe, Illinois: Free Press.

Duncan, S. D., Jr.
1972 Some signals and rules for taking speaking turns in conversations. *Journal of Personality and Social Psychology, 23*, 283–292. (a)
1972 Distribution of auditor back-channel behaviors in dyadic conversation. *Journal of Psycholinguistic Research.* (b)
1973 Toward a grammar for dyadic conversation. *Semiotica, IX*, 1.

Fillmore, C. J., & Langendoen, D. T.
1971 *Studies in linguistic semantics.* New York: Holt, Rinehart & Winston.

Garfinkel, H.
1967 *Studies in ethnomethodology.* Englewood Cliffs, New Jersey: Prentice Hall.
1972 Remarks on ethnomethodology. In J. Gumperz & D. Hymes (Eds.), *Directions in sociolinguistics.* New York: Holt, Rinehart & Winston.
1973 Lecture presented at the University of Manchester.

Garfinkel, H., & Sacks, H.
1970 On formal structures of practical actions. In J. C. McKinney & E. A. Tiryakian (Eds.), *Theoretical sociology.* New York: Appleton-Century-Crofts.

Goffman, E.
1955 On face work: An analysis of ritual elements in social interaction. *Psychiatry, XVIII*, 3.
1959 *The presentation of self in everyday life.* New York: Doubleday Anchor Books.
1961 *Asylums.* New York: Doubleday Anchor Books.
1963 *Behavior in public places.* New York: The Free Press.
1964 The neglected situation. *American Anthropologist, 66*, 6, part 2.
1967 *Interaction ritual.* New York: Doubleday Anchor Books.
1971 *Relations in public.* New York: Basic Books.

Goffman, E.
1974 *Frame analysis: An essay on the organization of experience.* New York: Harper & Row.

Goldberg, J.
1975 A system for the transfer of instructions in natural settings. *Semiotica, 14*, 3, 269–296.
1976 *Amplitude as a discourse affiliation mechanism in sequence construction.* Unpublished Ph.D. dissertation, School of Social Science, University of California at Irvine.

Isaacs, S.
1933 *Social development in young children.* New York: Harcourt Brace.

Jaffe, J., & Feldstein, S.
1970 *Rhythms of dialogue.* New York: Academic Press.

Jefferson, G.
1972 Side sequences. In D. Sudnow (Ed.), *Studies in social interaction.* New York: Free Press.
1973 A case of precision timing in ordinary conversation. *Semiotica, IX*, 1.
1974 Error correction as an interactional resource. *Language in Society, III*, 2.
forthcoming
A technique for inviting laughter and its subsequent acceptance/declination. In G. Psathas (Ed.), *Papers of the Boston University Conference on Ethnomethodology and Conversation Analysis.* Boston: Irvington Publishers.

Jefferson, G., Sacks, H., & Schegloff, E.

1973 Preliminary notes on the sequential organization of laughter. (Informal Seminars of the Ethology Research Groups, University of Pennsylvania.) Unpublished draft.

n.d. Some notes on laughing together. Forthcoming in M. Moerman (Ed.), *International Journal of the Sociology of Language*. The Hague: Mouton.

Jefferson, G., & Schenkein, J.

1977 Some sequential negotiations in conversation: Unexpanded and expanded versions of projected action sequences. *Sociology, 11*, 1. Reprinted in this volume.

Jordan, B., & Fuller, N.

n.d. The non-fatal nature of trouble: Sense-making and trouble managing in lingua franca talk. Forthcoming in *Semiotica*.

Katz, B., & Sharrock, W. W.

1975 Eine Darstellung des Kodierens. In E. Weingarten, F. Sack, & J. Schenkein (Eds.), *Ethnomethodologie: Beitrage zu einer Soziologie des Alltagslebens*. Frankfort, Germany: Suhrkamp.

Kendon, A.

1966 Some functions of gaze direction in social interaction. *Acta Psychologica, 26*, 1. 1–47.

Labov, W., & Waletsky, J.

1966 Narrative analysis: Oral versions of personal experience. In J. Helm (Ed.), *Essays on the verbal and visual arts*. Seattle: University of Washington Press. Pp. 12–44.

Matarazzo, J., & Wiens, A.

1972 *The interview: Research on its anatomy and structure*. Chicago: Aldine-Atherton.

Miller, G.

1963 Review of J. Greenberg (Ed.), "Universals of Language." *Contemporary Psychology, VIII*, 417–418.

Mitchell, J. C.

1956 *The Yao village*. Manchester: Manchester University Press.

Moerman, M.

1972 Analysis of Lue conversation: Providing accounts, finding breaches, and taking sides. In D. Sudnow (Ed.), *Studies in social interaction*. New York: Free Press.

1973 The use of precedent in natural conversation. *Semiotica, 7*, 193–218.

forthcoming

(Ed.), *The International Journal of Sociolinguistics*, The Hague: Mouton.

Moerman, H., & Sacks, H.

1974 On understanding in conversation. In *Festschrift for E. Voegelin*. The Hague: Mouton.

Pomerantz, A.

1975 *Second assessments: A study of some features of agreements/disagreements*. Unpublished Ph.D. dissertation, School of Social Science, University of California at Irvine.

forthcoming

Agreeing and disagreeing with assessments: Some features of preferred/ dispreferred turn shapes. In M. Moerman (Ed.), *The International Journal of Sociolinguistics*. The Hague: Mouton.

Ryave, A.

1973 *Aspects of story-telling among a group of "mentally retarded."* Unpublished Ph.D. dissertation, Department of Sociology, University of California at Los Angeles.

Ryave, A., & Schenkein, J.

1974 Notes on the art of walking. In R. Turner (Ed.), *Ethnomethodology*. Harmondsworth, England: Penguin Books.

Sacks, H.
   1963   On sociological description. *Berkeley Journal of Sociology*, *8*, 1–16.
   1967   The search for help: No one to turn to. In E. Schneidman (Ed.), *Essays in self-destruction*. New York: Science House. (a)
   1967   Transcripts of unpublished lectures. Department of Sociology, University of California at Los Angeles. (b)
   1968   Transcripts of unpublished lectures. School of Social Sciences, University of California at Irvine.
   1969   Transcripts of unpublished lectures. School of Social Science, University of California at Irvine.
   1970   Transcripts of unpublished lectures. School of Social Science, University of California at Irvine.
   1971   Transcripts of unpublished lectures. School of Social Science, University of California at Irvine.
   1972   Transcripts of unpublished lectures. School of Social Science, University of California at Irvine. (a)
   1972   On the analysability of stories by children. In J. Gumperz & D. Hymes (Eds.), *Directions in sociolinguistics*. New York: Holt, Rinehart & Winston. (b)
   1972   An initial investigation of the usability of conversational data for doing sociology. In D. Sudnow (Ed.), *Studies in social interaction*. New York: Free Press. (c)
   1972   Notes on police assessment of moral character. In D. Sudnow (Ed.), *Studies in social interaction*. New York: Free Press. (d)
   1973   On some puns with some intimations. In R. Shuy (Ed.), *Report of the Twenty-Third Annual Georgetown Roundtable in Linguistics*. Washington, D.C.: Georgetown University Press.
   1974   An analysis of the course of a joke's telling in conversation. In R. Baumann & J. Sherzer (Eds.), *Explorations in the ethnography of speaking*. Cambridge: Cambridge University Press.
   1975   Everyone has to lie. In B. Blount & R. Sanchez (Eds.), *Ritual, reality, and innovation in language use*. New York: Academic Press.
   n.d.   *Aspects of the sequential organization of conversation*. Unpublished manuscript.
   forthcoming *Collected works of Harvey Sacks*. New York: Academic Press.
Sacks, H., & Schegloff, E.
   1974   Two preferences in the organization of reference to persons in conversation and their interaction. In N. H. Avison & R. J. Wilson (Eds.), *Ethnomethodology, labelling theory, and deviant behavior*. London: Routledge and Kegan Paul.
Sacks, H., Schegloff, E., & Jefferson, G.
   1974   A Simplest Systematics for the Organization of Turn-Taking in Conversation. *Language, 50*, 4, 696–735. Reprinted in this volume.
Schegloff, E.
   1967   *The first five seconds: The order of conversational openings*. Unpublished Ph.D. dissertation, Department of Sociology, University of California at Berkeley, 1967.
   1968   Sequencing in conversational openings. *American Anthropologist, 70*, 4, 1075–1095.
   1972   Notes on a conversational practice: Formulating place. In D. Sudnow (Ed.), *Studies in social interaction*. New York: Free Press.
   forthcoming On some questions and ambiguities in conversation. In M. Moerman(Ed.), *International Journal of the Sociology of Language*.
Schegloff, E., Jefferson, G., & Sacks, H.
   1976   The preference for self-correction in the organization of repair in conversation. Unpublished draft.

Schegloff, E., & Sacks, H.
  1973   Opening up closings. *Semiotica*, *VIII*, 4, 289–327.
Schenkein, J.
  1971   *Some substantive and methodological issues in the analysis of conversational interaction.* Unpublished Ph.D. dissertation, School of Social Science, University of California at Irvine.
  1972   Towards an analysis of natural conversation and the sense of *heheh*. *Semiotica*. *VI*, 4, 344–377.
  1974   An introduction to the study of "socialization" through analyses of conversational interaction. Forthcoming in M. Mathiot (Ed.), *Semiotica*, special issue on socio-linguistics.
  1975   Letzte Bemerkungen zur Ethnomethodologie. In E. Weingarten, F. Sack, & J. Schenkein (Eds.), *Ethnomethodologie: Beitrage zu einer Soziologie des Alltagslebens.* Frankfort, Germany: Suhrkamp. (a)
  1975   Techniques in the analysis of verbal interaction. (Didactic Seminar of the American Sociological Association Seventieth Annual Meetings, ASA-43.) North Hollywood, California: Convention Seminar Cassettes. (b)
  1976   The radio raiders story. Forthcoming in G. Psathas (Ed.), *Papers of the Boston University Conference on Ethnomethodology and Conversation Analysis.* Boston: Irvington Publishers. (a)
  1976   Review of D. E. Allen and R. F. Guy, *Conversation analysis: The sociology of talk. Language in Society, 5,* 3, 387–389. (b)
  1977   *A videotape introduction to sociology.* Flushing, New York: Center for Instructional Development and the Queens College Portable Video Laboratory.
forthcoming *Introduction to conversational analysis.* New York: Academic Press.
forthcoming Sequential resources in natural conversation. In B. Butterworth (Ed.), *Language production.* London: Academic Press.
Sharrock, W. W.
  1974   On owning knowledge. In R. Turner (Ed.), *Ethnomethodology.* Harmondsworth, England: Penguin Books. (a)
  1974   The availability of culture. Unpublished manuscript. (b)
Stephan, F. F., & Mishler, E. G.
  1952   The distribution of participation in small groups: An exponential approximation. *American Sociological Review*, *19*, 598–608.
Sudnow, D. (Ed.).
  1972   *Studies in social interaction.* New York: Free Press.
Terasaki, A.
  1976   *A proposal on announcement sequence in conversation.* Unpublished Ph.D. dissertation, School of Social Science, University of California at Irvine.
Turner, R.
  1970   Words, utterances, and activities. In J. Douglas (Ed.), *Understanding everyday life.* Chicago: Aldine.
  1972   Some formal properties of therapy talk. In D. Sudnow (Ed.), *Studies in social interaction.* New York: Free Press.
  1974   (Ed.), *Ethnomethodology.* Harmondsworth, England: Penquin Books.
Yngve, V.
  1970   On getting a word in edgewise. In *Papers from the Sixth Regional Meeting of the Chicago Linguistic Society*, 567–577. Chicago.

A
B
C 8
D 9
E 0
F 1
G 2
H 3
I 4
J 5